About the Author

George Johnston is a New Testament scholar and United Church minister whose thought-provoking courses on the Bible have sparked the interest of students from all backgrounds.

Born in Scotland, he did his undergraduate work at Glasgow University and obtained his doctorate from Cambridge University. He has honorary degrees from several institutions. From 1940 to 1947, he was minister of the Church of Scotland Martyrs' parish, St. Andrews, Fife, and has served as interim pastor of two Charges in Mississauga and one in Montreal.

He lectured at Trinity College, Glasgow, and later was professor of New Testament at the seminary in Hartford, Connecticut, and Emmanuel College of the University of Toronto. Since 1959 he has taught at McGill University in Montreal, where he was professor of New Testament until 1981 and is now Emeritus Professor of Religious Studies. He also served as Principal of United Theological College from 1959 to 1970 and Dean of Religious Studies from 1970 to 1975.

His books include *The Doctrine of the Church in the New Testament*, *The Spirit-Paraclete in the Gospel of John*, and *Discovering Discipleship*, as well as *The Secrets of the Kingdom*, a book for senior high school students.

He lives in Montreal with his wife Nandy, who is the author of two books, has published devotional services for women's groups, and has been active in the United Church Women and in social work within the Church.

opening the scriptures

A Journey through the Stories
and Symbols of the Bible

opening the scriptures

A Journey through the Stories and Symbols of the Bible

George Johnston

THE UNITED CHURCH PUBLISHING HOUSE

Copyright © 1992 The United Church Publishing House

All rights reserved. No part of this book may be reproduced, stored in a retrieval system, or transmitted, in any form or by any means electronic, mechanical, or otherwise, without the written permission of The United Church Publishing House.

Canadian Cataloguing in Publication Data
Johnston, George, 1913 June 9-
   Opening the Scriptures

Based on lectures delivered at McGill University.
Includes bibliographical references and index.
ISBN 0-919000-81-9

1. Bible - Criticism, interpretation, etc.
2. Bible as literature. 3. Myth in the Bible.
4. Symbolism in the Bible. I. Title.

BS538.J63   1992   220.6'6   C92-094155-9

The United Church Publishing House
85 St. Clair Avenue East
Toronto, Ont.
M4T 1M8

Publisher: R.L. Naylor
Editor-in-Chief: Peter Gordon White
Editor: Robert Chodos
Book Design: Chris Dumas, Dept. of Graphics and Print
Cover Design and Maps: Nina Price
Printed in Canada by: Hignell Printing Ltd.

5 4 3 2 1   92 93 94 95 96

Cover Illustration
Christ the Redeemer is shown standing between the Greek letters alpha and omega, the first and last letters of the Greek alphabet. The book of Revelation is the source of this imagery. *"It is done! I am the Alpha and Omega, the beginning and the end. To the thirsty I will give water as a gift from the spring of the water of life"* (Rev. 21:6, NRSV). The Christ figure is shown holding a long staff-like cross in the left hand, a flower-shaped insignia lifted up in the right hand, both symbols of hope and resurrection. By maintaining bodily proportions and the penetrating eyes of the original, our illustrator has been faithful to the 800-year-old round, flat, silvered box on which the dramatic image is engraved. It is an example of French Gothic artistry, simple in design, rich in Christian convictions.

Contents

Preface   xii

1. Introduction   1
    The purpose of this book
    The joy and wonder of Bible study
    Translations of the Bible
    The biblical library
    Two problems about linguistic usage

2. Beginnings: Genesis 1–11   11
    The writings and the stories
    Four stories from the earliest times
    The later creation story
    Some spiritual lessons from Genesis 1–11

3. Patriarchal Legends: Genesis 12–50   18
    Tales of long ago
    Abraham: number one patriarch
    Jacob: the supplanter who made good
    Joseph — Rachel's son (Genesis 37–50)
    Human life in the light of eternity

4. Exodus: The Escape of Israel from Egypt   27
    The Liberation Story
    Memory and Hope
    The covenant at Mount Sinai
    Pilgrims of faith
    An ever-present God

5. Spirited Personalities in a Turbulent Age   39
    From Joshua to Saul
    The Judges
    Samuel: judge, prophet and seer
    Rulers of the ancient Near East
    The election of Saul
    The career of Saul

6. David: The Once and Future King   46
      A colourful character
      Historic David: from shepherd to outlaw
      Historic David: king of all Israel
      David, the ideal king

7. Schisms and Exiles   54
      Solomon: the wise or unwise king
      Break-ups and reunions
      Elijah and Elisha
      Exile: the fall of Samaria
      Judah conquered, the great Dispersion

8. The Development of Prophecy in Israel   62
      Why bother with the prophets
      What makes a prophet
      The passion of Jeremiah
      How Jeremiah's book was composed
      The new covenant
      The sins of Judah
      Hope in the midst of despair
      Ezekiel: his book and his call
      Visions of resurrection
      The contribution of the great prophets

9. The Era of the Second Temple   73
      Five centuries at a glance
      Apocryphal and Pseudepigraphical
         literature of Judaism
      Restoration to Judea
      The religion of early Judaism
      Some new elements of the Second Temple era

10. Daniel: Dreams and Hopes   84
      Heroes of faith
      A romantic figure
      An apocalyptic hero
      A fictional hero

11. Climax and Threshold: The Spiritual
    Achievement of Early Judaism   91
       Climax and threshold
       About "end-times"
       The different types of Messianism
       Second Isaiah: the poetry of vicarious suffering
       The legacy of early Judaism

12. Luke's Life of Jesus   105
       Getting a perspective on the New Testament
       How the Gospel of Luke was composed
       Part one of the content
       Part two of the content
       Major themes in Jesus' career and message,
           according to Luke
       The parables of Jesus
       Concluding comments

13. The Church Story in the Acts of the Apostles   127
       What we can expect to learn from Acts
       The Spirit motif
       The meaning of "Church" (ecclesia)
       The martyr motif
       The heroes of the faith
       The Christian message
       A power struggle?

14. Paul the Christian Jew   144
       A Hellenistic Jew
       A nationalist Jew
       A Jew arrested by God
       A Christian Jew
       The man who changed the world

15. Paul's Pastoral Advice to His Churches   154
       Some real-life moral issues
       On moral purity

      On charismatic gifts
      On rich and poor church members
      On church unity
      On sowing and reaping

16. The Christ as High Priest in "To the Hebrews"   160
      The symbolism of "Bethel"
      The meeting place
      The chief celebrant
      The benefits of worship
      A final blessing

17. John's Revelation: Dreams and Hopes   166
      Is the end of the world at hand?
      Background information
      To the seven churches of Asia
      John's visions
      The millennium
      The Christ-figure in Revelation
      The values and limitations of visionary prophecy

Conclusion   176

Appendix 1: The Forms of Biblical Literature   180
    A. In the Hebrew Bible   180
    B. In the New Testament   190

Appendix 2: The Signs and Symbols
    of the Bible: a Guide   196

References   213

Select Bibliography   221

A Guide for Study and Discussion   224
    As you read alone
    With a friend

In your living room
In your congregation
A weekend retreat
Advent study: preparation, expectation, hope, future
A Lenten study: parables to live by
An intergenerational event: ages 5 and up
Graphics and audiovisual resources
Where is that in the Bible?

Index   245

Illustrations

Maps
1. The Near East Today   4
2. The World of the Patriarchs   14
3. The Exodus from Egypt   30
4. The Empire of David and Solomon   49
5. The Assyrian Empire in Isaiah's Time   58
6. The Kingdom of Judah in Isaiah's Time   67
7. Palestine in the Time of Jesus   106
8. The Journeys of Paul   149

Plates
1. Rembrandt's *Moses with Tables of the Law*   29
2. Rembrandt's *Jesus with the Sick and the Poor*   104
3. Dürer's *Four Apostles*   129
4. Caravaggio's *The Supper at Emmaus*   143
5. Rembrandt's *The Descent from the Cross*   153
6. Dürer's *The Four Horsemen of the Apocalypse*   165

Charts and Timelines
1. A Biblical Timeline   6
2. The Kingdoms and Their Rulers and Prophets   56
3. Judaism in World History 538–4 B.C   76
4. New Testament Timeline   108
5. An Outline of the Contents of Luke   110
6. The Distribution of Parabolic Stories   121
7. A Grouping of the Parables   122

Preface

Nine years ago, at the suggestion of my colleague, Dr. Katherine K. Young, I instituted a course to help students to read the Bible for themselves, and to appreciate the extent and manner of biblical influence on the arts, literature and institutions of Western civilization. Two years ago, a student reported with enthusiasm to Dr. Peter Gordon White about the approach to the Bible presented in that course. Immediately, Dr. White proposed that I should produce a book on this subject for a wider public. *Opening the Scriptures* is the result.

For the working relationship that has transformed seminars into manuscript and manuscript into book, I am indebted to Peter White for assiduous editorial direction through early drafts, to manuscript editors Robert Chodos and Lynn Gresham, to John and B.J. Klassen for study guide material, and to the creative design team of The United Church Publishing House. For word processing, I am grateful to Samieun Khan.

The Faculty of Graduate Studies, McGill University, contributed substantially to the cost of preparing the manuscript.

As always in my career, my wife Nandy has had to listen to many drafts. She has shared in putting up with the difficulties endemic to an enterprise like this.

I would like to dedicate this book with gratitude and affection to my teaching assistants, students and colleagues in biblical studies and theology from 1947 to 1992 in the U.S., Scotland and Canada.

George Johnston
Montreal, Que.
June 1992

one

Introduction

I
The purpose of this book

My intention in producing this volume is to encourage people — women and men, young and old — to read the scriptures without prior commitment to a particular interpretation or theology. Scripture is worth reading, I think, if only because of the honoured place it enjoys in the cultural heritage of the West. From the time of Charlemagne, about A.D. 800, until about the end of the First World War in 1918, scripture dominated Western civilization. Its influence is found in Western literature, music, the visual arts, education and law. Not only is scripture still widely read in the major languages of the West, but it continues to make an impact globally through nearly two thousand other translations. As this second millennium comes to an end, it is entirely reasonable that biblical teaching could contribute a great deal towards solving the social issues that have to be faced. I want to let scripture come alive in fresh ways, providing a treasury of faith and wisdom that might stimulate hope for the future.

II
The joy and wonder of Bible study

A common experience of most people is that on certain occasions we find ourselves compelled to reflect on the very fact of being alive in a strange and sometimes daunting universe. How did that universe come to be? What are human beings and where are they bound — if anywhere? Is there an end, a goal to which the whole creation moves? Does existence have a built-in purpose? We know that there is Something — that it is real. The world and all that it contains, including ourselves, are not illusions. We are self-aware, blessed with a sense of the right and the good, the just and the unjust, the true and the false. The ability to make these moral distinctions has a real bearing on what we choose to do and whether we suffer as a consequence. But does the universe care?

In the human situation there is also evidence of inhumanity and undeserved suffering. Quarrels flare up: sometimes over trivial disputes, such as the way someone speaks; sometimes over significant issues such as the right of the strong to rule and enslave the weak. Do some people deserve to be poor, and is it perfectly all right for them to be exploited by the clever, the industrious and the ambitious? Can suffering ever be good? There seems to be no end to the questions that confront us.

All these existential questions were posed by ancient Israelites too. They faced such problems head-on, and some of their answers, as well as much of their poetry and religious beliefs, can be read in their sacred books. They produced documents of literary and spiritual power that deal with the human situation. It is because they did so that we turn to their scripture and seek to read it wisely.

Using recent discoveries from archaeology, history and linguistics, we can read the Bible in a fresh way. Increasingly, we have more accurate translations of the Bible and are able to interpret its message without being unduly constrained by creed or authority. Ancient creeds that are still accepted in some religious communities do not always sit comfortably with a contemporary approach to the Bible. We should not be compelled to submit to a religious authority that defines the truth about God and humanity so that all we have to do is add a signature to the answer. The Bible is no less sacred for being read afresh. For many, it may come alive if it is presented in a secular context and not in the format of what may be called a conventional piety.

Certainly it has been my experience that studying the Bible in this way has been liberating and inspiring. Understanding with the mind is one result of study, but another is inspiration and a sense of divine instruction. Even though there may often be no final answers, and even though God himself remains a mystery, life gains more meaning and joy.

III

Translations of the Bible

The first part of the scriptures, called the Hebrew Bible or the Old Testament, was written almost entirely in Hebrew; the second part, called the New Testament, in Hellenistic Greek. For many churches, there is a third section called the Apocrypha of the Hebrew Bible, comprising documents that are accorded only secondary religious and ethical authority. Some of them, too, were composed in Greek. Consequently, what most of us read is a translation, and the more accurate the translation the better. Fortunately, it can be said without fear of contradiction that, on the whole, one can fully depend on the available versions.

Three of them are pre-eminent:

Δ The Latin, the work of St. Jerome, is known as the Vulgate and was finished in A.D. 405. Since the sixteenth century, an edition of the Vulgate has been the official text for use in the Roman Catholic Church.

Δ The German, the work of Martin Luther, completed in 1534, is said to have created the modern German language.

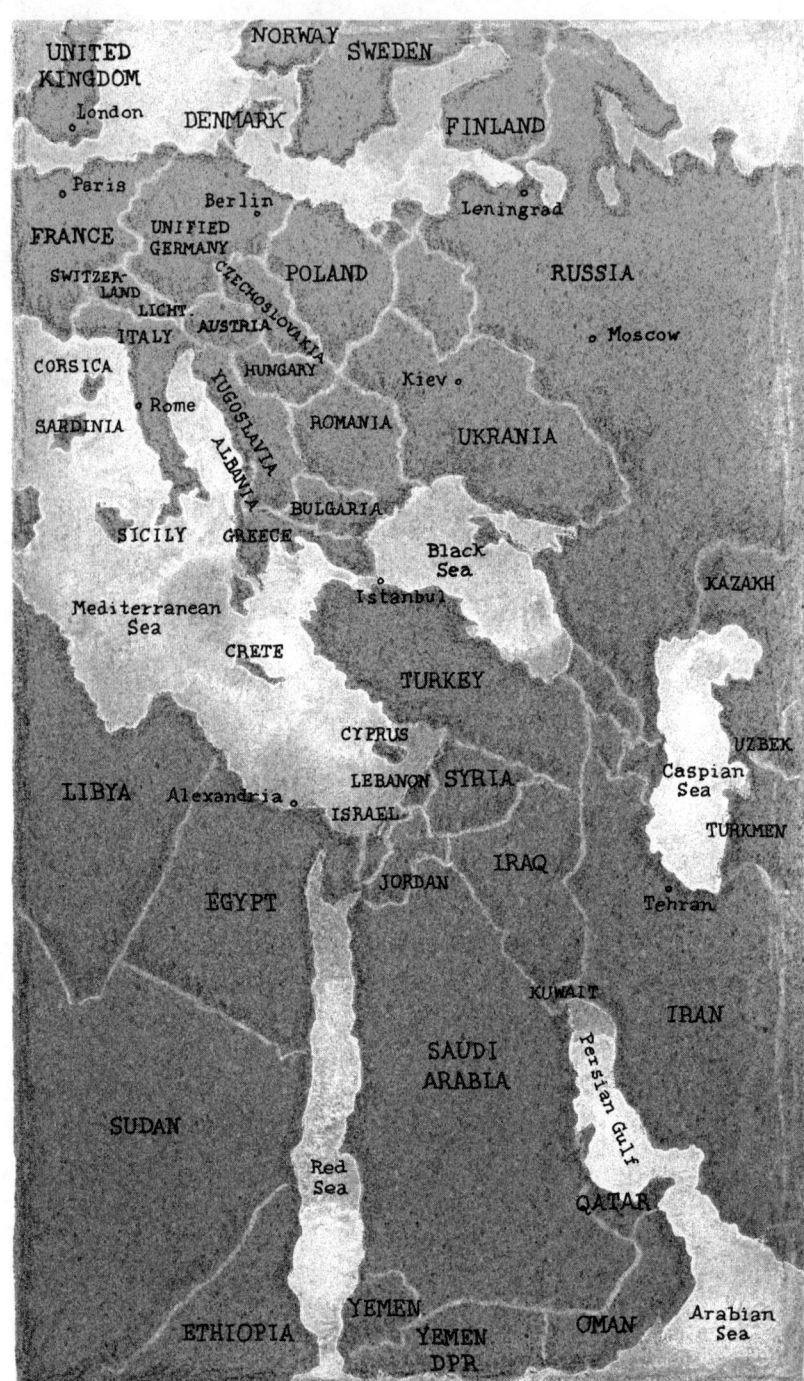

The Near East Today

This map is not drawn to scale. It is an impressionistic view of where our story takes place, as are the other maps in this book.

Δ The King James (KJV), or Authorized English Version (AV), was published in England by royal authority in 1611. It was a revision of several earlier English translations with which the name of William Tyndale is associated. A more up-to-date and accurate revision is the New Revised Standard Version (NRSV), which appeared in 1989. Alongside it one should set the Revised English Bible (REB) from the same year: it is a revision of the so-called New English Bible.

The KJV is the most famous of all English translations. Almost certainly, it is the one that has been most widely read throughout the world. It is a classic of English literature and, like the works of William Shakespeare, it is "full of quotations." This Bible has been a source of inspiration for poets from John Milton to T.S. Eliot and for prose writers from Henry Fielding and Charles Dickens to Margaret Laurence and Margaret Atwood.

The primary text that I use in this book is the classic KJV. I hope that my readers will use it too, but also have to hand either the NRSV or the REB. Both are excellent for style, accuracy and elegance.

IV

The biblical library

Even though you obtain a single volume when you buy a Bible, it is in fact a large anthology, a veritable library of sacred writings. It has a central place in the liturgies of Jews and Christians and belongs in synagogues, churches and homes as a resource for sermons about God and duty, for moral teaching and private devotion.

Bound together into this single volume is literature of great variety: collections of religious law, discussions of ethical problems, histories that are nonscientific because they have a theological tendency built in, myths, legends, miracle-stories, sermons and prophetic addresses or poetry, occasionally a real letter to someone together with semiofficial epistles that resemble encyclicals, many famous songs and the hymns known as psalms.

A Biblical Timeline

	B.C.
Creation	
Abraham	1800
Israel	
Exodus: Moses	1280
David	1000
Fall of Samaria	721
Exile: Fall of Jerusalem	587
Early Judaism:	
Torah and Prophets as the Hebrew Bible	398*
Death of Alexander the Great	323
Maccabaean Revolt against Syria	168
Hasmonaean Kingdom	142–63
Herod the Great (client king under Rome)	37–4
	A.D.
Ministry of Jesus	28–30
The Christian Church	
The Apostolic Age	30–150

(Many dates are approximate.)

*When we read the early parts of the Hebrew Bible, it is important that we position ourselves imaginatively with its editors in the fifth century B.C. The editors of the Hebrew Bible looked back to the origins of the people called Israel — and of the universe itself. Traditional stories were collected. Narratives described the story of Israel, with a viewpoint determined by the doctrine that they were the Chosen, covenant people of God (Yahweh). Judaism is the religion of the postexilic community, beginning with Ezra. The Torah is the first five books, ascribed to Moses.

The actual writing of many of the important documents probably began during the reigns of kings David and Solomon, soon after 1000 B.C., and ended at the close of the Christian Apostolic Age about A.D. 140 or 150. There is much imaginative literature that is based on very ancient tales that were passed on orally. Some of it looks back to the very beginning, the creation of the universe; some of it points forward to the end of time. It is interesting material, on the whole, requiring imaginative reading. To set it within the context of the ancient Middle East, from the Gulf to Egypt, maps are very useful. The eight maps in this book provide a graphic summary of the whole story. You will see that they have been prepared by an artist, not a cartographer. They are impressionistic. So too the designs. The drawings reflect ancient charts and works of art, some of which are identified briefly in the captions.

Although the Bible is, of course, a religious anthology still sacred to millions of people and canonical to churches (that is, authoritative for doctrine and ethics), it helps to remember that it is all the product of people very like ourselves. The setting is the secular world, where Israel and the Church lived, agonized and faced serious problems. In that secular order, people had to work, farm, trade, make war or peace and raise families.

V

Two problems about linguistic usage

Before we proceed further, it may be well to deal with some points that need to be clarified about references to the Deity and about the definition of "myth."

God-language

Typical biblical expressions about God include:

Δ "The Lord is the everlasting God, the Creator of the ends of the earth. He does not faint or grow weary."[1]

Opening the Scriptures

Δ "For the Lord is a great God, and a great King above all gods."[2]

Δ "When Israel was a child, then I loved him, and called my son out of Egypt ... for I am God, and not man."[3]

Δ They broke "the covenant that I made with their ancestors ... though I was their husband, says the Lord."[4]

Δ "When you pray, say: 'Father, hallowed be your name....'"[5]

From such passages it is clear that the writers were accustomed to employ masculine images in reference to God: he is Lord, King, Husband, Father. The writing originally came from the ancient societies of Israel and the Church which, being patriarchal in structure, gave women a subordinate role. To accommodate a more contemporary view of women's place, some of the most recent translations have tried to avoid sexist usage even if it meant making minor changes or additions to the original. Although there is good reason for change, it does the biblical authors an injustice if we radically alter their texts. For reasons that are important, especially in the case of Israel, it would be wrong to use feminine images for the God of Israel who is also God the Father celebrated in the Church. The original writing needs to be placed in its historical context.

The priests and prophets of Yahweh had to struggle for centuries against the infidelity of Israel itself. Despite its "covenant" to serve Yahweh only, the people frequented shrines of other deities. Those deities were both female and male. Leaders of the cult of Yahweh abhorred them all, but especially the female, for goddesses in the Canaanite and Middle Eastern world were often very influential and were associated with rituals such as those related to royal coronations. The embodiment of the deity was a cult-prostitute with whom worshippers had sexual intercourse. There were similar rituals in the worship of a fertility-goddess (among

Canaanites, it was Ashtoreth[6]) whose blessing was requested for fertile fields or fertile wives.

To separate the new cult of Yahweh from those of the other deities, feminine elements in the godhead tended to be played down and often eliminated. This was the case even though theology, both in Israel and in the Church, laid tremendous emphasis on God as lover and occasionally on Yahweh as husband. In the New Testament, Paul wrote that "anyone united to the Lord becomes one spirit with him."[7] In that verse the word for "united" in the original Greek is a verb used for sexual intercourse. It was audacious language to use about communion with the divine Redeemer. Yet Paul and early Christians in most areas would never call God or a Person of the Holy Trinity "Mother" or "Wife."

Hence, in this book, I use masculine nouns and pronouns, following the biblical usage. It may be helpful to keep in mind that our language about God has to be figurative because God is not a man, even if masculine idioms are to be found in discussions about God. The gender of the images that are employed is not a reflection of the essence of God but rather a product of the historical context of the original writing.

Myths and the mythological

Although language about God may be masculine in form, it is human language, for God does not "speak" Hebrew or Greek, English or French. When we use *speak*, it is to convey the religious experience of God's somehow communicating with responsive human beings. His spirit meets our human spirit. Insight, not physical sight, is appropriate to an encounter with the invisible Divine. Spiritual listening and attention, not physical hearing, are appropriate encounters with the Divine, who is best described in personal terms.

That is why our ways of speaking and writing about God have to include myths. The adjective that I use in this connection is mythological, though some continue to use mythical. Many people think that if something is mythical, it is untrue, false, not be taken seriously. But myths have to be taken seriously, for they are indispensable. God and the eternal world are beyond rational definition, so we need to fashion verbal clothes that are familiar to human life. Although words are inadequate, the inexpressible has somehow to be expressed. One must say something so as not to say nothing. The linguistic form of a myth has a sacramental relationship to a truth or truths that lie hidden in the mythological story. The outward and visible part is human, temporal, earthly; the truth to be uncovered is divine, eternal, heavenly.

The most famous myth in the Bible is the story of God's creating Adam and Eve in the beginning and setting them in a garden, Eden.[8]

For many it is a hallowed story, with profound spiritual perceptions about the origin and destiny of humanity and about our responsibility to the Creator and his will. It is also about temptation and the ease with which one may disobey that divine will. The myth and its sequel show the terrible legacy, known as "the Fall," that results from disobedience.

A myth in literature is a species of fiction, so that one reads it like a novel. The characters were invented by early poets and seers who tried in this way to explain the origins of sin, death and life. That is why the story of the first human pair and a talking serpent in the Garden of Eden is not to be read as if it were a historical documentary. No one recorded the beginnings. There was neither video nor CD — only an imaginative narrative that calls for our own imaginative response to the beliefs enshrined in it about the reality of a Creator-God and the inescapable duty of men and women to serve that Creator. It is the poetry of faith.

two

Beginnings: Genesis 1–11

I
The writings and the stories

As we start out on the journey that will take us to the final pages of the Bible, we can look at the beginnings that are the subject of the first eleven chapters in Genesis.

For the editors of the Hebrew Bible, Genesis was part of the prologue to the rise of the nation known as Israel. Israel did not emerge far back at creation or in the epic history of peoples in the Mesopotamian homeland. It did come out of that larger context, but its existence was realized in the tenth century B.C. with the call of Saul to be prince and war-leader and with his great successor, David.

Before the tenth century, the ancestors of Israel are linked to a patriarch who was called Abram or Abraham and more nearly to a remarkable man called Jacob (reported in the Bible to be Abraham's grandson). Jacob was given the new name "Israel" as a result of his encounters with God.[1] The edited story relates the adventures of Abraham, Isaac and Jacob. It tells why and how the family of Jacob entered Egypt, where

Joseph miraculously rose to one of the highest government posts. But then, some time after Joseph's death, the Jacob-people were enslaved by the Egyptians. Their liberation is ascribed to Moses, inspired by God, and is still celebrated by Jews each spring at Passover.

We are told in the book of Exodus that an epoch-making experience near Mount Sinai began to transform the ex-slaves into a real community. After several years, they joined with relatives and allies so that gradually they became a dominant factor in the land of Canaan, the land of promise. From about 1240 to 1020 B.C., Israelites were often at war with their neighbours, especially the Philistines on the coast. Israel was becoming a nation-state. Saul and David mark a decisive turning point in the process. The rest is history!

After Solomon, David's son, the kingdom was split in two. By 587 B.C., the two kingdoms of Israel and Judah had been destroyed, Israel by Assyrians and Judah by Babylonians. Not long after those disasters, in the aftermath of the Exile and restoration of some of the nation, the priests and lawmakers combined the five books of Moses, known as the Pentateuch, with a collection of prophecies to produce a sacred and authoritative Bible. By this time, Israel was what I describe as an ecclesiastical republic. Its name was Judea; its people were Judeans, from which they came to be known in other languages as "Jews."

II

Four stories from the earliest times

There are four stories dealing with humanity's beginnings on earth. The first tells how a human being *(adam)* was first created out of the dust of the ground *(adamah)*. Then a garden was planted, and the man became its gardener. To prevent his being lonely, the Creator fashioned a helper *(ezer)* from the man himself, whom Adam calls "woman" *(isha)*. Adam was then known as *ish*, a male, the husband of mother Eve.[2] This is not so demeaning to women as some today would have us believe. The myth implies that sex was devised by the Creator and must be good in itself. Men and women are to be partners for their mutual benefit.

Eden contained many trees, including two very special ones: the tree of life and the tree of the knowledge of good and evil. Presumably the fruit of the former would lead to more and more life, and the fruit of the latter to more wisdom and moral insight. But the fruit of the second tree was forbidden to the human pair, and terrible consequences followed after the serpent (whose place is never explained) tempted the woman to eat and the man followed her lead. When they were found out, cowardly Adam blamed Eve, while Eve blamed the serpent. That is a pattern of excuse familiar even today! Adam and Eve, the myth says, were driven out of the garden because of their disobedience. They had aspired to be godlike. Henceforth human life must be lived "outside of Eden," in disgrace.[3]

The second story is the account of a disgraceful episode in which Cain, the son of Adam and Eve, killed his brother Abel. Cain was not put to death for this crime, but was sent out to wander as a fugitive, bearing a mark that warned of a terrible vengeance if anyone were to murder him.[4]

Next we have a story that is familiar all over the world. Wickedness was so widespread that the Creator lost patience and resolved to destroy the earth in a universal flood.[5] Nevertheless, he recognized that one man, Noah, was a decent fellow. Noah, his family and representatives of the other creatures were allowed to survive in an ark. In the new age that followed, God set a rainbow in the sky to be a sign to humanity that never again would there be the disaster of a universal flood. "Seedtime and harvest, and cold and heat, and summer and winter, and day and night, shall not cease."[6] This promise by God may be called an "alliance." It was an agreement based on divine kindness, without specific conditions, though they may be implied.

After the flood, special powers were granted to human beings over the other creatures: "And the fear of you and the dread of you shall be upon every beast of the earth ... even as

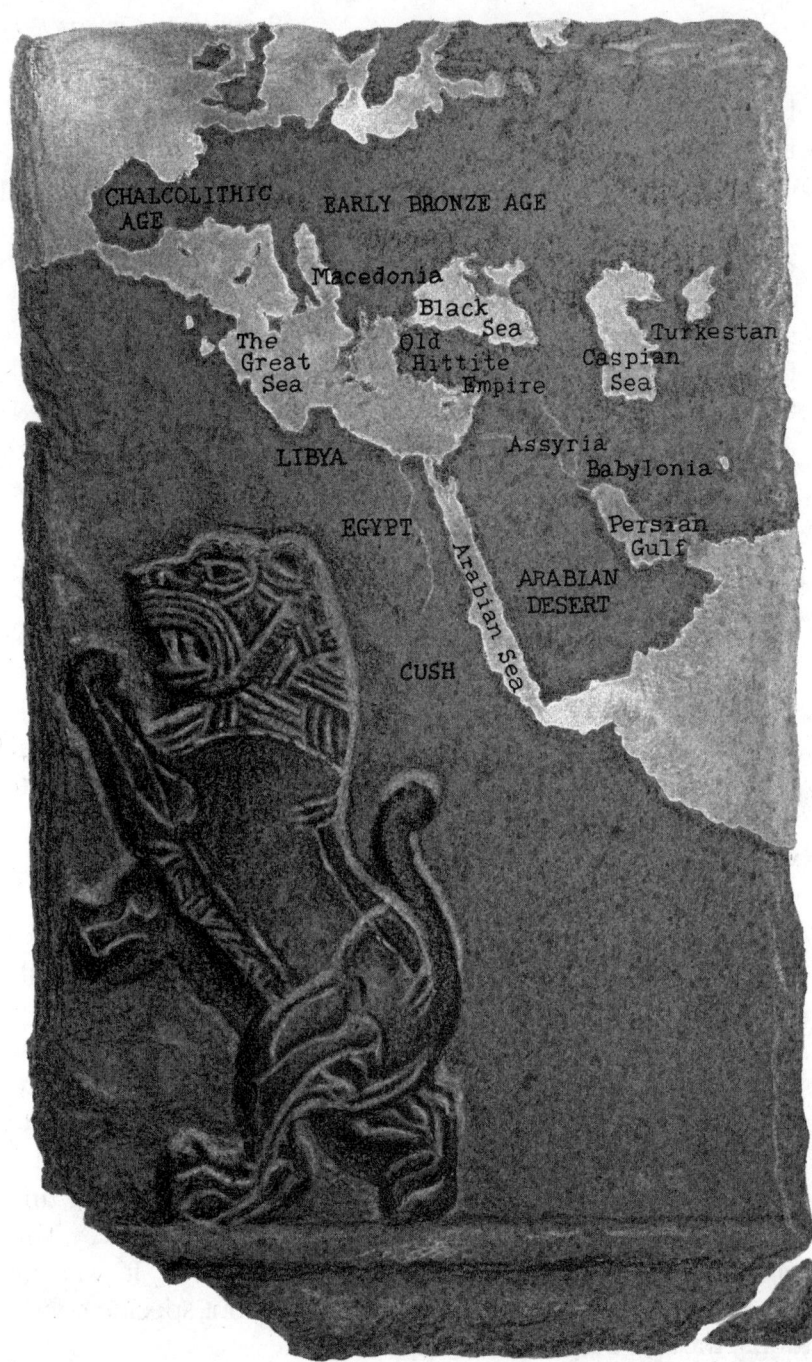

The World of the Patriarchs

The ancient world had regions rather than boundaries as we know them. The fiercesome lion design is from a ninth-century B.C. palace carving in stone.

the green herb have I given you all things ... be ye fruitful, and multiply; bring forth abundantly in the earth, and multiply therein."[7] These ideas are not acceptable in our own time to those who worry about ecology and the environment, and we must acknowledge that the earth is the Lord's. Human beings live in it by his permissive will, and they ought to be responsible stewards.

The fourth story, about the Tower of Babel, has to be compared to Genesis 10:5 where we read that each of the families descended from Noah had its own language. The Babel legend, however, assumes that originally there was one language for everyone. In this story, the people built a city and a tower that aimed to reach the sky (or heaven). The tower was probably modelled on the ziggurat, a mountain built by ancient Mesopotamians with a shrine at the top where they enacted rituals to link the earth to the abode of the gods. The building offended the divine beings: they felt attacked. So, to keep humanity from becoming too powerful, the tower was destroyed and communication among people was confused by different languages.[8]

Of course, linguists today would not agree that the variety of languages originated like that. It does not matter. The legend makes a powerful point about ambitious pride and the dire results that can follow when people live outside Eden, disobeying their Creator.

In the world's beginning, people were grouped under the three sons of Noah: Shem, Ham and Japheth.[9] At the end of this section of Genesis, we see that Abram's family was descended from Shem. From Abram, we can trace the origin of the people of Israel.

III

The later creation story

Before we trace the origin of the people of Israel, we have to backtrack to a second and much later story about the creation of the universe and humanity found in Genesis 1:1 to 2:3. It may have emerged from the editorial team in the fifth century that produced the Torah and the Prophets, the first authoritative written scripture for early Judaism.

In this story, creation happened when God spoke. First light came, with day and night; then the heavens appeared, separated from the flat earth below. Next the seas, vegetation and the many kinds of creatures emerged. And at last, on the sixth day, man and woman were created in the image and likeness of God himself. Here woman, too, was made in the divine likeness: the two sexes have equal roles in the ordering of life on earth. The seventh day was the sabbath of God, a day of rest.

IV
Some spiritual lessons from Genesis 1–11

There are many spiritual lessons to be learned from Genesis 1–11:

Δ We learn that knowledge can be dangerous.

Δ We learn that people are obstinate. Even when prohibitions are made for their good, they experiment with evil "for the hell of it."

Δ We learn that evil breeds more evil. Yet Genesis does not give us theoretical or philosophical answers to questions such as "How did evil get into the garden?" or "Why was there a tempter?" In some ways, evil and sin remain mysterious to us.

Δ We learn that selfishness and pride lead to conflict. If Cain was the founder of city life, that is, of civilization, then culture rests on an unstable foundation.

Δ We learn that there is a mystery about the death of human beings. The myths and legends adapted into the Hebrew Bible suggest that because humanity's disobedience gave them knowledge of good and evil, a divine prerogative, the Creator banished them lest they should eat from the tree of life and become immortal. Death is said to result from sin.[10]

In *Wisdom of Solomon* 2:23–24, we find that a later teacher did not accept this view but affirmed that "God created man to be immortal, and made him to be an image of his own eternity. Nevertheless through envy of the devil came death into the world." (There is a Christian comment in Paul's epistle to the Romans, 5:14–21). Both Jews and Christians believed that humanity had to be liberated from the powers of evil and redeemed for eternal life with the God who creates, loves and saves his people.

Although with today's medical advances it may seem that human beings are programmed to live to be a hundred, death is still inevitable. In many circumstances, it is to be welcomed as the divine ordering for the climax to life on earth. Even so, many people continue to fear death, which often occurs in distressing circumstances. In scripture, there are no theoretical answers to questions of life and death, nor were any intended. More important to the editors of Genesis was the desire to keep alive their faith in one God, the Creator, the God who is Providence, who had been revealed to them in the history of their nation and in the records of faith that became their sacred and authoritative scripture.

three

Patriarchal Legends: Genesis 12–50

I

Tales of long ago

Harvest thanksgivings are great occasions, not only for those lands where the climate is balmy and nature is bountiful but more especially and paradoxically for lands, like Palestine (also called Canaan), that combine fertile lowlands with rocky and mountainous uplands. At their harvest festival, the Israelites remembered a time when their ancestors had not lived in Palestine. "A wandering Aramean was my ancestor," they declared in an old ritual, apparently referring to nomadic and seminomadic migrations by their forebears.[1] Even though archaeological evidence cannot corroborate these migrations, we shall still follow the literary tradition found in Genesis.[2]

Imagine the children and young people listening to the heroic saga of the migrants on many different occasions: during siestas, around the camp fire and at oasis stops. The seers, teachers and priests would be the storytellers, and what they told animated the faithful to survive times of crisis and to celebrate the occasions of joy. Those honoured in the tales would include Abraham and Sarah, Isaac and Rebekah, Jacob and Rachel, and Joseph and Benjamin. The telling served to keep the memory of the ancestors alive and remind the people of the duty owed to the ancestral God.

II

Abraham: number one patriarch

The patriarch Abraham dominates many of the tales. Perhaps the first motif remembered about him was his covenant with God[3] and the circumcision ritual that made every small boy a member of Abraham's extended family.[4] Covenants are treaties or agreements in which two parties assume mutual obligations. In this case, on the human side, total obedience to God's commandments was promised. On the divine side, a monumental promise was made of which there are several versions.[5]

Even though Abraham's wife Sarah was barren, they were guaranteed children and innumerable descendants. They were also promised that the land between the rivers Nile and Euphrates would be their homeland forever, and through their offspring all the nations of the earth would be divinely blessed. In due course the promised son, Isaac, was born. Repetitions are common in the saga. Sometimes this is a result of using diverse sources, all precious and maybe sacred; sometimes the point is to emphasize the material.

Abraham is remembered too for the audacity wed to humility he displayed in "conversations" with God. God is reported as saying: "How great is the outcry over Sodom and Gomorrah! How grave their sin must be! I shall go down and see whether their deeds warrant the outcry reaching me. I must know the truth."[6] Abraham, whose nephew Lot lived in Sodom, realized that the people in the two cities were about to suffer dire punishment for their sin. So in the most daring manner, he interceded with God, who is the judge of all the earth and must therefore be just and not destroy the righteous along with the wicked. He proceeded to bargain. God agreed to spare a city with fifty decent folk in it. Then God accepted that forty would be enough. Abraham concluded: "Oh let not my Lord be angry, and I will speak yet but this once: Peradventure ten shall be found there. And [God] said, I will not destroy it for ten's sake."[7]

Alas, according to Genesis 19:24–25, God overthrew the two cities and all their inhabitants. Sodom became a byword for sexual vice. The editors of Genesis clearly labelled that vice as some form of homosexual rape, and one ought not to disguise that by suggesting, as some contemporaries do, that the sin of the Sodomites was merely lack of hospitality. Of course, a passage like this may not, of itself, settle the difficult questions about homosexual practice that are now in the public arena.

Perhaps the most memorable story about Abraham, yet for many a very distressing and difficult one, is the *Akedah* or Binding of Isaac, told in Genesis 22:1–14. Abraham was commanded to take Isaac, his beloved only son, the son of the Promise, and offer him on a mountain in the land of Moriah as a burnt offering: a human sacrifice.

Why did Abraham not question God as he had about Sodom: "Is this worthy of the Judge of all the earth? Of my God who made covenant with me?" True, the story highlights the obedience of Abraham, but was it blind obedience? Perhaps the story was intended to teach that in Israel human sacrifice was intolerable, for the account ends with Isaac's being spared when an angel appears and points to a ram to be substituted. The story has haunted the imagination of artists from Rembrandt to George Segal and provided them with subject matter. Segal's powerful sculpture, which depicts a modern Abraham, provoked tremendous controversy in Israel when it was unveiled in Tel Aviv in 1973. The tale of Abraham and Isaac remains one of the most moving stories among all the patriarchal legends and profoundly affects many people.

Abraham, however, is not depicted as a plaster saint. Twice, Abraham benefited by practising deceit about his beautiful wife Sarah, saying she was his sister. On one of these occasions, he excused his action by claiming that she was his half-sister (same father, different mother).[8]

To have a child, Abraham followed Sarah's suggestion and took his wife's Egyptian servant, Hagar, as concubine. But later, because of Sarah's complaint, he allowed Hagar and their son, Ishmael, to be banished into the wilderness where they might well have perished. They were saved, providentially, and Ishmaelites survived to become a great nation.[9] They are sometimes regarded as half-brothers and half-sisters of the Israelites, but their relation to Arabs, Bedouin and other Semitic families is unclear.

The stories of Abraham and Sarah have had great impact. The influence of the Hagar story, for example, can be seen in the important novel by Margaret Laurence, *The Stone Angel.*

The stories also raise questions about the land claim defined in the narratives. This claim arises from a revealed communication according to which the Israelites were promised the lands of the Kenites, Kenizzites, Kadmonites, Hittites, Perizzites, Rephaim, Amorites, Canaanites, Girgashites and Jebusites.[10] The revealed communication is basic to Israel's status as a distinct society in the Middle East. However, it is not clear how Israel was to occupy and enjoy the land of Canaan; were the other peoples living there simply to vacate the land? The land claim implied in the promise to Abraham (Genesis 15:18) appears to be a later Israelite party line, enacted by military conquest and sanctified by attributing it to a revelation by Israel's God. Accordingly, it must have been disputed in ancient times, and it will still be disputed in our own day.

III

Jacob: the supplanter who made good

Only sparse material in Genesis is devoted to Abraham's son, Isaac. This may be because of the relative insignificance of the shrine at Beersheba with which he appears to have been associated. So his story had little to offer the first collectors of the saga, or the later editors of the Torah, except as a plausible link between Abraham and Jacob.

Isaac was the father of Esau and Jacob. According to the

narrative Esau, the firstborn, was his father's favourite, while Jacob was his mother's. That situation contained the seeds of disaster. Jacob bargained for Esau's birthright in exchange for a mess of lentil soup.[11] Later, by conspiring with his mother, Jacob tricked old Isaac into giving him the blessing that was rightfully Esau's.[12] Etymologically, "Jacob" may enclose the meaning of "supplanter."

There is yet another tale of deception in the Jacob cycle. Fourteen or fifteen years later, Jacob was the husband of sisters Leah and Rachel. Jacob had twelve sons in all: six by Leah; two, Joseph and Benjamin, by his darling Rachel; another two by Leah's maid, Zilpah; and two more by Rachel's maid, Bilhah.[13] Only one daughter, named Dinah, is mentioned.[14] In Mesopotamia, Jacob and his huge entourage of people, cattle and sheep fell into disfavour with his father-in-law, Laban. So he planned to escape. Before they did, Rachel stole her father's *teraphim*, or household gods.[15] It is a merry tale and may seem to be unedifying, but the possession of household gods gave a son-in-law the right to inherit land and property, even if there was already a legitimate son as heir.

To some extent, the saga presents Jacob as a successful adventurer who prospered exceedingly. He was not allowed to get off scot-free, however. For it is equally significant that Jacob had at least three major religious experiences that transformed him. In these encounters with God in dreams and in a peculiar mystical battle, Jacob met himself. He discovered conscience and faced his own insufficiency, at least in a rather elementary fashion. Despite his youthful follies, he is depicted as a man of faith whose life was changed by the grace of God who blessed him.[16] He was not godless.

The first episode happened at Bethel, when Jacob was a fugitive from Esau whom he had hurt and offended. He dreamt of a ladder or ziggurat that reached from earth to heaven, and he bargained with God.[17] In his kindness, God granted Jacob the same promise as Abraham had received: that he and all his progeny would prosper. Jacob, in turn, vowed that if he escaped with his life and returned in peace to his home, he would give God a tithe of everything that he received.

The second encounter occurred on his way back from Laban's country, before he met his brother Esau again. At the brook Jabbok, Jacob "wrestled" with a man who turned out to be both an angel and God. "I have seen God face to face, and my life is preserved," said Jacob.[18] As daybreak came, the divine being fought to get away. But Jacob insisted on receiving a blessing first and was given one, although he failed to discover the name of his opponent. In the ancient world, knowing the secret name of a god gave one power. After this encounter, Jacob's name was altered to Israel.[19]

The third encounter may be a duplicate of the first. Jacob was met by God at Bethel, though in this version there is no reference to a dream nor to a ladder with angels ascending and descending. The Abrahamic promise was repeated and Jacob was again called Israel.[20]

Because he was called Israel, his descendants and the nation they created are also "Israel." Through him, they are all one person: Israel could be called the Seed of Abraham. This is a very Semitic and biblical way of describing the unity of a national community. Eventually this unity was transferred to Adam, which came to mean humanity, in an affirmation that all human beings belong to one family. That Adam is identified by Paul as Christ.[21]

The tale continues with the adventures of Jacob and Rachel's son Joseph, leading to the migration of Jacob's family, numbering sixty or seventy people,[22] to Egypt.

IV

Joseph — Rachel's son (Genesis 37–50)

The story of Joseph, son of the beloved Rachel and a favourite of his father Jacob, is remarkable for its tantalizing plot, pathos, reversals of fortune and comic ending.

The story begins when Joseph was seventeen. Jacob gave Joseph a long robe with sleeves (NRSV) or a tunic ornamented with long sleeves (the 1926 translation by James Moffatt). This display of favouritism resulted in Joseph's half-brothers hating him. The crisis came when Joseph told them of his dreams in which all his family and even the sun, moon and stars bowed before him.[23] What followed was a kidnapping.[24]

Joseph had been sent out to find his brothers, who had gone to Dothan shepherding Jacob's flocks. Seeing the dreamer coming, the brothers resolved to humiliate him. They took off his ornamental robe and dipped it in blood as proof to old Jacob that the lad had been killed by an evil beast. Jacob was devastated and, rejecting the sympathy of all his children, wept sorely for his lost son. "Surely he is torn in pieces; and I saw him not since."[25] Joseph was not killed, however. The brothers threw him into a pit and later sold him as a slave to a passing caravan of Midianites.

The next episode in Joseph's adventures finds him sold again, this time to an official or priest in Egypt called Potiphar. There he was successful in the administration of Potiphar's household and business affairs. He drew the attention of Potiphar's mistress who tried, but failed, to seduce him. Finally, in frustration, she falsely accused Joseph of rape, and he was jailed.[26]

In jail he was well treated, for God seemed to bless him specially: he had the gift of interpreting the dreams of others. First, he correctly interpreted the fate of his fellow prisoners: the emperor's butler and baker. Then he interpreted for the emperor (Pharaoh) himself. He prophesied and planned for seven good harvests that would be followed by seven bad ones, causing terrible hardships in Egypt and neighbouring lands. As a result of his abilities, he was released to serve in the royal administration.

In the exercise of his new power, Joseph proved to be something of an autocrat and, in the interests of his royal master, a clever exploiter of distress.[27] The next part of the story deals with the effect of the famine in Canaan.

Jacob was forced to send ten of his sons to buy grain in Egypt. He kept Benjamin at home, fearing that he would come to harm as Joseph presumably had. In Egypt, the brothers had to deal with a haughty and powerful administrator they did not recognize as Joseph. Although he recognized them, he accused them of lying about their situation and insisted that they come again and bring his full brother Benjamin to prove their story. After they returned to Egypt, Joseph could not refrain from identifying himself. The scene in which this occurs is a very moving piece of writing.[28] The lost son was found. The naive youth had become, after the Pharaoh himself, the most powerful person in Egypt. Joseph's whole family was brought to Egypt where old Jacob was cosseted and, not much later, died peacefully. The story of the patriarchs as told in the book of Genesis ends with Joseph and his brothers highly regarded in the empire of Egypt.

It is not left without a moral. Joseph sums up the events when he speaks to his brothers: "God sent me before you to preserve you a posterity in the earth, and to save your lives by a great deliverance.... Ye thought evil against me; but God meant it unto good, to bring to pass, as it is this day, to save much people alive."[29]

V
Human life in the light of eternity

In summarizing Genesis, there are a few points to consider. In the myth of Eden and in the more sophisticated first chapter, Adam can be taken as a symbolic prototype, first for humanity and then for the male. Eve is the generic female, wife and mother. In the later social development of Israel, some priority and superiority were assigned to men. Any doctrine arising from that context that places women in an inferior position to men can be set in an historical context. Unless it is thought that such a view is the actual revelation of the Creator's intention, we need not commit ourselves to that patriarchal attitude.

Genesis also describes how human beings can be tempted to disobey the Creator's will, and it may be implied that the pattern of the first Fall is typical. It is a universal fact, many would claim, that human beings are not able to resist the forces of evil. They tend to become proud, greedy, contentious and exploitive, not only of other creatures and earth itself but also of one another. It seems as if might, not meekness, is right. Self-assertion is more typical than unselfish service to others. It must be said, however, that though temptation is inescapable, one should not assume that it is inevitable that people should yield.

In the Genesis saga, we read of people on their travels seeking a land of promise, stability and prosperity. Even if much of the saga consists of myth and legend, there is a great deal that rings true not merely to the experience of the people who came to be called by Jacob's new name, Israel, but to the life circumstances of all humanity.

Genesis in particular, and the scriptures as a whole, perceive human life in the light of eternity and of the divine. The central doctrine points to a wise and caring Providence. That doctrine may commend this material to men and women as they live through a major transition in world affairs.

four

Exodus: The Escape of Israel from Egypt

I

The liberation story

Happy days in Egypt for the family of Joseph and his relatives lasted for a considerable time, though we do not know specific dates. Then a Pharaoh arose "who knew not Joseph."[1] The presence of the Hebrew aliens provoked antagonism that resulted in their enslavement. The conditions were pitiful, and the heavens echoed with their cries to God for redress.

The story of how Israel escaped from Egypt emerged as fundamentally important after the nation had become secure in its own territory and teachers and priests in the Second Temple era edited the traditions into sacred scripture. As heirs of that Jewish tradition, Christians too have always understood the special significance of the themes in the book called Exodus: liberation, covenant, pilgrimage and the creation of a nation. These themes can be applied to the life situation of individuals as well as groups. At the heart of the liberation story are Exodus 1–3, 12–15 and 19–34 and Deuteronomy 5, 6 and 33.

The call of Moses

We begin with the romantic story of a Hebrew baby who was saved from an Egyptian death decree by being hidden in an ark of bulrushes and laid among the reeds on a riverbank. An Egyptian princess found him, took him home to be a prince and gave him an Egyptian name, "Moses." His own mother was brought in to be his nurse.[2]

By and by, Moses discovered his Hebrew birth. When he killed an Egyptian who was assaulting a Hebrew, he was forced to flee to the land of Midian. There he became a shepherd to Reuel (or Jethro), whose daughter Zipporah he married. All this time Providence cared for him. One day Moses encountered the divine Presence. He saw a bush that seemed to be on fire "and yet it was not consumed."[3] On that sacred ground he "heard" the divine voice, was told to liberate Israel, and was taught that the God he had encountered was the ancestral God of the patriarchs Abraham, Isaac and Jacob.

Though reluctant, Moses, aided by his brother Aaron, faced the Pharaoh and demanded that the people of Israel should be freed so that they could worship their God "in the wilderness." The Pharaoh refused.[4] He rejected the demand repeatedly in spite of disasters that the Hebrew leaders said were divine punishment for his stubborn refusal. The worst disaster was the last, and it produced results. The Pharaoh was told that the God of Israel would pass through Egypt one night and smite all the firstborn in the land, both human and animal. The gods of Egypt would utterly fail to prevent the slaughter.[5]

All the Hebrews were assembled and led out by Moses, Aaron and their sister Miriam. They crossed the sea of reeds without getting wet because their God worked a great miracle. When the Egyptian warriors and chariots tried to follow, the waters rushed back and drowned them. Israel had escaped. Their liberation had begun and they sang for joy.[6]

Rembrandt (1606 –1669), *Moses with the Tables of the Law*, 1659. Berlin, State Museums.

Rembrandt is possibly the greatest illustrator of biblical material. Rembrandt's Moses pictures well his image as the "First Redeemer," the intermediary through whom Yahweh enacted the covenant with Israel, fulfilling earlier promises to Abraham and Jacob. He is the leader who has been venerated as the source — and traditionally, but wrongly, as the author — of the sacred canon of the Torah or Pentateuch (Genesis to Deuteronomy).

Moses is represented as mediator of the *torah* (the Law) communicated to him by Yahweh on Mount Sinai. The second Table, seen here, contained regulations for the morality of Israel as the "chosen" nation. The first Table affirmed Yahweh's sole sovereignty over Israel and warned against every sort of idolatry and blasphemy (see Exodus 20:1–17, 31:18).

It is sometimes thought that Moses is about to break the tablets because of Israel's worship of the Golden Calf (Exodus 32:15, 32:19, 34:1).

Reproduced by courtesy of Gemäldegalerie Staatliche Museen Preußischer Kulturbesitz, Berlin.

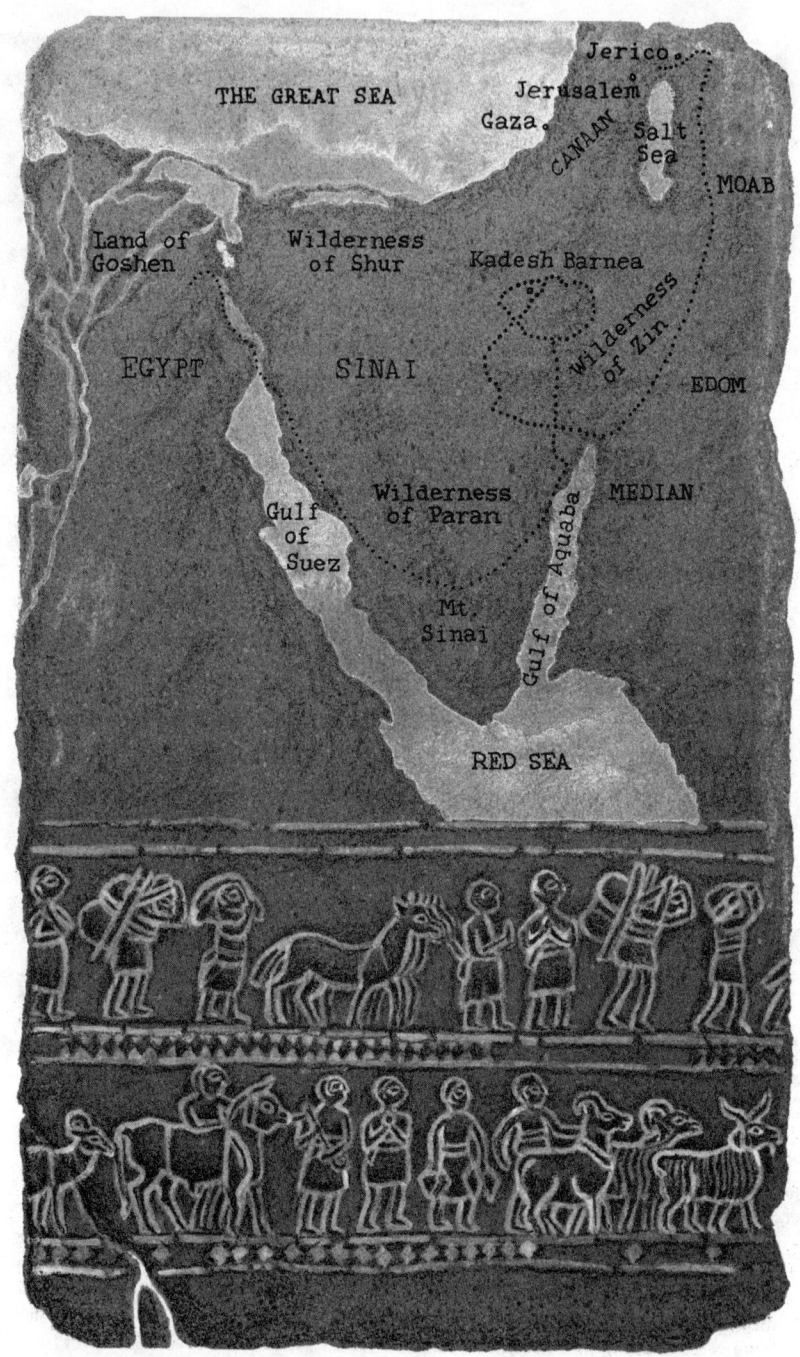

The Exodus from Egypt

Migrations of people make their way through geographic and other obstacles. From the royal tomb of Ur, about 2500 B.C., we drew these images of mass movements.

Passover

According to the Exodus story, the Israelites were commanded to prepare for liberation on the night that the divine agent would slay the firstborn of Egypt. They were to mark their doorposts specially. Then with "their loins girded, sandals on their feet, staff in hand"[7] and eating in haste, they were to feast on unblemished lambs. This became the annual Jewish celebration called Passover. Moses gave specific instructions to the head of the household for the Passover meal: "And it shall be when thy son asketh thee in time to come, saying, what is this? that thou shalt say unto him, By strength of hand the Lord brought us out from Egypt ... This is done because of that which the Lord did unto me when I came forth out of Egypt."[8] The story of the escape is repeated each year in terms of "me" and "us." What happened in 1280 B.C. (the date of the Exodus, in my view) continues to happen for each succeeding generation as the liberation is remembered.

II

Memory and hope

It is a distinguishing characteristic of people that we live simultaneously in the *present*, the *past* and the *future*. Our *present* always includes a living past. Memories of the past are linked to hopes for the future as the present becomes the future. The liturgy of worship and commemorative religious festivals play a special role in helping people to connect both with their past and with their future.

Comment: The name of God revealed to Moses (Exodus 3:14)

We will digress here to consider the name of God revealed to Moses. The name consists of four Hebrew consonants rendered as YHWH or JHVH, to which at a much later time the vowels suited to the word "Lord" or "my Lord" were attached, because the name was too sacred to be uttered aloud. Originally the form may have been *Jah* as in the word *Hallelujah*, "praise ye Jah." Today, opinion has settled on Yahweh or Jahveh. The familiar "Jehovah" is regarded as an earlier and now outmoded attempt to render the word. I prefer the form Yahweh.

Its derivation may be from the verb *to be*: so either, "I go on being", "I am the Eternal"; or alternatively, "I cause to be", "I am the Creator." Older names for the God worshipped by the patriarchs at different shrines in Israel are found in scripture. It is interesting that the Jewish people have maintained such a profound reverence for the name of God that they will not pronounce it. It is potent with authority, power and holiness. God is thought of as a transcendent and awe-inspiring reality, both apart from and closely concerned with the life of men and women.

The use of the name is significant. Prophecy, if it was genuine, was delivered in the name of Yahweh.[9] Blessings were bestowed in that name.[10] Oaths were taken in the name of Yahweh.[11] Sometimes "the Name" appears in place of "Yahweh" or "God," as if the divine Name lived in a temple, a city or a person.[12] One of the psalmists sums up the faith of Israel: "Thy name, O Lord, endureth for ever; and thy memorial, O Lord, throughout all generations."[13]

III

The covenant at Mount Sinai

After the crossing of the sea of reeds, the refugees, probably consisting of the clans connected with Joseph and Levites like Moses and his family,[14] made their way to a sacred mountain, Horeb or Sinai. There, amid strange and alarming indications of the divine presence, they awaited instruction about their duty in the service of the God Yahweh. Instruction is *torah*, which since it came from God in numinous encounters may also be translated as *revelation*. Moses, it is said in Exodus, was the chosen mediator of this *torah* from Yahweh. It came to the people in the form of commandments, and there are several traditions about the exact content.

We find ten prohibitions in Exodus 20:1–17 and Deuteronomy 5:6–21. But at Exodus 34:11–26, there seem to be four negative and five positive injunctions. What happened, I think, is that as time went on, the religion we know as Yahwism continued to define and refine the regulations for maintaining the covenant, or *berith*, with Yahweh. To be witness to his wisdom, power and grace, Israel had to remain distinct from other nations. Many efforts have been made to produce the earliest possible form of the Ten Words, as the teachers defined the Commandments. The best I know follows:

The First Table of the Law:
1. No images were to be set up in a shrine, so as to be certain that God would be present there spiritually.
2. No worship of idols that represented other gods was permitted.
3. No serving of other gods was to be tolerated.
4. No unnecessary oaths in the Name of Yahweh were to be uttered.
5. No working on the Sabbath was allowed.

The Second Table of the Law, dealing with morality:
6. No killing was allowed where the right of asylum was not possible.
7. No sexual violence was to be done.
8. No stealing (or kidnapping) was permitted.
9. No false accusations were to be brought against a neighbour.
10. No seizure of a neighbour's house was allowed.[15]

By combining 2 and 3 in the above list, one can add as the fifth commandment, "Honour thy father and thy mother."[16]

It may be of interest that the Ten Words (as they are known in Judaism) comprise two "handfuls," two fives. In Celtic and other ancient lore five represents a whole. Hence, here is a double wholeness: five about service to God, five about social ethics. The religion of Israel is distinct in linking ethics to worship in this way. There is no philosophical system about duty, about right and wrong, about sanctions imposed for breach of the law. The regulations in this Sinai covenant are theological, originating from God himself and received by his servant Moses. The Hebrew Bible presents law differently from our own civil codes or common law systems. The covenant is a gift from the Lord who cares for his people.

The biblical law is less like a commercial transaction or contract than it is like the agreements built into a marriage ceremony. Love defines the duties of each partner as a matter of grace and favour. Human beings, being what they are, however, still require legal sanctions to warn of the consequences of failure. In the prophetic literature, Israel's failure to obey the law of God is compared to sexual offence: idolatry is a form of immorality. The sacred marriage of Yahweh and Israel is tarnished by serving idols and by social injustice.

Comment: *The Second Law — Deuteronomy*

Besides the legal sections found in Exodus, Leviticus and Numbers, there is a second major compilation in Deuteronomy. It is composed chiefly of speeches and sermons given by Moses and also mentions his death.[17] A famous passage from it is sometimes called the Creed of Israel. It begins with the Hebrew word *shema'*, meaning hear or listen.

> *"Hear, Israel: the Lord is our God, the Lord our one God; and you must love the Lord your God with all your heart and with all your soul and with all your strength. These commandments which I give you this day are to be remembered and taken to heart; repeat them to your children, and speak of them both indoors and out of doors, when you lie down and when you get up. Bind them as a sign on your hand and wear them as a pendant on your forehead; write them on the doorposts of your houses and on your gates."*[18]

There is also a famous prophecy about a future time of blessing. God said, "I will put my law in their inward parts, and write it in their hearts; and will be their God, and they shall be my people."[19] In the Second Law, too, there is a promise of a future prophet like Moses.[20] This has become more interesting because of passages in the Dead Sea Scrolls of the Qumrân Community. A reference there to the Moses-like prophet in the "Messianic Anthology"[21] is echoed in John

6:14 and Acts 3:22–23 in the New Testament which refer to Jesus as "the Prophet who was to come into the world." Acts 3:22–23 explicitly quotes Deuteronomy 18:15 about that prophet. Therefore, some people think that Jesus was regarded as the new Moses, the promised messianic Prophet.

In whole or in part, Deuteronomy is identified nowadays with the Book of the Law found in the Jerusalem Temple area by the high priest Hilkiah about 622 B.C. According to 2 Kings 22–23, this book led to a reformation in the kingdom of Judah and a covenant-renewal ceremony led by the king, Josiah.

IV

Pilgrims of faith

The people who had escaped from Egypt and set their sights on the new world, the land of promise, may be described as pilgrims of faith. They may have stayed for a long time at a place called Kadesh-barnea.[22] Traditional stories, found in several chapters of the book of Numbers, tell how Israel wandered for many years in the wilderness. From this period of wandering come a number of stories.

One of these is a poignant tale of how the people, feeling abandoned by Moses when he was on the sacred mountain for forty days and forty nights, compelled Aaron to produce an idol in the form of a golden bull, typical of some Canaanite cults. Moses was incensed and smashed the tables on which the Ten Words were inscribed. Yet Moses interceded for Israel with Yahweh. He received a second version of the *torah* and assurance that Yahweh would journey with his people to the Promised Land. It is a remarkable doctrine: the God of Israel was a fellow-traveller, a constant presence, a God who would shelter his wandering people by day and lighten their way by night.[23] This is a God who heard the cries of men and women, who came down, and who did something about the plight of his chosen ones, even though they were often disobedient.

It is doubtful that as many as six hundred thousand men plus their womenfolk and children (as Exodus 12:37 [REB] claims) arrived in the promised land. Nor is it possible that everything now found in Exodus 20–24 and 34 can be assigned to a sojourn in the wilderness of Sinai. The regulations apply to a settled agricultural nation and so came from an era much later than that of Moses. Parts, however, may be traced to his leadership. His contribution to the group was unquestionably remarkable.

Liberation can be conceived in secular terms as national or group freedom or in religious terms as salvation from bondage to the powers of evil and sin in the past, hope for the divine pardon and longing for a heavenly home with God in the world to come. In ancient Israel, secular and religious ideas of liberation were combined.

The themes of liberation and wilderness wandering have proved very powerful in the imagination and struggles of different groups of men and women. The English Pilgrims escaped to the new world of North America, seeking freedom from the tyranny of royal regimes and church establishment. Many of them carried the texts about Israel's pilgrimage. They used biblical names for their offspring and for the names of settlements in the New England wilderness and, later, all across the United States. In literature, the most significant use of the pilgrim motif is John Bunyan's *Pilgrim's Progress* (published in 1678). It was not difficult for Bunyan or for Christians in general to connect their discipleship as individuals and as congregations with the distant experiences of old Israel. For they were themselves members of a "New Israel," and for them the Hebrew Bible had become part of the Christian Bible.

These same themes have continued to exert an astonishing influence in the emancipation of slaves in North America and the development of their faith in God through Christ. As Mark A. Noll has written, "Blacks sang about Adam, Eve, and the Fall, about 'wrestlin' Jacob' who 'would not let God go', about Moses 'going down' to Egypt, about Joshua possessing the Promised Land.... The stories of the Old Testament in particular lent slave use of the bible its special social dimension. For slaves, the figure of Moses loomed especially large as the one raised up by God to free his people."[24]

Another image from the wilderness story of Israel is the "highway" or "way." In Second Isaiah, it is used when Yahweh clears "a way in the wilderness, and rivers in the desert,"[25] making possible the trek of the exiles home to Judea. Similarly, the appearance and mission of John the Baptist is foretold: "In the wilderness prepare the way of the Lord, make straight in the desert a highway for our God."[26] The image was also applied by the people of the Dead Sea Scrolls to their own vocation. The "way" has become a symbol about human life, playing a part in art, literature, religion and ethics in many lands over the centuries.

V

An ever-present God

Another theme was taken from the Exodus narratives by some of the New England Congregationalists and given preeminence in the organization of both religious and secular life. It was the notion of "covenant," the agreement between God and his elect people, which also bound the people together as members within the same covenant relationship. Some interpreters have held that we should read the Hebrew Bible with that concept as the central theme, watching to see the rise and fall of Israelite fidelity. That focus, though, is debatable, even though it is clear that the Ten Commandments, as a primary clause in the covenant, have continued to be central in Israel's understanding of its moral duty.

An attractive alternative is to focus on the proclamation of Israel's God revealed to Moses and mediated through him to the nation in the generations that followed. The *torah*, as edited in the Pentateuch or Five Books of Moses, is instruction or revelation about the living God who is creator, redeemer and guide. He is forever a present reality, Israel's teachers said, a very present help in time of travel. As the psalmist sang, "The Lord is my shepherd; I shall not want."[27]

It can be argued that ancient Israel as represented by its seers, saints and prophets had eyes for invisible facts. In the New Testament, it is said of Moses that he was "resolute, as one who saw the invisible God."[28] Israel therefore challenged the rest of humanity to see what Moses saw and to hear what he heard: communications or revelations that can make life new, set people free from slavery to the past and inspire the faithful to do great things for one another and thus for God himself.[29]

"Hearing" and "sight" of that kind make a useful definition of "faith." The Hebrew Bible, then, is a testimony to faith, one might say a multiform parable. Readers are to look and listen for divine realities and, through faith, to confront the chances and changes of the world.

By faithful adherence to the *torah* of Yahweh mediated by Moses, the refugees in the wilderness would have been on the way to becoming the people Yahweh destined them to be: "Now therefore, if ye will obey my voice indeed, and keep my covenant, then ye shall be a peculiar treasure unto me above all people: for all the earth is mine. And ye shall be unto me a kingdom of priests, and an holy nation."[30]

So Israel could fulfil the promise made to Abraham and Jacob that their descendants would be a blessing to nations. Certainly during the centuries since the rescue of Israel from Egyptian slavery and their dedication to Yahweh at Mount Sinai, this people has in many ways proved a blessing: in religious teaching and liturgy; in music, literature and the arts; and in the heroic acceptance of terrible suffering.

At the close of the book of Exodus, however, the refugees in the desert were far from having become an organized national society. They had still to reach the Jordan River and cross over into Canaan. The conquest of the new land and the growth of a nation-state lay in the future. It is to that story that we now turn.

five

Spirited Personalities in a Turbulent Age

I

From Joshua to Saul

The period from the crossing of Jordan River under Joshua to the occupation of much of Canaan in the time of Saul is some two hundred years, about 1240 to 1020 B.C. The accounts given in Numbers and Joshua are called into question by recent archaeological evidence. It is now regarded as probable that most of the Twelve Tribes were part of the mixed population that lived in Canaan from the fourteenth to the late twelfth centuries. The escaping refugees from Egypt may have been composed mainly of Levites and the tribes of Ephraim and Manasseh, descendants of Joseph. There is no archaeological evidence to corroborate the tale of a miraculous victory at Jericho in the time of Joshua.[1] It is therefore doubtful that there was a renewal of the covenant with Yahweh as described in Joshua 24.

Numbers offers a late account that devotes special attention to priests and Levites.[2] It retains some interesting traditions about the northward push of the people who crossed the Jordan.

We shall pay little attention to the military campaigns. Instead, we shall look at the heroic people whose deeds are recorded in Judges 1, 2:16–23, 4:4–5:31 and 13:2–16:31 and 1 Samuel 1–7. These heroes can help us appreciate how important godly leadership is for the wellbeing of a nation or organization.

II

The Judges

The Israelites settled mainly in the hills, though they faced competition from Edom, Moab, Ammon and other clans. The fertile coastal lands were possessed and controlled by people called Philistines, who were descended from Peoples of the Sea, invaders of Egypt many years before. The Israelites were not an organized confederacy. The different bands had to learn how to assist each other and to ally themselves with Canaanite relatives.

To accomplish these aims, certain leaders were summoned to undertake temporary roles as guerrilla commanders: male leaders like Othniel, Ehud, Shamgar, Gideon, Jephthah, Barak and Samson, and an outstanding and spirited woman, Deborah, who may have been a prophetess and inspired Barak. There are exciting narratives about each of them. Other tales include a sorrowful one of Jephthah's daughter who was sacrificed as an offering of thanks.[3] Samson's superhuman deeds, his entanglement with Delilah, his betrayal and his terrible acts of vengeance on the Philistines are also related.[4]

Wars with the Philistines dragged on. For several months, the enemy held the sacred box or "ark" that symbolized the presence of Yahweh and may have contained tables of the *torah* given at Sinai. Deborah and Barak waged war against Jabin, king in Hazor, whose field commander was called Sisera. The Israelite victory is described both in prose and in a powerful poem thought to date from the very time of Deborah.[5]

One of the central passages of the poem tells of another woman who was not an Israelite: Jael, the wife of Heber the Kenite. The defeated Sisera sought refuge with Jael, trusting to the peace that prevailed between king Jabin and Heber.[6] "He asked water, and she gave him milk; she brought forth butter in a lordly dish. She put her hand to the nail ... and with the hammer she smote Sisera, she smote off his head.... At her feet he bowed, he fell, he lay down: at her feet he bowed, he fell: where he bowed, there he fell down dead."[7] They were tempestuous times indeed, but the nation of Israel looked back to them as times when Yahweh had empowered great leaders to deliver the tribes and win their independence.

III
Samuel: judge, prophet and seer

The last of the Judges, according to the biblical narrative, was the son of Elkanah and Hannah who worshipped Yahweh at the great shrine in Shiloh.[8] Hannah was barren, but after much prayer she conceived. She had a son, called him Samuel ("Name of God"), and dedicated him for life to the service of the cult in the shrine. Hannah sang for joy, "My heart rejoiceth in the Lord."[9] Samuel was to be instrumental in the inauguration of a state system that had some of the features of a monarchy.

IV
Rulers of the ancient Near East

Long before the emergence of Israel as a community, the empires and nations of the Near East each had a deity who was deemed to be its sovereign ruler. Invisible gods, though, required human visibility. That was provided by princes and, in the case of Egypt, by pharaohs. Such rulers were regarded as divine representatives, viceroys of the god; sometimes they were designated as sons of god.

There is some confusion about the origin of kingship in Israel. In Judges it is related that although Yahweh was indeed the King of Israel, yet "in those days there was no king in Israel: every man did that which was right in his own eyes."[10] Rule by an unseen God merely meant chaos and anarchy in the body politic. In due course, Samuel emerged as the leading priest for all the tribes, a charismatic seer and prophet who brought peace with the Philistines for a while. When Samuel was old, the tribes of Israel, more united than they had been, spoke against letting his dissolute sons succeed him in leadership. One account says: "The elders of Israel gathered themselves together, and came to Samuel unto Ramah, And said unto him, Behold, thou art old and thy sons walk not in thy ways: now make us a king to judge us like all the nations."[11]

V

The election of Saul

There are two versions of how Saul was elected. In one source, Samuel was inspired to anoint the young man. In another, he resists the demands of the people and submits only at the urging of Yahweh himself.

The early source is in 1 Samuel 9:1–10:16, possibly 11, and certainly 13 and 14. Young Saul the Benjaminite had been sent out to find his father's lost asses. He met the seer Samuel and, to his amazement, was secretly anointed "to be captain"[12] over Yahweh's people Israel and save them from the old enemy, the Philistines. Saul was thus the choice of Yahweh himself, his vicar among the community and commander of the next campaign for freedom. On his way home, he fell into an ecstasy. He was "spirited," for leadership was impossible apart from the Spirit of God. Saul, however, did not live up to his divine vocation, so he was rejected. In this source, the immediate cause of the rejection was that, like a priest, he offered a burnt offering, thus contravening his appointment by Yahweh.[13]

A later source, or at least a different form of the story, is to be found in 1 Samuel 8, 10:17–27, and 12. Here we read about the dissolute sons of Samuel and the request of the people that Samuel give them a king. When the old seer protests to Yahweh that the request insults Yahweh as the King of Israel and Samuel as the viceroy of God, he is told by Yahweh: "They have not rejected thee, but they have rejected me, that I should not reign over them ... shew them the manner of the king that shall reign over them."[14]

So Samuel told the people how rulers would behave. He said that sons would be conscripted to be servants of the monarch. Daughters would have to serve as confectioners, cooks and bakers. A tenth of everyone's goods would be exacted. The people refused to listen, however, and still demanded a monarch.

What follows reads strangely.[15] The tribes assembled, and a sacred lot was cast to reveal the elect warrior-commander. The lot fell on Saul. But Saul had hidden himself among the baggage. When he was found, the tallest man among them all, he was acclaimed with the cry, "God save the king!"[16] Samuel could not let this go without a warning, however. He calls on Yahweh to send thunder and rain in order to remind the people of their duty to Yahweh. Although the tribes were on the way to becoming a nation, a state comparable with others in Canaan, they were still the people of Yahweh: "For the Lord will not forsake his people for his great name's sake.... Only fear the Lord, and serve him in truth with all your heart."[17] Samuel himself continued to pray for them and played a very important role in the new order of society.

VI

The career of Saul

Saul had mixed success as a military commander. He was not consistently inspired in leadership. He seems to have been moody, jealous, insecure in a position of authority and depressed, perhaps because of religious infidelity. Yahweh needed a better agent, for not even the inspiration of being an anointed person could work automatically. The burgeoning nation needed wise government, and there is little evidence to indicate that Saul knew how a state government should operate. He made mistakes.

As observed earlier, Samuel remained on the scene. In his eyes, Saul's great fault was his failure to obey an injunction from God himself, given through Samuel, that the Amalekites should be exterminated.[18] Saul had taken Agag, the king of the Amalekites, alive, "and the best of the sheep, and of the oxen, and of the fatlings, and the lambs, and all that was good, and would not utterly destroy them."[19] But Samuel had no compunction about completing the work: he "hewed Agag in pieces before the Lord in Gilgal."[20]

There are two versions of the eventual downfall of Saul. It is written in one source that, after a terrible defeat at Gilboa, Saul died by his own hand.[21] In another it is said that a young Amalekite slew him at his own request: "Stand, I pray thee, upon me, and slay me: for anguish is come upon me, because my life is yet whole in me."[22] The deaths of Saul and his charming son Jonathan, the best friend of David of Bethlehem who would succeed Saul as king, are mourned in David's memorable lament:

> *The beauty of Israel is slain upon thy high places:*
> *how are the mighty fallen!*
> *Tell it not in Gath, publish it not in the streets of Askelon;*
> *lest the daughters of the Philistines rejoice,*
> *lest the daughters of the uncircumcised triumph....*
> *Saul and Jonathan were lovely and pleasant in their lives,*
> *and in their death they were not divided....*
> *How are the mighty fallen in the midst of the battle!*
> *O Jonathan, thou wast slain in thine high places.*
> *I am distressed for thee, my brother Jonathan:*
> *very pleasant hast thou been to me:*
> *thy love to me was wonderful, passing the love of women.*
> *How are the mighty fallen,*
> *and the weapons of war perished!*[23]

Saul and his family were rejected, for there was no crown, no throne, no dynastic setup. The spirit of the Lord clothed itself with certain heroes and prophets, but it was never a permanent possession or endowment. Once received, it could nevertheless be lost. A proper monarchy was not to emerge until the enthronement of David.

Comment: questions of interpretation

The passage about Saul's refusal to exterminate the Amalekites raises difficult questions. It has been argued that Yahweh required the extermination of the Canaanites, the Hittites and other people to ensure that Israel would gain possession of the land of promise. But this seems to be sanctification of a policy after the event, claiming that conquest was the will of God. That was, of course, the party line in Israel, but one need not accept it as an adequate explanation for the place of Israel in the Middle East.

A problem with the definition of revelation is at stake, since religious experiences may be interpreted in a variety of ways. There are different criteria for determining when the human language about God can be accepted as a statement of the truth of God. Adherents to the Hebrew Bible accept the teaching of the great prophets about divine holiness, mercy and lovingkindness. Christians believe the spirit of Jesus is to be discovered in the Gospels. There is bound to be ambiguity because there is no infallible revelation from above and no uniformity of response to the Word of God. God was not created in the image of human beings: his are not human emotions and intentions. Rather, people respond in faith to the pressures of the Divine who demands honesty, truth in the inner person, and commitment to the Highest as the spirit within answers to the Spirit above. Faith is a responsibility to be godlike within the limits of a human life.

six

David: The Once and Future King

I

A colourful character

David, the son of Jesse of Bethlehem, is one of the most colourful characters in world history. He is well known through biblical narratives of his career and from certain psalms that may be his compositions: for example, Psalms 8, 23, 34 and 63.

People of his calibre inspire other people to fulfil their potential as human beings. He developed from obscurity to become a great warrior, statesman and poet. Lovely, intelligent women and resolute, wise men were loyal to him. Few could have been indifferent, for he was a heroic figure. Although his fortunes fluctuated, his confidence in his God and his destiny did not falter. One may not feel impelled to emulate him, since his time and place were so utterly different from ours, but his exploits lift the heart, quicken the pulse and stir the imagination. The narratives catalogue his passionate loving, his bursts of ecstatic joy, his magnanimity and his moments of profound sorrow and penitence. The best stories about David are in 1 Samuel 16:14–23, 16:1–13 and 17–31; 2 Samuel 1:1–27 and 2–24; and 1 Kings 1:1–2:11.

The place of David as an ideal figure for Israel and the Church may be traced in prophecy and liturgy by consulting Hosea 3:5; Isaiah 55:3; Jeremiah 30:9; Ezekiel 34:24; *Psalms of Solomon* 17 (in the Greek version of the Hebrew Bible called the Septuagint and dating from about 50 B.C.); Matthew 1:1; Luke 3:31; Romans 1:3; 2 Timothy 2:8 and Revelation 3:7 and 22:16.

II

Historic David: from shepherd to outlaw

David was one of the seven sons of Jesse, a descendant of Boaz and the Moabitess Ruth, whose romantic marriage is described in Ruth 4. He also had two sisters. When Saul was suffering from spiritual depression, it was suggested that he send for David. So Saul's message was relayed to Jesse: "Send me your son David who is with the sheep."[1] He became armour-bearer to Saul, who loved him greatly, for David could rally or soothe him by playing on the harp or lyre.

In the verses preceding the passage just quoted, there is a narrative that seems to follow from 1 Samuel 15:26 and 15:35, where we read that the Lord had decided to depose Saul. Samuel was despatched to Jesse in Bethlehem to discover the successor whom Yahweh had already selected. Much to Samuel's surprise, all six of the fine, upstanding sons were passed over and the choice fell on the youngest boy, the sheep herder: "Now he was ruddy, and had beautiful eyes, and was handsome. The Lord said, 'Rise and anoint him; for this is the one.'" So David was (secretly?) anointed "in the midst of his brethren."[2]

The narrative then describes David's prowess as a warrior and his relationship with Saul and his family. David slew the Philistine giant Goliath and became the dearly beloved friend of Jonathan, Saul's heir. David's success in battle against the Philistines provoked Saul's jealousy when the singing and dancing girls announced that "Saul hath slain his thousands, and David his ten thousands."³ David wished to marry Saul's daughter Michal, but was able to do so only after successfully gathering a hundred foreskins of the uncircumcised Philistines as the bride price.

Saul pursued a persistent vendetta against David, causing him to become an adventurous outlaw. He even went to the point of seeming to fight with and for the enemies of Israel. But once or twice, he spared the life of Saul, his hunter, because Saul had been anointed by the Lord. It is interesting, however, that no mention is made of the fact that the outlaw was also the Lord's anointed! It is also interesting to note in passing that when Saul was desperate, he resorted to a witch in Endor and conjured up the ghost of Samuel, only to be reminded that Yahweh had definitely disowned him and given the kingdom to David.⁴

Stories tell how David was revenged on certain Amalekites and how, at last, his exile ended when Saul and his sons fell at Mount Gilboa. Not many years had passed since the youth with his lyre had come to entertain his prince. Chosen by God, David was the first real monarch and organizer of the nation-state. His reign marks a decisive turning point in history.

III

Historic David: king of all Israel

David's reign lasted from about 1000 to 960 B.C. He started by consolidating good relations formed earlier with Judah, the people in the south, and became king in Hebron for seven and a half years. During that time, he showed diplomatic skill and political sagacity. He also demanded and got the return of his first wife, Michal, whom Saul, in his spite, had given to one Palti.⁵ His status as Saul's son-in-law gave him a claim to leadership in the northern realm of Israel, where Ishbosheth, Saul's son and heir, was ineffectual and was soon murdered,⁶ leaving only lame Mephibosheth, Jonathan's son, who had no pretensions to leadership. When David was thirty years old, he received and accepted an invitation from the northerners to become their king. He was "bone of their bone and flesh of

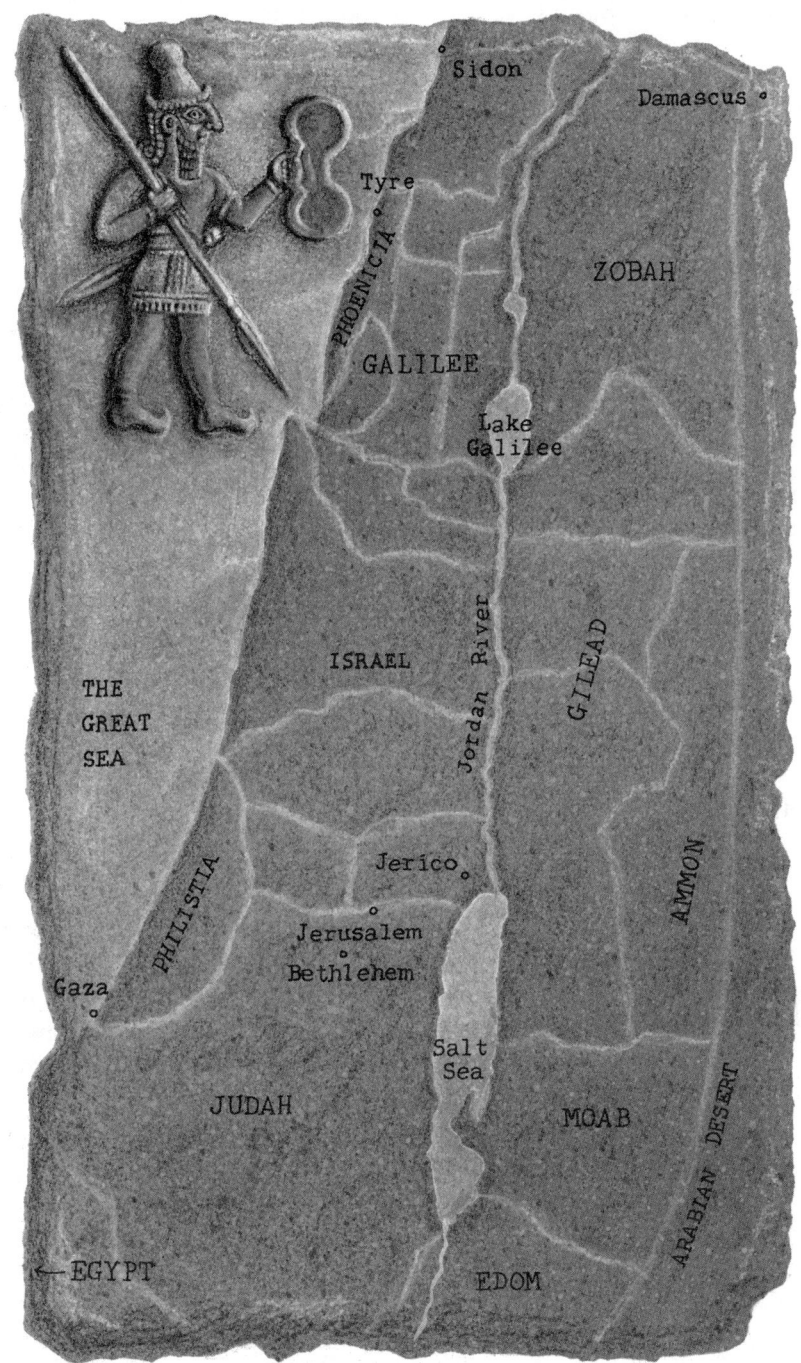

The Empire of David and Solomon

The story becomes more focussed, closer to "historical" events. The Hittite warrior, 1200 B.C., was ancient even in David's time. His shoes with upturned toes were Phoenician.

their flesh",[7] even if he did come from Bethlehem, and he was Yahweh's choice.

David's sagacity was proved by his seizure of the Jebusite city called Jerusalem. On neutral ground, between the north and the south, and high above Mediterranean sea level, it commanded much of the country. David made it his capital and the site of his palace and chapel, to which he brought the sacred Ark.

King David was a military genius. He defeated the Philistines, Moabites, Ammonites and Edomites, enlarging the territory so that it stretched from the Egyptian border to the Euphrates River. At the height of his strength, Israel was a great power. He was, however, less successful at home. David did institute a civil service, possibly on Egyptian models, and take a census. He also began the process of organizing the kingdoms into a single state, although he did not complete the project.

Part of the weakness in his reign may be put down to his sexual affairs and fierce struggles within his polygamous family. The harem had eight wives and several concubines. Eighteen or nineteen sons are listed, as well as unnamed daughters.[8] The most significant woman in his life was probably Bathsheba, the wife of Uriah the Hittite, one of the king's special guardsmen. David committed adultery with her and then arranged that Uriah would be killed in battle, fighting for David and Israel. It was a terrible crime, and his penitence may lie behind the words of Psalm 51. As a result of Yahweh's displeasure, their first son died.

The court prophet Nathan pointedly advised the king of God's anger in a moving parable. A man rich in flocks and herds was neighbour to a poor man whose sole possession, the joy of his family, was one little ewe lamb. One day the rich man stole the lamb to make a feast for a guest. David was furious: "As the Lord lives," he cried, "the man who has done this deserves to die; he shall restore the lamb four-fold ... because he had no pity." "You are the man!" said Nathan. And, he added, as punishment, the sword shall never depart from your family and your wives shall be taken by neighbours. You acted secretly, he said, but this shall be done in the sight of all Israel.[9] David repented in total abasement and gained a respite for himself and Bathsheba. She later bore Solomon, the son who succeeded David through a conspiracy in which Nathan and Bathsheba played leading parts.

Under David, priests and prophets were established in Jerusalem and at other shrines. Songs of praise and prayers may well have been composed and performed by David, "the sweet psalmist of Israel."[10] Every tradition emphasizes not only Yahweh's favour towards him, but also his loyalty to Yahweh. Yahwism, the faith in Israel's covenant-God and moral obedience to his will, was a religion that continued to develop during the conquest and the monarchy, although it was not followed strictly by much of the population. Canaanite influence was powerful. David the Yahwist had a special place in the chronicles of the latest stages of Yahwism, when it had become monotheistic.

Near the end of David's life, palace intrigues centred on his third and favourite son, Absalom, probably the intended heir. Absalom rebelled, seized the throne and the harem, and almost won the kingdom. In defiance of express orders, David's military commander Joab killed Absalom, and the old king lamented as he had for his beloved Jonathan: "And as he went, thus he said, O my son Absalom, my son, my son Absalom! would God I had died for thee, O Absalom, my son, my son!"[11]

"And the days that David reigned over Israel were forty years: seven years reigned he in Hebron, and thirty and three years reigned he in Jerusalem. Then sat Solomon upon the throne of David his father."[12]

IV

David, the ideal king

It is not surprising that heroic David became a symbol of the once and future king who is to be the viceroy of Yahweh, ruling over the nations. In the postexilic era, it was predicted that Israel's fortunes would be restored under another David: God's anointed agent, his servant and prince, his Messiah.

> *"The people that walked in darkness have seen a great light: they that dwell in the land of the shadow of death, upon them hath the light shined.... For unto us a child is born.... Of the increase of his government and peace there shall be no end, upon the throne of David.... And there shall come forth a rod out of the stem of Jesse, and a Branch shall grow out of his roots...."*[13]

Such passages, however, probably belong to monarchical times long before the Exile and refer either to an actual prince of David's dynasty or to an ideal prince still to come.

There is another important prophecy about David's dynasty.[14] David was told that Yahweh would not allow him to build a temple as a permanent dwelling place in Jerusalem, for Yahweh is a journeying deity, not to be confined to any human-made shrine. Nevertheless a promise is given: that the throne and dynasty of David would last forever. No wonder later expectations of a new Golden Age or the Kingdom of God became linked to the coming of a new and greater David, as in the full-fledged messianic hope to be discussed in chapter 11.

In conclusion, it may be noted that through his poetry, David has become important in the music and liturgy of synagogues and churches. We do not know whether, in fact, he directed the ritual and music of the Jerusalem cult, or how many of the psalms in the scriptures are his authentic compositions. Nevertheless, David's prayers, confessions of sin and songs of praise and thanksgiving have all been incorporated into the sacred literature of Jews and Christians. The works are chanted by cantors or choirs in prose versions, either in Hebrew or translated into English, Scots or French. They are paraphrased — sometimes not successfully. They are sung to touching melodies like *Crimond*, the popular composition by David Grant, or to more contemporary music.

Whatever the form, the sentiments, petitions and meditations to be found in the psalms of David and the other psalms that are now attached to them lie deep in the cultural consciousness of Western people. Many collections of devotional literature are based on their themes.

David was old and respected when he died. The throne and empire then went to Bathsheba's son Solomon who became a legendary source of wisdom.

seven

Schisms and Exiles

I
Solomon: the wise or unwise king?

Comparatively little is written about the reign of David's successor, Solomon: what there is can be found in 1 Kings 1:32 to 11:43. In that narrative, his work is shown to have produced a great building programme, and special honour is given to the Temple in Jerusalem that he built with the help of foreign skilled craftsmen. It was not the only shrine, although later, in the reign of Josiah, it did become the only centre for the worship of Yahweh.

At first, the youthful Solomon humbly prayed to God for wisdom in government. He was promised riches and honour: he was to be Solomon the Incomparable.[1] And indeed, wisdom was attributed to him, although without adequate evidence: he was wrongly reckoned the author of Proverbs, Ecclesiastes, the Song of Solomon and *Wisdom of Solomon*. Alas, he went on to assemble an enormous harem of seven hundred wives and three hundred concubines, some of whom, being foreigners, were disliked by the loyal priests and prophets of Yahweh. It is likely that Solomon permitted the cults of foreign deities to be practised because of these women. His failure to promote Yahwism became a warning to later generations.

II

Break-ups and reunions

Although the disintegration of nations is often unsettling for people, it is a common occurrence throughout history. Nations have sometimes broken apart and reformed with new boundaries and new names. For example, it was heartbreaking for Christians like St. Augustine of Hippo when, in the fifth century, the western Roman Empire fell apart under the onslaught of the Vandals, Goths, Huns and other barbarians (even though some of them were Arian Christians, considered heretics by Augustine). In more recent times new frontiers for Poland were drawn after the First World War, and new states like Czechoslovakia, Syria and Iraq came into existence. In 1990 the two Germanies were reunited, and in 1991 the old Soviet Union broke up. Similar upheavals took place in the tenth century B.C.

After the death of Solomon, the empire of Israel broke apart. As we have seen, the south and north had been united by David, but because of the poor policies of his grandson, Rehoboam, the two regions were sundered again. The south became the kingdom of Judah; the north, the kingdom of Israel (using the ancient name for the group of ten tribes). Jerusalem was the capital of Judah and Samaria the capital of Israel. This split was not mended. In 1948, a new version of a nation called Israel was created, and it continues to have a somewhat precarious existence. A chronological table of the kingdoms and their rulers and prophets may be helpful.

It is almost certain that the tensions between Judah and Israel had roots in the distant past. In the south, we find the Joseph tribes, called Ephraim and Manasseh, allied with Benjamin, a name said to mean "southlander." In the family trees of Genesis, they are all traced to Rachel, Jacob-Israel's

The Kingdoms and Their Rulers and Prophets

United kingdom

Solomon, 960–922 B.C.

South: kingdom of Judah	North: kingdom of Israel
Rehoboam 922–915	Jeroboam I 922 – 901
	Omri 876 – 869
	Ahab 869 – 850
	Prophet Elijah 855
Uzziah 783 – 742	Jeroboam II 786 – 746
Prophet Isaiah 742 – 701	Prophet Amos 755 – 745
Jotham 742 – 735	Prophet Hosea 747 – 736
	Hoshea 732 – 724
	Fall of Samaria to Assyria 722 – 721
	EXILE: first Dispersion
Manasseh 687 – 642	
Josiah 640 – 609	
Deuteronomic Reform 622 – 621	
Prophet Jeremiah 626 – 587	
Jehoiachim 598 – 597	
Prophet Ezekiel 593 – 573	
Zedekiah 597 – 586	
Fall of Jerusalem to Babylonia 587 – 586	
EXILE: in Babylon. The great Dispersion (Diaspora)	

favourite wife. Rachel's symbol was a ewe. These clans, then, claimed descent from Jacob.

During the years of guerrilla war and conquest, these people joined six tribes — Reuben, Levi, Simeon, Judah, Issachar and Zebulun — that traced their lineage to another wife of Jacob, Leah, whose symbol was a cow. But it appears that Levi ceased to be a tribe like the rest. Hence there were eight clans in south and north. Four more were added: those that could claim Jacob-Israel as ancestor through Bilhah (Dan and Naphtali) and through Zilpah (Asher and Gad). The linking of all those families or clans may be late and artificial.

It may well have been military and economic policies pursued by Solomon and his son Rehoboam that precipitated the rupture of north and south. Israel and Judah remained suspicious and often at cross-purposes for two centuries, and each was rendered weaker by the loss of the other. The story is told in 1 Kings 12 to 2 Kings 25.

III

Elijah and Elisha

During the two centuries of division, Yahwism had to struggle to gain supremacy within the chosen nation. The story of Elijah is an exciting episode in that struggle. Elijah was a charismatic prophet and priest in the north about 855 B.C. He waged war on the Canaanite and Israelite worship of *baal*, a title meaning "lord" that was applied to several deities. King Ahab's foreign queen, Jezebel, fostered the cult of her own baal and persecuted the Yahwists. Her name became a byword for cruelty and tyranny. In a secular history, Ahab and his father Omri are described as great kings, but they were not Yahwists.

Elijah rallied the Yahwists on Mount Carmel in an encounter that is vividly described, devastating in its irony and, for some readers, incredible in its miraculous elements. The baalist priests failed to persuade their god to answer their prayers for fire to consume the sacrifices. Elijah taunted them, then proved the greatness and power of Yahweh. After soaking his sacrifice in water, he prayed to Yahweh. In answer to his

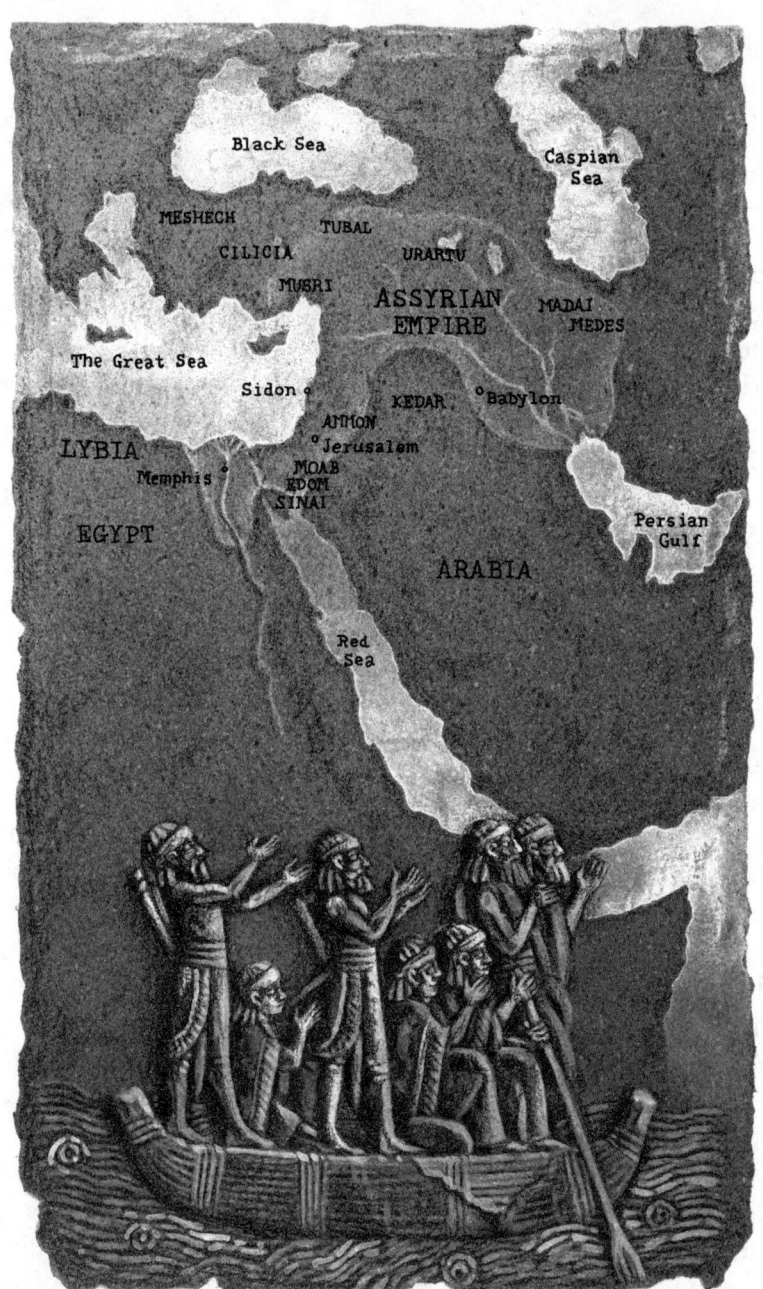

The Assyrian Empire in Isaiah's Time

Great military powers of the world can be callous to people and prophets. The impression here shows a family of refugees captured in the marshes of southern Babylon.

prayers, all the water and the sacrifices were consumed in fire from heaven. The result was a slaughter of the baalist priests, led by Elijah himself. Then, because of the wrath of Queen Jezebel, he had to flee the country.[2]

Elijah fled in a sort of ecstasy until he reached the sacred Mount Horeb (perhaps another name for Sinai). There he met his God not in volcanic eruption or in thunder and lightning but "in a faint murmuring sound" (REB) or "the sound of a fine silence."[3]

Yahweh rebuked him for leaving: "I have left me seven thousand in Israel."[4] You are not, as you say, the only one left who is loyal to me. Then Elijah was commissioned to instigate a political revolution in Syria by anointing Hazael to be king there and to do likewise in Israel by anointing Jehu to be king. Finally, since his time of service was up, he was to find his disciple Elisha and anoint him to be prophet.[5]

There is something odd about this passage, for 2 Kings 8:13–15 ascribes the accession of Hazael to a prophecy of Elisha. In 2 Kings 9:1–3, it says that Elisha sent a young man to Ramoth-gilead to find Jehu and take him to an inner room. The man was instructed to "take the box of oil, and pour it on his head, and say, Thus saith the Lord, I have anointed thee king over Israel. Then open the door, and flee, and tarry not."[6] This latter story seems more credible.

The climax to Elijah's career comes with the appearance of a chariot and horses of fire that carried Elijah in a whirlwind into heaven.[7] It is thought that he will come again, or that a new prophet, endowed with his spirit, will come to usher in the age of the Messiah. It could happen at Passover any year. So each year, faithful Jews pour a cup of wine at the Passover table for Elijah, who may come to presage a new Exodus, liberation, salvation and divine rescue.[8] In Christian tradition, the new Elijah was John the Baptist.[9]

IV

Exile: the fall of Samaria

Israel, the northern kingdom, lost its independence in 722–21 B.C. when it was conquered by the Assyrians and some of its inhabitants were dispersed. Thereafter, many native Israelites and an unknown number of Assyrian colonists occupied the northland. Over the next six hundred years, the northerners (Samaritans) and the postexilic community in the south (Judeans) grew apart in customs, economic life and religion. To this day, Samaritans claim to be Israelites. They have their own version of the Torah and their own temple, priesthood and sacrificial system centred at Mount Gerizim near modern Nablus. Jewish tradition disputes the claim and tends to regard Samaritans as little better than Gentiles.

V
Judah conquered: the great Dispersion

Judah was a rather tiny state in the midst of great powers, and as such it was sometimes a pawn in the conflicts between Egypt and Assyria or Babylon. One of Judah's important rulers was Uzziah, who reigned from 783 to 742. He is sometimes called Azariah, perhaps because he was a leper for many years and thus unfit to rule: his son Jotham was the regent. In Uzziah's time, Judah reached the height of its power as a state. In the year of his death, Isaiah, the son of Amoz, was in the Temple and had a vision that led to his entry into one of the most significant prophetic missions in the history of Israel.[10]

During the reign of Josiah, the Second Law was discovered and a religious reformation undertaken (see chapter 4). But after Josiah's death, the fortunes of Judah quickly faded. Its end came in 587–86 B.C. when it fell to the Babylonians and the inhabitants were moved en masse. This was the beginning of the Exile, a historic turning point.

Hereafter the word "Israel" no longer refers to a northern kingdom or to the people of the distant patriarchal age. Israel becomes associated with the history and doctrine belonging to people who affirmed their divine vocation as the children of Abraham. They often asserted their right to be a distinct society, the chosen people, with an assurance that helped to breed antisemitism. The sacred title "the Israel of God" is claimed later by the Christian Jews and Christian Gentiles who preached a new order inaugurated by the appearance of Jesus of Nazareth.

The experience of Exile in Babylon left its mark everywhere in the life of the people we must now call Jews. They must have wondered if Yahweh had, at last, deserted them and whether the promises to Abraham and Jacob would be fulfilled. Sometimes the mood was one of desolation: the longing of the exiles was always for Jerusalem, the holy city, the city of David. One of the psalms reflects that mood. It ends with a call for divine vengeance on Edom and Babylon in language that cannot be condoned. The first six verses, however, are moving poetry of sadness in an alien land:

By the rivers of Babylon —
there we sat down and there we wept
when we remembered Zion.
On the willows there
we hung up our harps.
For there our captors
asked us for songs,
and our tormentors asked for mirth, saying,
"Sing us one of the songs of Zion!"
How could we sing the Lord's song in a foreign land?
If I forget you, O Jerusalem,
let my right hand wither!
Let my tongue cling to the roof of my mouth,
if I do not remember you,
if I do not set Jerusalem
above my highest joy.[11]

eight

The Development of Prophecy in Israel

I
Why bother with the prophets?

It could be argued that among all of old Israel's contributions to religion and culture, the messages in the collected prophecies are of paramount importance. The messages are relevant in all situations: sanctuaries, schools, homes, government offices and shops.

The prophets (Amos, Micah, Hosea, Isaiah of Jerusalem, Jeremiah, Ezekiel and Second Isaiah, the poet of the Exile) addressed their contemporaries between roughly 750 and 550 B.C. Yet what they had to say was influential when Constantine founded Constantinople, when Joan of Arc defied the English and when Christians laughed and cried at the Reformation and the Counter-Reformation. Since then, the writings of the prophets of Israel have fed the spirit and challenged the behaviour of Jews, Christians and humanists. The prophets' writings about the nature and purpose of God and about the obligations of his followers have been important for both individuals and institutions. One famous text reads: "He has told you, O mortal, what is good; and what does the Lord require of you but to do justice, and to love kindness, and to walk humbly with your God?"[1]

II

What the prophets were

The prophets were not fortune-tellers, though they did speak about events in the immediate future. They looked to both the past and the future. They had meditated on their nation's past and the divine favour to their ancestors; they perceived its significance. They saw clearly how future conflicts, solutions, disasters and dangers cast their shadows in advance. The job of the prophets was to make the people aware. They used rebukes, threats and promises. Their admonitions, warnings and encouraging words had to be communicated in a variety of forms. Sometimes secular material was adapted to religious use in elegies, taunting songs, prayers and proverbs.

The most significant fact about prophets, however, was that they were Yahweh's representatives, ambassadors and spokespeople. A person could not decide to be a prophet: Yahweh "called" chosen people. A classic account of such a call is in Isaiah 6:1–8. Isaiah and his like, for example Amos, were a different breed from Elijah and earlier charismatics. Hence Amos demurred even at the word prophet: "I am no prophet, nor a prophet's son; but I am a herdsman, and a dresser of sycamore trees, and the Lord took me from following the flock, and the Lord said to me, 'Go, prophesy to my people Israel.'"[2]

The occasion when such a call might come was likely to be one of personal or social crisis. The time when Nathan confronted David about his affair with Bathsheba was one such moment. Similarly, prophets arose when the schismatic kingdoms of north and south were in disarray, and corruption, folly in foreign policy, wickedness among the rich and powerful, and blatant hypocrisy in religion were endemic. God was not pleased: "I spurn with loathing your pilgrim-feasts; I take no pleasure in your sacred ceremonies.... Spare me the sound of your songs; I shall not listen to the strumming of your lutes. Instead let justice flow on like a river and righteousness like a never-failing torrent."[3]

One feature of prophetic careers, sometimes predicted in advance, was that the audience might hear the message but not understand, might see but have no spiritual insight.[4] It seems to be the fate of spiritual teachers and prophets that they may be despised and rejected, especially if their message sounds judgmental. Passages that might be read in the NRSV or REB are Hosea 1–3, 11 and 14; Isaiah 1–23, 28–33 and 36–39; and Amos 5–9.

III
The passion of Jeremiah

Jeremiah is deservedly regarded as one of the supreme spiritual figures in the Hebrew Bible. Born about 650 B.C., he was the son of a priest and, therefore, a priest himself, although he did not practise in that capacity. A lonely man, passionately devoted to Yahweh, Jeremiah was probably called to prophesy in 626. He was realistic about the international situation and the threat from Babylon in the north, and so, to the dismay of the government and the religious establishment, he was a pacifist. After the capture and destruction of Jerusalem in 587–86, he was taken to Egypt, and his fate there is unknown. Jeremiah's messages and a short biography, edited after his death, were incorporated into the sacred list of authoritative books. Later editors thought him so sorrowful that they wrongly attributed to him the book called Lamentations.

IV
How Jeremiah's book was composed

The book of Jeremiah is confusing because of revisions and editing. When Jeremiah received a divine command to write down the Word of Yahweh (36:1–4), he called on his friend and secretary, Baruch, to produce the required scroll. But when the prophecies were made public in the royal court, King Jehoiakim, son of Josiah, had the scroll defaced and burned. Baruch and Jeremiah were able to hide and to produce another edition. It was dangerous then to be a preacher, just as it was dangerous in Nazi Germany to read and preach from the Hebrew prophets. Analysis provided by some contemporary interpreters is needed to read authentic Jeremiah. There are three major groupings.

Δ Poetic oracles are found in 1–18, 20:7–15, 21:11–14, 23 and 25:14–38. These probably appeared in the material dictated to Baruch about the year 605, at a time when Nebuchadrezzar of Babylon defeated the Egyptian Pharaoh Neco II.

Δ Prose memoirs of Baruch are in 19:1–20:6, 21:1–10, 26, 27:2–6, 27:15–20, 28, 29:1–9 and most of 30. These were written some time after 605.

Δ Later authentic prophecies are in 32:1, 32:7–15, 33, 34:1–7, 35:1–11, 36:1–27, 37:3–21, 38:1, 38:3–22, 38:24–26, 39:3, 39:14, 42:1–6 and 43.

There are many verses where it seems that revisions were introduced by editors influenced by the Second Law (Deuteronomy).

V

The new covenant

Special notice must be taken of Jeremiah 31, particularly verses 31–34. The style and some of the vocabulary of this passage may not be genuinely Jeremiah's, but the doctrine is his. He predicts a time to come when Yahweh shall make a new covenant with Israel and Judah different from the Sinai covenant, known to us from Exodus and Deuteronomy. Jeremiah's spiritual wisdom includes the following concepts:

Δ That the *torah* of God, his instruction and law, will be set inside men and women by being written on their hearts.

Δ That everyone, from the least to the greatest, will know Yahweh as his or her own God. No one will have to teach a sibling or a neighbour, for true faith and worship will be universal within the people of God.

Δ That this will be a covenant in which the forgiveness of sins will be central.

Jeremiah's concept of religion transcends old ideas of agreements made formally between a superior Deity and an inferior congregation. His is very personal, meant to be true for everyone.

His view was idealistic, however. In reality, neighbour deceived neighbour: "Brother supplants brother as Jacob did, and friend slanders friend.... Wrong follows wrong, deceit follows deceit; they refuse to acknowledge me. This is the Word of the Lord."[5] It is not surprising that the prophet cried out in his agony: "O that my head were a spring of water, and my eyes a fountain of tears, so that I might weep day and night for the slain of my poor people! O that I had in the desert a traveller's lodging place, that I might leave my people and go away from them! For they are all adulterers, a band of traitors."[6]

VI

The sins of Judah

Jeremiah's accusations were against priests and prophets as well as the ordinary people. Those who should have interpreted the law of Yahweh did not even have direct experience of their God, pastors transgressed and prophets were inspired by a baal, not by Yahweh. One case can be cited. According to the covenant, Hebrew slaves should have been liberated by their owners after six years, but were not. God therefore decided to punish the people of Israel with war, famine and

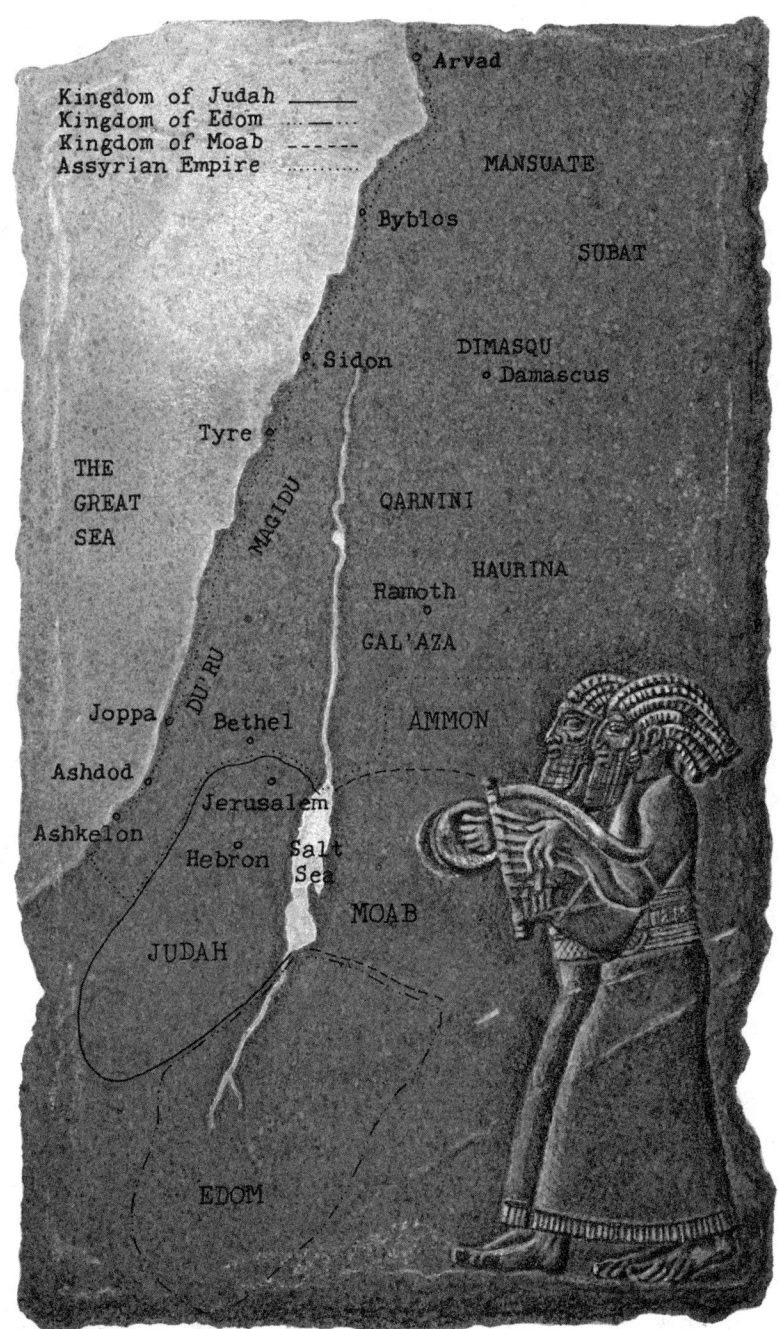

The Kingdom of Judah in Isaiah's Time

People preserve their stories and legends in song. This sketch of musicians (from Nineveh) reminds us of realities not captured in maps and literature.

disease. The Babylonians would take the holy city and its king, princes and inhabitants.[7] Elsewhere Jeremiah gave a message to those who had defiled the Temple by worshipping a Canaanite baal: their city would be destroyed.[8]

The words that the Lord had Jeremiah say appalled his sensitive soul and tempted him to abandon his vocation altogether: "You have duped me, Lord, and I have been your dupe; you have outwitted me and prevailed. All the day long I have been made a laughing-stock; everyone ridicules me.... Whenever I said, 'I shall not call it to mind or speak in his name again,' then his word became imprisoned within me like a fire burning in my heart. I was weary with holding it under, and could endure no more."[9]

VII
Hope in the midst of despair

Not everything in the scrolls of Jeremiah is pessimistic doom-saying. When he was in jail in the besieged capital, he had the chance to buy back a field in his native Anathoth that his cousin offered to him. Jeremiah did so, knowing that the offer was a divine sign that in spite of imminent disasters, it was safe for him to invest in the future.[10]

Though he became a refugee and witness to the terrible fall of Jerusalem, Jeremiah stands out as a messenger of hope, a prophet of tenderness and gentleness. His witness has impressed generations within the Judeo-Christian tradition.

VIII
Ezekiel: his book and his call

Ezekiel was a contemporary of Jeremiah. He too was a refugee priest but was, it seems, taken to Babylon. His book is postexilic, though no precise date can be given for its publication. It was skilfully edited, especially by the addition of chapters 40–48, which are concerned with the Temple, priesthood and cult in the time after the return from exile in Babylon and the rebuilding of the Temple.

Three themes dominate the main parts of the book of Ezekiel:

Δ the certainty of Israel's doom (1–24);

Δ the changing fortunes of seven nations: Ammon, Moab, Edom, Philistia, Tyre, Sidon and Egypt, with special sections on Tyre and Egypt (25–32);

Δ the restoration that is sure to come for Israel (33–39).

Ezekiel's call to become a prophet is recounted twice.[11] The first passage tells of a whirlwind, a fantastic vision of Yahweh on a throne and four winged creatures bearing the faces of a man, a lion, an ox and an eagle. In the New Testament, the creatures are echoed in John's Revelation, and later they became the symbols for Matthew, Mark, Luke and John. According to the narrative, Ezekiel was given a scroll to eat: that is, he had to hear, learn and inwardly digest the Word of the Lord. In his mouth, it was as sweet as honey. Ezekiel fell into strange spiritual states and was "carried back and forth" between Babylon and Jerusalem — if not in reality, then certainly in his imagination.

In the second account of Ezekiel's call, Yahweh informed him that he was to be a watchman who blows a trumpet in order to warn the people of Israel. If a wicked person died without being warned of his sins, then the sentinel would be accountable. But if Ezekiel did his duty and people still failed to repent, then he would not be answerable. It was not the will or desire of Yahweh that anyone should die; therefore, his prophet had to plead with them to repent, so that they could be pardoned.

IX

Visions of resurrection

There are wonderful passages of hope in Ezekiel 34 and 37. In chapter 34, we read in the REB that because the official guardians and governors had let God and the nation down, God himself would be their Good Shepherd, governor and guardian. He would seek them out to rescue them from exile in an alien land. He would feed them on the mountains of Israel and by her streams, searching for the lost and the stragglers, caring for the sick and giving them all their proper food: as for those who are healthy and strong, they would be left to play. (There is a slight divergence in the NRSV and the KJV.)[12]

In a collection of prophecies that often read strangely, it is refreshing to come across such a wonderful message about the God who cares, the God about whom David sang, "The Lord is my shepherd,"[13] and of whom Second Isaiah said:

He will feed his flock like a shepherd;
he will gather the lambs in his arms,
and carry them in his bosom,
and gently lead the mother sheep.[14]

In chapter 37, there is a tale of Ezekiel's being carried in the spirit and put down in a valley full of bones. "Can these bones live?" God asked him. Ezekiel replied, "Only you, Lord, can tell!" Then a transformation was accomplished by the spirit of Yahweh the Creator. With his powerful energy, he alone could give breath to his creatures, the dead as well as the living. The dead in this vision represent a people or its army that had become decadent and lifeless, "as good as dead." The prophet saw that Yahweh would resuscitate the dead Israel who had been exiled for their folly and sin; they would be restored to their homeland and given another chance. God promised that "a David my servant shall be king over them ... they shall also walk in my judgments, and observe my statutes, and do them.... I will be their God, and they shall be my people."[15] (I have altered "David" to "a David" because the postexilic nation hoped that a new king as devout and successful as David would arise.)

X
The contribution of the great prophets

Passages like Jeremiah 31, Ezekiel 37 and Second Isaiah 40–55 (see chapter 11) show the importance of prophecy to everyone in the Judeo-Christian tradition. Earlier, the eighth-century prophets preached:

Δ about the lovingkindness of Yahweh (Hosea),

Δ for social justice to be emphasized as much as or even more than liturgies of religious observance (Amos);

Δ about Yahweh, the all-merciful, who expects his people to be kind and merciful too (Micah);

Δ about the holiness of Yahweh, God on High whom one comes to adore, a just, loving and merciful God who will not forsake his people forever (First Isaiah).

To such doctrines there were corollaries. Worshippers were to be holy because God is holy; but holiness had come to mean personal integrity and decent moral behaviour instead of only transcendent and miraculous power. People, therefore, should be fair in commercial dealings and gracious to the outcast, even the sexual deviant.

Their religious experiences taught the prophets that Yahweh was the only God to be served by Israel. He was the best of rulers, the best of judges, the best of fathers and, if one may dare to say so, the best of mothers (for the qualities of their God do seem to be maternal as well as paternal). Isaiah 58 makes clear that, as Amos had said, Yahweh would not be served well by fasting and other rites. The *Shema'* noted earlier sums up their faith: one was to love God wholeheartedly and also love one's neighbour as oneself. Unless efforts were made to set the oppressed free, to clothe the naked and to feed the hungry, the cult would be a farce. The same message is repeated in Isaiah 61 and Matthew 25:31–46.

That message, however, is not acceptable to everyone. Some people think that prophets should address religion, not politics, economics, foreign policy and social welfare; that their business should be with heaven, not earth; that it should be with the next world, not this one. Nazi politicians held that view, and it is still heard in some quarters.

Some religious leaders may devote themselves to the traditions of faith: the buildings, the art treasures and the sacred music. Some do emphasize the joys and ceremonies of the liturgy — its words, music, songs and dances — to the exclusion of concerns about social conditions outside the sanctuary. The prophets of Israel, however, insisted that religion is a way of life, that while morality without the graces of worship lacks what Paul Tillich used to call one's "ultimate concern," religion without moral earnestness scarcely deserves anyone's concern.

nine

The Era of the Second Temple

I

Five centuries at a glance

The period that concerns us now as we follow the story line of the Hebrew Bible is sometimes called the postexilic period or, as Jews prefer, the era of the Second Temple, because the return to Jerusalem from exile in Babylon was marked by the rebuilding of the Temple as the centre of religious life.

The prophets, poets and other biblical writers wrote about Judea and the Babylonian, Persian, Macedonian and Roman empires to which the Jews were subject in succession from 538 to 63 B.C. In our reading, we must try to take account of the different social customs, trade, tax laws, humour and religious observances of those centuries and cultures. What follows is a glance at the history and geography, so that the remaining parts of the Hebrew Bible and its Apocrypha may be set in proper context.

We shall quickly note the major events. Babylon fell to Cyrus the Persian. The Persian Darius was defeated by Alexander the Great, who died in 323 B.C. and left a splintered empire: the Antigonids ruled Macedon and Greece; the Seleucids ruled Syria and Persia; and the Ptolemies ruled in Egypt. It was not peaceful. Syria and Egypt fought for control of Judea, the strategic land-bridge between Africa and Asia. So the Jews were buffeted by both powers and, at least in part, influenced by both in several aspects of culture. Early in the second century B.C., a new power erupted on the stage of the Middle East: Rome. In 63 B.C., the quarrelling Hasmonaean princes in Judea called in Rome to settle their dynastic dispute. Rome annexed them and their land!

The era that followed the accession of Alexander the Great in Macedon is known as the Hellenistic Age, for Greek became the *lingua franca* as a result of his conquests. Greek philosophy and moral teaching were influential, for Aristotle had been Alexander's tutor and teachers moved throughout Alexander's empire spreading Greek ideas and customs. In Alexandria, the Hebrew Bible was translated into Greek about 250 B.C. This translation is called the Septuagint (LXX) because the number of the translators was reputed to be seventy. Jews lived in most of the cities and towns around the Mediterranean, and other Jewish writers composed in Greek during this time of the Dispersion. The area was partially unified under Greek authority initially; later it came under Roman control.

Under these circumstances, people were isolated from one another, and there was a greater emphasis on the individual than there had been. The general unrest of the times and the health problems that followed civil wars caused some people to feel that life had no meaning and that religious cults could provide no real consolation. People experienced alienation and hopelessness, although some high-spirited individuals, aware of their own genius, asserted themselves and created niches of power. Individuals increasingly saw themselves as citizens of the world, not just of a city-state or small kingdom. Marcus Aurelius, the stoic Roman emperor, wrote in his Confessions: "Man, thou hast been a citizen in this World-City."[1] Thus, he affirmed that he was a cosmopolitan, as earlier Stoics had also said. One is reminded of the proud claim by the Jewish Christian, Paul of Tarsus, that he was a Roman citizen by birth.[2]

One custom that originated in Egypt and the Persian world was adopted by Alexander and the Roman Caesars: the cult of kings and emperors. Jews, and later Christians, could not accept the idea and suffered for their obstinacy. In particular, when a Syrian tyrant tried to force the Jews to conform to Greek customs, rebellion broke out, leading to a major war: the Maccabean War of Liberation.

The timeline on page 76 may help to place events.

II
Apocryphal and Pseudepigraphical literature of Judaism

From the arrangement of the Hebrew Bible in Christian versions in English, one might well conclude that Malachi was the last book chronologically. That is not so. Daniel can be dated to 166 or 165 B.C. To complete documentation for the period from the end of the Exile in Babylon to the coming of Jesus, one needs to examine the Apocrypha and the Pseudepigrapha (so called because the authors are unknown and their books never became authoritative and biblical) as well as the *Histories of Josephus*, written after A.D. 65.

In the Pseudepigrapha, the important books are *Jubilees, I Enoch,* the *Assumption of Moses,* the *Psalms of Solomon* and the *Scrolls* from the Qumrân Caves by the Dead Sea. In the Apocrypha, the *Wisdom of Ben Sirach* (also known as *Ecclesiasticus*) is spiritually superior to Esther and Proverbs. The *Wisdom of Solomon*, belonging to the Greek period of the second or first century B.C., is far superior to the Song of Songs which has been attributed, wrongly, to King Solomon. *Wisdom* is a most interesting and significant treatment of moral and religious issues, not in the mode of Greek philosophy but rather in that of Hebrew prophecy blended with Greek rationalism. *I Maccabees* is important for the history of the War of Liberation. Many editions of the Bible include the Apocrypha, but it can also be obtained separately. Interesting

Judaism in World History
538–4 B.C.

538 Return from Exile   Cyrus II of Persia 559–529

ERA OF THE SECOND TEMPLE

Malachi

                           Attica's Golden Age 490–347

444 Nehemiah

                           Artaxerxes I of Persia 465–424

398 Ezra
Nehemiah-Ezra

                                       Stoicism 330
                 Death of Alexander the Great 323

Jews under Egypt

                                    Ptolemies in Egypt

? *Proverbs*

                                    Steleucids in Syria

? *Ecclesiastes*

                                    Antigonids in Greece

200 Jews under Syria
? *Ecclesiasticus (Wisdom of Ben Sirach)*
166 *Daniel*
Maccabean War of Liberation
142 – 63 Hasmonaean Ethnarchs and Kings
Pharisees and Essenes
? *Wisdom of Solomon*
63 Jews under Rome

                                            Pompey
                                     Julius Caesar
                                         Octavian

37 Herod the Great   (Augustus)

8 ? Birth of Jesus
4 Death of Herod the Great

passages include *Tobit; Wisdom of Solomon* 1–3, 6–9, 18 and 19; *Ecclesiasticus* 1, 10, 15, 19 and 24–26; and *I Maccabees*.

Within the Hebrew Bible itself, 1 and 2 Chronicles also belong to the postexilic era: they present a rewriting of Israelite history with a theological bias. Joel, Jonah and Job are also late. A special place has to be given to the wonderful poems and oracles collected in Isaiah 40–66, which will be discussed in chapter 11. Nehemiah and Ezra should also be read. Another late document is the prophetic apocalypse ("revelation") of Daniel, which is the subject of the next chapter.

III

Restoration to Judea

As noted earlier, King Cyrus of Persia allowed some Jews to return to Judea from exile in 538 B.C. Though there is still controversy about this, it seems that his successors permitted the rebuilding of Jerusalem's defences between 515 and 450. The Temple too was rebuilt and became known as the Second Temple or the Temple of Zerubbabel. Much later, it was enlarged and transformed by Herod the Great. Gradually a new system of priests, Levites and laity reorganized the worship of Yahweh. Haggai and Zechariah 1–8 tell part of this story.

Ezra the priest, "a scribe skilled in the law of Moses,"[3] arrived in Jerusalem in 398, about forty years after Nehemiah. He is credited with leading a renewal of the ancient Sinai covenant, enforcing customs like Sabbath observance, and promulgating new regulations aimed at ensuring the purity of the Jewish people: "Then Ezra the priest stood up and said to them, 'You have trespassed and married foreign women, and so increased the guilt of Israel. Now make confession to the Lord the God of your ancestors, and do his will; separate yourselves from the peoples of the land and from the foreign wives.' Then all the assembly answered with a loud voice, 'It is so; we must do as you have said.'"[4]

The rhetorical form of this passage suggests that the assembly shouted out its response on cue, but there is no doubt that the decrees of Ezra produced some consternation in families and social life generally. It has been said that the kind of religion espoused by Ezra was at once universalist and separatist: in going beyond the specifics of the Mosaic law, he tended to inculcate a narrow-minded spirit. Given Israel's belief in Yahweh and its especial mission to serve him among the nations, it can be argued that the separatism legislated by Ezra and the postexilic community may have been necessary. But it also had its dangers, and it must be contrasted with the more universalist message of the Second Isaiah.

The people restored to Judea should not be described as a Jewish church or a nation-state. It was not a cultic association based on national identity only, but rather a Volk: a kinship-group knit together by a notable tradition, a great history and a special faith. The Judeans or Jews were, therefore, a distinct society in the Middle East. For a while, there were twin heads of the community: a civil governor, because it was part of a province in the Persian empire, and a high priest who was in charge of the liturgy. Two such leaders were Zerubbabel and Joshua. The description that fits this community of the Second Temple era, then, is either a religious republic or an ecclesiastical state. Apart from the short period of 142–63 B.C., the Jews were a subject people. Sovereignty eluded them until A.D. 1948.

IV

The religion of early Judaism

At the beginning of this book, it was noted that the Hebrew Bible in its primary elements came into existence after a series of collected traditions was available and after editing by priests in the fifth century B.C. Much of the postexilic literature did not acquire sacred, authoritative or canonical status until near the end of the first century A.D. Nevertheless it is valuable for understanding the development of Judaism.

There is a secular Jewish festival called Purim that seems to have originated in Persia before the return from exile. It was, and has remained, a very joyful occasion, marked by giving presents and alms to the poor. At first it included nothing that could be regarded as specially religious. In some way, it is related to a tale that is retold in the book of Esther about a Jew called Mordecai and a man named Haman who was the chief minister of a Persian emperor. Hence *2 Maccabees* called the day of Purim "Mordecai's Day."[5] The book of Esther also lacks religious elements: Yahweh is never mentioned, and there is no reference to worship other than to fasts and lamentations.[6] The book is also confused about the royal customs and the chronology of the Persian empire. It is, therefore, a piece of historical fiction that conveys only one message: that persecution of the Jews is a crime and that Jews were, and presumably will be, revenged in terrible fashion against their enemies.[7] The tale of how Haman was hanged on gallows that he had intended for Mordecai is a nice example of irony and a good read. This book remains as a protest against antisemitism.[8]

A short story that is usually regarded as taking an opposite stance to the particularism of Esther is Jonah, which tells a well-known story. The prophet Jonah was reluctant to go from his Hebrew homeland to pagan Nineveh as spokesman for Yahweh so that the population of that great city might have an opportunity to repent their sins and be forgiven. The sailors in whose ship he was fleeing cast him into the sea to propitiate whatever god he had offended. In a reference to the Jonah story in the Gospel of Matthew, the KJV speaks of a "whale's belly" into which Jonah fell, while NRSV and REB translate the passage as "a sea monster."[9] The reference in Jonah itself is, in fact, to "a great fish."[10] Eventually Jonah was compelled to visit Nineveh: the city's people repented and were forgiven. Jonah, though, was very displeased and angry with his God.

The traditional interpretation of this story is that because Israel's God was interested in pagans too, Jews should not be narrow-minded or isolationist: the opposite lesson to those in Ezra and Esther. The story raises questions, especially about the relevance of the prayer offered up by Jonah while he was in the belly of the fish,[11] but also about the ending where Jonah's rest under a climbing gourd was ended by God. It is possible that the tale emphasizes not merely a universalist spirit in the people of God but also a divine prerogative that may well be taken too lightly by his worshippers. It was Yahweh who commissioned Jonah. It was he who brought the fish and then made possible the prophet's escape. A second time, he bade Jonah to preach in Nineveh. He prepared the plant that would shelter Jonah in the midday sun. He caused a worm to wither the plant. The lesson for Jonah was surely that his primary duty was obedience to his God.

The book of Job, also from the era of the Second Temple, is concerned with what kind of deity God is. The book questions why the innocent suffer. Job is memorable for its marvellous poetry and the character of Job the sufferer. It begins with a prose prologue, in which a reference to Satan — as the prosecuting counsel in the council of heaven rather than the devil — may be a later addition. Poetic dialogues between Job and each of three friends, in chapters 3–31, are important. In chapters 32–37 (probably another addition by editors), there are speeches by a conventional youth called Elihu. Finally there is an address by Yahweh to Job that is so overwhelming in its assertion of the magnificence and power of God that Job is sent to his knees in abject surrender (38–41). Job makes a brief reply in 42:1–6.

The denouement is in chapter 42, where verses 12–17 may also have been added. God rebukes the friends of Job, and Job intercedes for them. Then there is an astonishing reversal of fortune: "The Lord gave Job twice as much as he had before. Then there came to him all his brothers and sisters and all who had known him before, and they ate bread with him in his house; they showed him sympathy and comforted him for all the evil that the Lord had brought upon him; and each of them gave him a piece of money and a gold ring."[12]

In the story, the author asserts that the evil Job endured was brought on him by his God. If the prologue is genuine, we are to understand that Job suffered because God had wagered with Satan that, no matter how terrible the evil and suffering Job might be forced to endure, Job would not curse God or do evil. His integrity and goodness were such that he had been "eyes to the blind, and feet ... to the lame."[13]

The problem is that good, innocent people like Job do suffer terribly in this world. They suffer not only from the inhumanity exhibited in torture and the denial of human rights but also from natural disasters like earthquakes and diseases. If creation was good, why did a tempter get into the garden of Eden? Why did the Holocaust of 1939–45 happen if there is a God who is just and caring? Do we not require a theodicy, that is, a defence of the Creator as trustworthy, wise and gracious?

There is no theoretical answer in the scriptures. Amos wrote, "Shall there be evil in a city, and the Lord hath not done it?"[14] A distinction needs to be made between the actual will of God — what he would wish for humanity and the entire creation — and the permissive will of God, by which he lets people and the universe be. In other words, there is a possibility that creation was self-limiting, even for God. If any other way had been possible to allow human beings, with reason and conscience, to come into existence, the Creator would have done it. Risks had to be taken, and one risk is that people must have freedom of choice: to obey God or to rebel against him. It is in the context of human freedom that we have to set at least part of the suffering of the innocent. At the same time, there is something in the universe that is irrational or beyond our reason, so that accidents do happen. We are a very small part of the vastness of creation. Yet what other creatures think God's thoughts after him and believe, in spite of evidence to the contrary, that there is an ultimate goodness, that a divine heart pulses unseen and that God shares somehow in the sorrows and sufferings of women and men? Job raises such questions but does not fully answer them. The book stimulates faith and feeds a hope that evil will be overcome, sin will be defeated and the kingdom of God will come.

V
Some new elements of the Second Temple era

△ There is an emphasis on the individual, traced sometimes to Ezekiel's teaching of each person's responsibility before God for sins.[15] There is a similar concept in the Psalms: "Nevertheless I am continually with you; you hold my right hand. You guide me with your counsel, and afterward you will receive me with honor."[16]

△ Related to this is the growing faith in a life to come. The concept was not immortality, like that in Greek thinking: it was resurrection. Jews could not easily sunder body and spirit or think of a disembodied spirit. So we read: "Your dead shall live, their corpses shall rise. O dwellers in the dust, awake and sing for joy!"[17] A passage in the *Wisdom of Solomon* is famous: "God created man to be immortal.... Nevertheless through envy of the devil came death into the world.... But the souls of the righteous are in the hand of God, and there shall no torment touch them ... their hope is full of immortality."[18]

△ There is conflict between the isolationism and legalism of the Ezra renewal and the more universalist spirit of Jonah and, as we shall note later, the poetic prophecies of Second Isaiah. The underlying theological question was whether the God of Israel is the one and only God of the whole world (monotheism). Related to this question was the problem of defining the character of the adherents to early, postexilic, Judaism. Were they, as the people of God, a kingdom or republic of priests who functioned in one centre only, the rebuilt Temple of Jerusalem? Or was this renewed community really to be the representative of all nations, a true Abraham-family that should be a blessing to all and through whom all others would be blessed? The difference of opinion is longstanding and has continued.

Δ Finally, it may be remarked that although the experience of the Exile disillusioned many Jews, some found refuge in apocalyptic expectations. The future of the nation might still be pictured in terms of the David ideal, and some time later there emerged what is known as the messianic hope. To messianism and apocalypse we must devote further space, and first we turn to the apocalyptic dreams and hopes in the book of Daniel.

ten

Daniel: Dreams and Hopes

I

Heroes of faith

One can well imagine pious Jews in Auschwitz, Buchenwald and Dachau in the 1940s mulling over their faith in Yahweh as they awaited their fate at the hands of the Nazis. No doubt their musings turned to the memory of the scriptures and to some of their forebears who had suffered, especially those who had heroic qualities.

Early Christians also faced similar questionings, fears and hopes in the years of persecution. We can tell how their courage and faith were sustained as we look at the frescos they painted in the catacombs: their subjects were Noah in his ark, Moses striking a rock and miraculously finding water, Samson slaying Philistine enemies and David fighting Goliath armed only with a sling. These are illustrations of heroism, of life rescued from the jaws of death, of the faithful redeemed by the brave servants of the one God.

Moreover, after several hundred years, when the persecution had become a distant memory, the same images appeared in the panels of the medieval Irish High Crosses (e.g. at Clonmacnoise, Moone and Monasterboice) and on some of the Pictish cross-slabs of northeast Scotland. Faced by the same problems, people turned to the same biblical examples of trust, hope and life from the dead. Among the heroes of the Hebrew Bible who fostered such hopes were the Three Children and Daniel, whose witness to God's goodness and saving power is described in the book of Daniel.

Daniel was a Judean youth who was captured and taken to the court of the Babylonian king Nebuchadrezzar (605–562 B.C.). In Babylon he received a new name, Belteshazzar,[1] but no one ever thinks of him as such. In that alien land, his commitment to Yahweh did not waver: he would not willingly eat the Gentile food of his royal master[2] and he refused to abandon prayers of petition to Yahweh in spite of a decree by King Darius that no one should petition "any god or man for thirty days" on pain of being cast into a den of lions. Three times a day Daniel continued to say his prayers, "his windows being open toward Jerusalem."[3] Such courage and fidelity inevitably brought dire penalties upon him, and it was only by a miracle that he escaped with his life.

There were also three other young Jewish heroes, called "children" in the KJV. Their Babylonian names were Shadrach, Meshach and Abednego, and this time it is these names that became familiar. They too insisted on eating kosher. They too would worship no god but Yahweh, and their trust in divine protection was boundless. When it was decreed that refusal to worship a golden image erected by Nebuchadrezzar would be punished by their being thrown into a fiery furnace, they replied:

If it be so, our God whom we serve is able to deliver us from the burning fiery furnace, and he will deliver us out of thine hand, O king. But if not ... be it known unto thee, O king, that we will not serve thy gods, nor worship the golden image which thou hast set up.[4]

It is that daring "if not ...," as I have punctuated the text, that describes their unshakable confidence in the providence of Yahweh. The story ends with their amazing rescue. When the king came to see them, expecting to find that they had been incinerated in his "Buchenwald," he saw four men loose in the furnace: not one of them hurt, "and the fourth," he said, "has the appearance of a god."[5]

II

A romantic figure

Daniel is pictured as more than a youthful pious hero. He may have been modelled on Joseph, a similar hero of the Torah, for at 9:11–13, there is a reference to what is written in the law of Moses (that is, the Torah). Like Joseph, Daniel was inspired to be an interpreter of dreams and rose to become the ruler of a kingdom.[6]

Later, in the reign of Belshazzar, the son of Nebuchadrezzar, Daniel was called to interpret strange words written by "the fingers of a human hand [that] appeared and began writing on the plaster of the wall of the royal palace, next to the lampstand."[7] This phenomenon took place during a royal banquet for a thousand of the king's lords. The words were MENE, MENE, TEKEL and PARSIN. They represented weights that had a monetary value: a mina, a shekel and a half-shekel. Daniel announced that the king had been "weighed in the balances, and ... found wanting."[8] He interpreted the words as a warning that the empire of Babylon was doomed and would pass to the Medes. He was proved right.

The most romantic story told is of Daniel in the lions' den. Once again, it is claimed that an angel came and shut the mouths of the lions so that Daniel was quite unhurt. The king was utterly astonished.

III

An apocalyptic hero

The stories we have reviewed are fascinating in themselves and significant in the spiritual lessons they teach. Daniel is both the central character and sometimes the narrator of the document. His real significance, however, lies in the fact that he had visions. They purported to unveil the future, not just the immediate future in the era of Nebuchadrezzar and Belshazzar but also a much more distant future, generations ahead. These revelations or apocalypses belong to a category of religious literature that is called apocalyptic.

Apocalyptic may be defined as prophecy that is geared to a truly momentous time in the future, called a *kets* in Hebrew. When that comes, it was claimed, an extraordinary intervention by God would change the course of history: perhaps it would end an historical epoch, perhaps it would be the end of the world as we know it. Some apocalypses were relatively sober; some carried extravagant dreams and hopes.

Like more conventional prophecies, apocalyptic was directed to contemporaries of the writer, but the message itself concerned a future time that might seem far off by chronological reckoning and yet, for believers, was a time that had always to be "soon." The *kets* was always imminent. One could not be sure when Yahweh would strike or how he would accomplish his designs. An apocalyptic prophet gave the impression, though, that he knew the secrets of Yahweh.

In the case of the book ascribed to Daniel, the hope was that there would be a new era when the Israel of God, the religious republic of Judaism represented by the Three Children and the inspired Daniel, would be liberated from bondage and once more glorified throughout the world. They are defined as "the saints of the most High."[9] Universal sovereignty would be awarded to them, not to the Babylonians, Medes, Persians, Greeks, Syrians or Romans (who at 11:30 are called "Chittim"). Israel is embodied, in chapter seven, in a man or an angel, perhaps its guardian angel Michael; to him "was given dominion and glory and kingship, that all peoples, nations, and languages should serve him. His dominion is an everlasting dominion that shall not pass away, and his kingship is one that shall never be destroyed."[10]

The book of Daniel is composed of two parts: the tales of

heroism (1–6) and the dreams and hopes of a universal Israelite kingdom (7–12).

IV

A fictional hero

A legend about a man whose name seems to be virtually the same as that of the biblical Daniel comes from the ancient city-state of Ugarit in northern Syria. There is also a verse in Ezekiel that reads, "What, are you wiser than Daniel? Is no secret beyond your grasp?"[11] So this name circulated in certain quarters. But the content of the book of Daniel compels us to hold its hero Daniel as an invention, part of what might be called an historical novel (except for its literary form as an apocalypse). In ancient times, the name of a character from a previous era was often used as either the author of or the main character in what purports to be a divine revelation. The name does not make the document the true word of God.

A major clue to the dating of the book is in the succession of empires just mentioned: from Babylon to Syria and the Romans. The time span involved is at least four hundred years. Specifically, one text speaks of "the abomination that maketh desolate."[12] This is known to be a reference to an action by the Syrian king, Antiochus IV Epiphanes, in 168 B.C. He polluted the Temple in Jerusalem by setting up an altar there to Zeus. This outraged the Jews. They had been continually oppressed by the Syrians who had tried to force Hellenistic Greek customs, fashions and religion on the Jews.

Syrian policy and actions provoked the Maccabees to make war on the Syrians, and the book of Daniel has to be seen in that context. Its date is, therefore, a year or two after the defilement of the Temple but probably before it had been cleansed (on Kislev 25, mid-December, 165 B.C.), hence 166 or 165 B.C. *I Maccabees* in the Apocrypha tells the tale of the Maccabean revolt. From the point of view of the Syrian government, the book of Daniel was no better than subversive propaganda disguised in the trappings of religion and prophecy.

The discovery of this context for the book of Daniel opens the way to an appreciation of its encouraging message for the resistance fighters and for the entire Jewish community; it also allows us to refuse to interpret the document as an infallible revelation of world history. Certainly Daniel was a rallying cry of hope and faith. Predictions of victory are put into the mouth of the angel Gabriel, the "Interpreter Spirit" who was later to be known as the angel of the Annunciation. Moreover, this fresh way to see Daniel means that one should not spend time trying to unravel the book's secrets such as the "weeks and weeks of years"[13] that are somehow related to Leviticus 26:14–34 and Jeremiah 25:11–12 and 29:10. Rather, a few historical facts should be kept in mind:

Δ The Maccabees did defeat the Syrians. The message of Daniel was effective there and then, and its predictions were never intended to reach out to our own century.

Δ The Hasmonaean family, to whom the Maccabees belonged, set themselves up in Judea as ethnarchs and later as kings and even as high priests. The claim to the high priesthood was very dubious and produced grievous disputes. There was no universal sovereignty over all peoples, nations and languages.

Δ Jewish independence lasted for some eighty years and came to an end in 63 B.C.

Δ There is no likelihood that there ever will be a worldwide empire of Israel. That would not be desirable, and it should be dismissed as a piece of Jewish nationalism from an age that is gone.

A compelling argument against wrestling with the predictions and secrets of Daniel is that it is not reasonable to think that a Jew in the time of Nebuchadrezzar had prevision of the imperial succession over the next four hundred years. That would imply that those empires existed in advance and could be spotted from afar. Before he was born, Cyrus would have already conquered Babylon. His destiny was written in the stars, as the astrologers would say. But that view is a denial of a personal God who allows considerable freedom to people. Morality cannot abide a predetermined plan whereby people travel in time along rigid lines.

That is not the end of the story, however. For Daniel has, in fact, stimulated hope and encouraged the faithful in their trust and faith. Their God is Daniel's God, who hears the cry of the tortured, the enslaved and the troubled and who finds his own spiritual means to comfort and assist them. He raises up human agents to be comforters, "paracletes" as they may be called because they are inspired by the Paraclete who is the Holy Spirit of God.

In Daniel 7, the powerful empires are represented by bestial figures: a lion with eagles' wings, a bear, a leopard and a terrifying beast with iron teeth.[14] These are all dream likenesses, but they have symbolic meaning. The fierce qualities of the heraldic beasts point to the nature of imperialism. Such symbols still appear in the insignia of certain powerful nations today.

According to Daniel, when world empire passes to the saints of God, his Israel, it is to be represented by a man: "As I watched in the night visions, I saw one like a human being coming with the clouds of heaven.... To him was given dominion."[15] The promise in this symbolic man is that the true kingship of God's people and of God himself is to be exercised in a humane community. Perhaps, therefore, one can say that when a nation-state changes to a more godly community, its logo (so to say) will be a person who is at once human and a very icon of God, the ruler of all nation-states. That seems to be the message being conveyed by Daniel's vision and expectation.

eleven

Climax and Threshold: The Spiritual Achievement of Early Judaism

I

Climax and threshold

In both world and Jewish history, a significant moment was reached in 63 B.C. when the Roman general Pompey arrived in Palestine. About twenty-six years later, the Romans set Herod on the throne in Jerusalem. He was the son of Antipater, an Idumaean whose Jewish credentials could be, and were, challenged. Although the story is not told in the Hebrew Bible, Herod established himself only after a struggle. His territory comprised Trachonitis, in the northeast; Galilee, the central area that had once been the kingdoms of Israel and Judah; and Peraea on the east bank of the river Jordan. Herod ruled with distinction until 4 B.C.

Jesus of Nazareth was born during Herod's reign, as early as 8 B.C. or perhaps about 6 B.C., as may be inferred from Matthew 2:16. For Christians, therefore, the final years of the

Second Temple era were a threshold leading into the age of the new covenant and the Church.

In the postexilic period, Jewish life had to be reorganized. During this time, many synagogues sprang up throughout the Dispersion since ten males constituted the quorum for their establishment. Synagogues were gathering places for worship, the study of the Torah and mutual encouragement. Each local synagogue functioned as a law-court for certain cases. In Palestine, after the resettlement, there was also a central court or Sanhedrin whose origins are obscure. The Sanhedrin, led by priests with the high priest as its president, interpreted the legal provisions of the Torah and helped to regulate social and political life under the various military occupations.

Probably during the second century B.C., different parties emerged within Judaism: a priestly caste known as Sadducees and groups of devout people called the *chasidim*. From the *chasidim*, both the Pharisees and the Essenes may have descended. The Pharisees were mainly lay folk interested in applying the rules of the Sinai covenant to their own daily circumstances. The Essenes were dominated by priests who may have rebelled against the corruption and power struggles of the official priesthood.

Many traditions had been collected and edited to produce what now constituted scripture:

Δ the Torah, with the massive authority of Moses attached and with Deuteronomy added to Genesis, Exodus, Leviticus and Numbers;

Δ the Former Prophets or, as we would say, the Histories;

Δ the Latter Prophets;

Δ perhaps a collection of Psalms.

This scripture was the core of religious education. It was to be studied as divine revelation feeding the hopes and dreams of the population. It had to be interpreted by the learned so that it would be relevant to the daily life of Jews within the Roman Empire.

As was noted above, belief in life after death and a new stress on the worth of the individual were features of religion at this time. Jewish faith reached a climax in the poetic prophecies of Second Isaiah and through teachers who had been influenced by them. In this period, new expectations, called messianic, were developing; it was to them that the Christian Church turned to find material that would identify its recognition of Jesus as anointed by God.

Passages that may be read include Psalms 2, 13, 18, 22, 27, 34, 72, 89, 130 and 146; Zechariah 6:9–14 and 9:9–13; and Isaiah 9:1–7, 11:1–9, 40–55, 60, 61 and 65:17–25.

II

About "end-times"

A Christian reading of the scriptures, especially as referring to Jesus, has been coloured by a particular interpretation of Hebrew prophecy and hope. For Christians, Jesus is regarded as the Lord's anointed — his "Christ" or "Messiah."

A specific hope of a Messiah in the "end-times" did not mature in time to be incorporated in the Hebrew Bible, however. There are, in that Bible, a host of references to the coming of a new, ideal "David" and these were exploited in the interest of the later messianic expectation. The following passages have been understood by both Jews and Christians as messianic:

Δ "The people that walked in darkness have seen a great light ... For unto us a child is born" (Isaiah 9:2,6).

Δ "And there shall come forth a rod out of the stem of Jesse" (Isaiah 11:1).

Δ The throne of David will be established for ever and his dynasty will survive likewise (2 Samuel 7:16).

Δ "I have found David my servant; with my holy oil have I anointed him [so that he is a Messiah of sorts].... I will make [this David] my firstborn.... His seed also will I make to endure for ever, and his throne as the harp of heaven" (Psalm 89:20–36).

Psalms 2 and 72 were similarly taken in this way.

But the primary allusions of these texts were to hopes for a time in the near future, not for something that was to happen in a world to come. The reading of them gets confused because both the community of Judaism and the early Christians reinterpreted the prophecies and songs, applying them to an "end-expectation" of a universal Day of Judgment and a reversal of the fortunes of God's faithful people. It's as if the libretto for Handel's *Messiah* had already been written into the Bible: the text would have been transformed to Christian belief and its original place in the history of the Jewish nation would have been banished.

It is very debatable how much reinterpretation to allow, though literature of this kind may very well suffer change because of new events and new insights. When that happens, one says that there has been "fulfilment" of the ancient expressions. The point to be made here is that true Jewish Messianism, as a systematic expectation, developed at a comparatively late period. It was linked to earlier hopes defined in terms of a revival of the Davidic kingdom. Sometimes one reads of a "new age" or sometimes of a "world to come." Yet it is unclear what precisely was hoped for. God had to fulfil his purposes. Evil had to be overcome. A judgment was placed at the end of time or, alternatively, at the end of that time when God's people were in bondage, as world-weary, anxious and fretful they pictured the eternal blessedness of a kingdom of God. As a result, there was great diversity in the Messianic hope and no clear statement about a new world either on earth or in heaven.

III
The different types of Messianism

Δ The Lord's "anointed" was by definition a "Messiah," for that is what the Hebrew word means. That person was a prince or a king and so the Messiah of the "end-time" was often viewed as being a king. Davidic prophecies follow this view.[1]

Δ Occasionally a prophet, like Elisha, could be said to be anointed.[2] "Anointed," in both his case and as it is used in Isaiah 61:1 ("The Spirit of the Lord God is upon me; because the Lord hath anointed me to preach good tidings"), is not to be taken literally, however, as if oil had been poured on their heads.

Δ More important is the discovery that the promise in Deuteronomy 18:15-18 of "a prophet like Moses" was taken seriously in some messianic sense by the Qumrân community.

Δ Priests, especially the high priest, were always anointed.[3] Once again, the Qumrân community seems to have been looking for a messianic high priest who would take precedence over another messianic figure, a prince of the congregation.

Δ In Psalm 105:15 (NRSV), God spoke of "my anointed ones." This could mean variously the patriarchs (Abraham, Isaac and Jacob), perhaps their families or possibly the entire nation of Israel. Probably this has no bearing on the developed messianic hope.

The fact is that the messianic hope was never systematically set out. There was faith that it would be fulfilled somehow, sometime, but devout imagination had a free field to speculate. Indeed, since Yahweh was the true King of Israel and kings were only his sacred representatives, one occasionally finds evidence of an expectation that God himself would come down to settle world affairs and liberate the nation: he would be his own Messiah, in person.[4]

Moreover, in keeping with later Jewish thinking about the Spirit of the Lord, any servant of God (prophet, priest or king) would require an endowment of that spirit, the Holy Spirit of Christian faith.[5] It was in relation to a permanent or plenary endowment of the Spirit that many of the texts cited above were applied by Jews to the coming Messiah and by Christians to Jesus as one who had been baptized with the Spirit and who healed and preached by the power of the Spirit, a theme of great importance in the New Testament gospel-books.

IV

Second Isaiah: the poetry of vicarious suffering

I wrote earlier that Jewish faith reached a climax in the poems and preaching of the unknown genius we call Second Isaiah. It is fitting to examine more closely his contribution to the faith of Israel, for his legacy has had the most profound effects both in Judaism and in Christianity.

Poems and sermons from the exilic period

In the book of Isaiah, chapters 1–23, 28–33 and 36–39 (with some exceptions) belong to the monarchical time of the eighth century, while chapters 40–66 have as backdrop the exilic and postexilic predicament of Israel. It is agreed by many today that chapters 40–55 derive from a single great poet living at the time of the Exile or soon after, while 56–66 comprise pieces of diverse origin, some of them perhaps stemming from the great poet himself or from a close disciple. In the poetic preaching of the Second Isaiah, we are reading work of a very sensitive genius of the spiritual life. This poet penetrated deeply into the mind of the God he worshipped as Lord, Creator and Redeemer.

Chapters 40–55 as an anthology

The actual collecting of the anthology that is chapters 40–55 was not the work of the poet himself. It was assembled and edited at a later time when all the biblical prophecies were given final form and put alongside the Torah (Pentateuch) to become the Bible. To find one's way around in an anthology is not easy, so the following analysis may be helpful:

Δ In 40:1–41:29, the glory of the Lord is to be revealed.

Δ In 42:1–49:12, the Lord acts and will act in time through his servant people.

Δ In 49:13–53:12, the servant of the Lord is saintly and innocent, but he must suffer for the guilty.

Δ In 54 and 55, the restored Israel will be a just and good society, and the word of God will be accomplished.

The major themes of Second Isaiah

As stated in the introduction, it is a primary purpose of this book to persuade you to take up the Bible, in the classic King James Version but with the use also of the New Revised Standard Version or the Revised English Bible, and discover its values for yourself. For the poems in this anthology, the KJV is preferred for the beauty of its language, but even here you may wish to consult one of the new translations. I shall outline the primary themes of Second Isaiah with some quotations.

Δ It is a notable feature that Zion, the hill of Jerusalem or Israel as a people may be summoned to shout and sing for joy. This is a gospel-book. "O Zion, that bringest good tidings, get thee up into the high mountain; O Jerusalem, that bringest good tidings, lift up thy voice with strength ... say unto the cities of Judah, Behold your God!"[6]

Δ The prophet promised divine pardon for Israel's sins: "Comfort ye, comfort ye my people, saith your God. Speak ye comfortably to Jerusalem, and cry unto her, that her warfare is accomplished, that her iniquity is pardoned."[7]

Δ It was the divine intention to bring back the exiles from Babylon and resettle them in their own land. The doom of Babylon was certain. "Come down, and sit in the dust, O virgin daughter of Babylon, sit on the ground: there is no throne, O daughter of the Chaldeans ... none shall save thee."[8] Next, using powerful images, the passage tells us that the word of the Lord declared that God would do wonders never seen before, that there would be a way in the wilderness and rivers in the desert, that the dragons, the owls and the beasts of the field would honour Yahweh, and his people would praise him: "I will make all my mountains a way, and my highways shall be exalted. Behold, these shall come from far: and, lo, these from the north and from the west."[9]

Δ The idea of universalism is evident. It is very significant that in one of the poems, about Israel as the servant of the Lord or, more probably, about a single person as the embodiment of Israel, it is said that his mission cannot be confined to Jacob and Israel, to his own kinsfolk. He is also to guide the gentile nations: "I will also give thee for a light to the Gentiles, that thou mayest be my salvation unto the end of the earth."[10] The NRSV clarifies: "that my salvation may reach to the end of the earth."

It must be confessed, however, that there is part of this expectation that is grating to me. In 45:14 (REB), it says that "toilers of Egypt and Nubian merchants and Sabaeans bearing tribute will come into your power and be your slaves, will come and follow you in chains." This is a reference to a nationalist victory when the other nations will be subject to Israel, as forecast later (Daniel 7:14). Not even Second Isaiah was exempt from this hope that Israel would one day be a world empire. It is all too easy to make sacred the life and hopes of the Jews in exilic and postexilic times while forgetting that they took part in the power politics of the Middle East, were involved in its economic affairs and were related in many ways to other societies.

Δ It is not surprising that a nation that believed in divine law as an essential element in the *torah* of its God should conceive of God as judge and, because of their inevitable involvement in international relationships, that they should think nations would sometime be summoned before the judgment seat of God: "Produce your cause, saith the Lord; bring forth your strong reasons, saith the King of Jacob."[11] "Behold my servant, whom I uphold; mine elect, in whom my soul delighteth; I have put my spirit upon him: he shall bring forth judgment [justice] to the Gentiles."[12]

Δ Nothing is more impressive in this poetry than the concept of God. Yahweh alone is God: that is monotheism. He is the universal judge and the final victor over all his foes. He is, of course, the helper and saviour of Israel and, presumably, also of the Gentiles to whom Israel is sent. He is the incomparable creator, a conviction that provides the poet's imagination with some of his grandest verse: "Hast thou not known? hast thou not heard, that the everlasting God, the Lord, the Creator of the ends of the earth, fainteth not, neither is weary?.... Even the youths shall faint and be weary, and the young men shall utterly fall: But they that wait upon the Lord shall renew their strength; they shall mount up with wings as eagles; they shall run, and not be weary; and they shall walk, and not faint."[13]

This Yahweh is the God of the Exodus who divided the sea; his name is "the Lord of hosts."[14] He is conscious of his status and will not allow his glory to be given to another; thus, one must never revere any other as god or serve an idol of any

Opening the Scriptures

kind, neither a wooden image nor some great cause that is not a cause ennobled by the spirit of the Lord.

Δ I have left to the end of this outline of major themes that of the Servant, though it is of the first importance for the theology of Second Isaiah and his view of Israel's mission.

As long ago as 1892, it was suggested that there are four songs of the Servant and that they were put into the anthology of Second Isaiah's poetry. They are (1) 42:1–4, (2) 49:1–6, (3) 50:4–9 and (4) 52:13–53:12.

The more these passages are studied in the context of the whole anthology, however, the more one notices that other references to the Servant abound. If they are songs, then they cannot be regarded as alien intrusions. Everything hangs together, as can be seen by reading 41:8–10, 43:8–13, 44:1, 44:2, 44:21, 45:4 and 48:12. In any case, it is not at all certain that four songs have been correctly isolated.

The identity of the Servant varies. In one poem, it is clear that the Servant is to recall Jacob-Israel to the service of Yahweh. But in the others, the community called Israel is the Servant whose mission is to the Gentile world, just as it is for the individual in 49:6. The Servant is at once the whole people and also a single embodiment or incarnation of it. The latter may have been someone known to the poet, such as Jeremiah; but it might be Moses, who is called the servant of Yahweh in Exodus 14:31 and Numbers 12:7.

Vicarious suffering

Isaiah 52:13–53:12, which contains passages about vicarious suffering, is a section of unusual interest and significance. *Vicarious* means that something is done in lieu of something else, or that someone acts or accepts a state of life on behalf of others, as a martyr does, for example. In Christian theology, it is often suggested that the death of Jesus makes him a voluntary martyr. He gave his life because of love for God, to save people from evil and sin. In the religious teaching of many Jews, suffering and sin were connected: this may be seen in the drama of Job. Vicarious suffering may lead, then, to a doctrine of atonement effected when one person assumes the guilt of others and suffers the penalty for it in their stead.

There is a group of Psalms in the Hebrew Bible (13, 18, 22, 27, 34, 119:169–176, 130 and 146) that tell of the afflictions of worshippers and their cries to their God for relief. Had he forgotten them? "My God, my God," cried one, "why hast thou forsaken me?"[15] These are notable confessions and protestations, and without being self-righteous they assume the basic goodness and religious loyalty of the nation and the psalmists.

Hebrew poets and teachers did not try to provide philosophical answers to the problem of innocent suffering, but they echo the defiant words of the Three Children, who said that their God "will deliver us.... But if not ... be it known unto thee, O king, that we will not serve thy gods."[16]

In the faith of postexilic Judaism, the response to the questions posed by terrorism, persecution and the mad enmity of imperialist powers went along the following lines:

Δ Much suffering is brought about by people and should be cured by them.

Δ Suffering may, indeed, be undeserved and unfair. Nevertheless, when it is endured out of love and obedience to God, believing that he has permitted it and trusting that others will benefit, suffering can transform night into morning.

Δ This world of our common everyday life is a world that is "outside of Eden." In it, people do not understand one another in the babbling of a thousand tongues. Noise is produced by the clash of armour and worldly empires (some of it still in the same areas of the Middle East as before), by the laments of the wounded and the permanently disabled and by the raucous verse of the insensitive who live to make money and enjoy the pleasures of the flesh. There is an example of the devilish nature of persecution of faithful Jews in *2 Maccabees* 7: a mother and seven sons were arrested and the sons tortured brutally before the mother's eyes. It is the prototype of a recurring pattern that culminated in the Nazi holocaust.

Δ If an innocent servant of God suffers for the sake of others, he will indeed feel distress, yet the Lord will heal him who gave himself as a sacrifice for sin: "After his suffering he will see light and be satisfied."[17] For God is not indifferent. He is deeply involved in the misfortunes and sins of his people and rescues them. As at the Exodus, he will be among them, leading them through desert places, informing them that there is forgiveness for them and seeking their return to his obedience. One may ask, finally, which is the spiritually greater: the suffering human servant who gives his life as a ransom for the congregation or the loving God who will so act in the history of the congregation that he and they will together enjoy the blessedness of eternal life?

V

The legacy of early Judaism

From reading the Hebrew Bible, one comes to realize that the spiritual achievement of Judaism is remarkable. It is customary to define it in religious terms, for the Bible is a sacred anthology that speaks of God the Maker and Redeemer of humanity and the universe. In assessing the legacy of Israel, however, one should remember that its people lived in the central highlands of Canaan. They had olives to tend, sheep and goats to herd, grain to sow and reap, trade to fill their working days, relationships to build and sustain and children to raise. Their economic and social developments have become the subjects of study only recently and add greatly to the comprehension of Hebrew life and thought. History must not be confined to tales of battles long ago, political infighting and religious controversies.

When we pay attention to social history, the scriptures become more relevant to our own times. The Hebrew Bible teaches that duty is paramount: duty to love and serve the Creator first of all and duty to love and serve all one's neighbours as well. Such a love is a caring attachment, not a romantic one. It is meant to be a godly, sacred love, not earthly, materialist or self-centred. For the sacred is what is worth dying for and what is worth living for. The answers to Israel's existential problems were not theoretical or wrapped up in pious verbiage. They were expressed in songs of praise, in petitions and intercessions of prayer to God, in joyful feasts, in disciplined fasting, in worship and in myths of great beauty and profound truth. It is a legacy to be grateful for.

Rembrandt (1606 – 1669), *Jesus with the Sick and the Poor*, etching, 1st state, 1649. London, British Museum.

    This wonderful etching is known as "The Hundred Guilder Print" from the auction price paid for it soon after it was finished.
    The sick and poor crowd around Jesus to be blessed in healing and teaching (see Luke 5:17, 5:21 and other places in the first three Gospels). Skeptical and nasty-minded scribes and Pharisees appear, none too clearly, to the far right of Jesus. Rembrandt makes us aware of the miserable condition of the folk who came to see and hear the new prophet out of Nazareth; he understands them as human beings, real people. And his Jesus too is a properly human healer and teacher, yet one in whom divine light shines. He is the Saviour who illumines, exposes and comforts the children, the men and women who come to touch him and listen to his words of life.

Reproduced by courtesy of the Trustees of the British Museum.

twelve

Luke's Life of Jesus

I
Getting a perspective on the New Testament

We come now to read the second main division of the scriptures, the New Testament, which tells about the career of Jesus and the first hundred years of the Christian Church.

A fact to remember is that Jesus and the first disciples did not possess a New Testament; there was none until the latter half of the second century. They did, however, have a Bible: the Torah, the prophets and the psalms. Some of their preaching was devoted to Christian interpretation of that Bible, since they believed that there were many forecasts in it of the coming of the Christ who is Jesus.

To begin with, the new movement was spread by word of mouth, announcing the significance of Jesus, his mission, ministry, death and resurrection. That oral tradition seems to have sufficed until about the year 70, the year that the Romans defeated the Jews and partially destroyed Jerusalem. By then, the three most important leaders, Peter, Paul and James the Lord's brother, were dead. So it became essential to record the reminiscences of

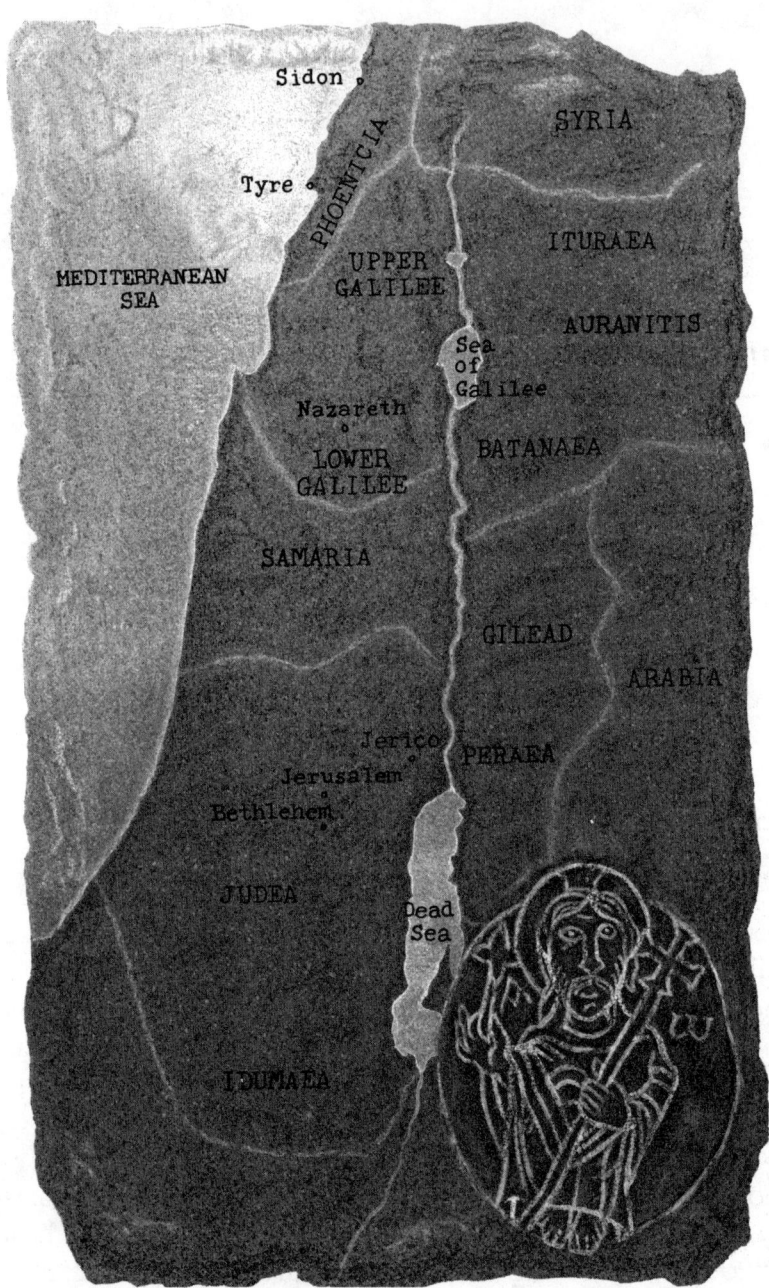

Palestine in the Time of Jesus

Some 1,200 years after Jesus, the story and its meanings were condensed and captured in the engraving of Christ used here and described in the opening pages of this book.

the apostles and others who had been eyewitnesses of Jesus' life (see Luke 1:1–4).

The first Christians may have thought that their Lord Jesus would return very soon from heaven to reign in glory on earth or to take his faithful to a heavenly kingdom (there is a reference to this in Acts 1:6). If that were the case, written records would not be necessary. Nevertheless, teachers and evangelists may have found it useful to collect and write down, in Aramaic (a language related to Hebrew spoken in Palestine) or in Hellenistic Greek, the teaching of Jesus. The material could have been used for their work outside the congregations, in the effort to convert people, or within the congregations, for the task of educating. For Jesus' teaching was even more valuable to them than the writings in their Hebrew Bible.

Paul's advice to local churches and his powerful theology became authoritative and influential. At some time late in the first century or quite early in the second, his letters were collected, circulated and studied; before long, they had been annexed to the Bible. Once begun, that process continued: various gospel-books about Jesus, letters, tracts and sermons by other leaders were assembled. It took time for the Christian bishops, elders and people to determine which of the documents made available should be accorded authoritative status and thus transformed into scripture. Of all the gospel-books in circulation, only four received that status; of various Acts, only the Acts of the Apostles (the second volume of Luke's Gospel) was accepted; and of letters and miscellaneous items, only 1 Peter and 1 John were originally incorporated. By A.D. 367 in Egypt and 405 in Italy and the West, the rest of the documents that are now part of our New Testament had all been accepted.

The process of making a New Testament, as a supplement to what then became known as the Old Testament rather than the Hebrew Bible, was quite long. It did not come down from God out of heaven! Its authors were fallible people like ourselves, and the language was always human language, though it pointed to divine and eternal realities.

Opening the Scriptures

New Testament Timeline

Literature	Christian events	Roman Empire
		Augustus, 30 B.C.–A.D. 14
	8 or 6 B.C. Birth of Jesus	
		Death of Herod, 4 B.C..
		Tiberius, A.D. 14–37
	A.D. 27–28 Ministry of John the Baptist 28–30 Ministry of Jesus 30 (April 7) Crucifixion of Jesus 35–37? Conversion of Paul 37–60 Pauline Missions	
A.D. 50–62 (roughly in this order): letters of Paul to Salonica; Galatia, Corinth; Rome; Colossae?; Philemon; Philippi		Nero, A.D. 54–68
	60–62 Paul imprisoned in Rome	
	64 Martyrdoms of Peter and Paul	Fire of Rome Persecution in Rome
65–70 Gospel of Mark		First Jewish War
	70 Temple destroyed	
80–100 Ephesians; Matthew; Luke-Acts		Domitian, A.D. 81–96
100? Gospel of John; 1, 2, 3 John Hebrews, Revelation, James		Trajan, A.D. 98–117 Persecution of Christians in Bithynia, 112
112 1 Peter		Hadrian, A.D. 117–135
120? Jude		Second Jewish War
130? 1, 2 Timothy; Titus 140–150 2 Peter		

There is no certainty about many of the dates assigned to the New Testament literature.

It is always helpful in matters of this kind to have a timeline that sets the literature and events in context.

In the New Testament, there is a twin orientation: upward, as people then thought, to the heavenly realm where Jesus lived in glory with God the Father, and forward to that future when the good news of Jesus is spread from its beginning in Jerusalem[1] to the very ends of the earth. At the end of the Acts of the Apostles (henceforth called Acts) Paul, the great missionary, was in the capital city of the empire, apparently unhindered in his work though under house arrest.[2]

It is an astonishing story: for Christians, the greatest story ever told. It inspired the spiritual conquest of the Roman Empire by A.D. 380 and the creation of a Christian civilization that has lasted until our own times. There is a unifying theme in Luke-Acts that bears on that impressive movement. It can be stated either as "teaching and preaching the Word of God, as it was clothed in the gospel of Jesus the Christ" or as "the movement of the Spirit of God in the first two or three Christian generations."

II
How the Gospel of Luke was composed

It is almost certain that Mark's was the first gospel-book. Most of it was incorporated into Matthew and Luke, although it was somewhat reduced to make room for new material. Matthew and Luke (to use the usual names for the authors or editors) each had access to material particular to himself or, occasionally, written by himself. Such material for Luke is called "Special Luke" or sometimes "L."

There was also a common source, mainly of the sayings of Jesus, referred to as "Q." To find Q, one must be able to see two almost identical citations in the Greek texts of Matthew and Luke of material that occurs nowhere else, or nowhere in precisely the same form. Q is situated at very different locales in the two Gospels.

Luke's special material gives his book its distinctive flavour. Included in Luke are his infancy stories, his account of the

Opening the Scriptures

walk to Emmaus and fourteen parables of Jesus. His interest in women who were in the company of Jesus is also evident. He gives an unusual place to the activity of the Holy Spirit.

Chapters 1–2	Chapters 3–23	Chapter 24
Special Luke	Marcan Material + Q + Special Luke	Special Luke

An outline of the contents of Luke shows that, after the infancy stories of chapters 1 and 2, there is a very precise statement of the date when the mission of John the Baptist began (3:1–2a). This is followed by four sections:

Δ Jesus' Galilean ministry (3:2b–9:50), including some reference to the activity of the Baptist;

Δ Jesus' journey to Jerusalem (9:51–19:27);

Δ the Passion narrative (19:28–23:56), including the entry into Jerusalem, Jesus' sometimes controversial teaching, a "cleansing" of the Temple, predictions about the "End," the Last Supper, the plot against the life of Jesus, the betrayal, the arrest and trial, and the crucifixion;

Δ stories of the resurrection of Jesus (24).

III

Part one of the content

The infancy stories tell about two boys: one was John, the other Jesus. John was the son of a priest, Zacharias, and his wife Elisabeth. Because Elisabeth had been barren and was "well stricken in years,"[3] bearing a child was a miraculous event, so there was an annunciation by the angel Gabriel. Jesus was the son of Mary, as it says in Luke. Jesus is called "son of God" because as the same angel, Gabriel, told Mary, the Holy Spirit would come upon Mary and "overshadow" her. It may be observed that no hint is given that Mary could not have had a baby in the normal way: she was not too old.

After telling the reader that Jesus was "supposed" to be the son of Joseph,[4] the husband of Mary, the editor provided a genealogy of Jesus (Luke 3:23–28) that is traced through that same Joseph to king David and eventually to "Seth, son of Adam, and Adam, son of God." Thus, Jesus was really a prince of the family of David, and as such, he might be the promised Messiah. There are complications, however. For at 2:48, in the story of the twelve-year-old Jesus visiting Jerusalem with his parents, Mary said, "thy father and I." Perhaps another supposition underlies this: formally Jesus is represented as the son of Joseph. Complications arise because of 1:27 — "The angel Gabriel was sent from God ... to a virgin ... and the virgin's name was Mary" — and 1:34 — "How shall this be, seeing I know not a man?" Of course she was a virgin until the act that brought conception and then birth!

But Luke is often read not in his own terms but with Matthew 1:23 in mind, where Isaiah 7:14 is quoted from the Greek translation (LXX). The Greek is an error! The Hebrew of Isaiah is *'almah*, a young woman of marriageable age; Isaiah did not intend that this should be taken as "virgin" (Greek *parthenos*). It was Matthew and his tradition that tried to prove a supernatural, miraculous birth for Jesus by reference to the Septuagint.

There are several places in the Hebrew Bible where Israel, as a whole, is called "son of God" (Hosea 11:1). The king too is called "my son" (Psalm 2:7), which is quoted as a proof-text at Acts 13:33. It was understandable that, when the early Church wanted to proclaim that Jesus was no mere Hebrew prophet or even a messianic prince but rather a God-man, the incarnate only-begotten Son of God, it had to find biblical proof. The proof is faulty.

This does not mean that God should be excluded from the birth of Jesus and his subsequent mission. We have read of barren women (Sarah, Hannah, Rachel and Elisabeth) giving birth. In every case, conception came about in answer to prayer. Hebrew thinking, not scientific in the matter, did allow for the providential ordering of family and national life. So the birth of Jesus was no accident. God was truly involved in it, and it was God's gospel and purpose that Jesus served. No "virgin birth" was required.

There are lyrical songs of praise within the infancy stories:

Δ the Magnificat (1:46–55), usually ascribed to Mary;[5]

Δ the Benedictus or Song of Zacharias (1:68–79) in which the reference to David is not to the family of a priest and so must refer to Mary's child (1:32);

Δ the Nunc Dimittis, the swan-song of old Simeon in 2:29–32 ("Lord, now lettest thou thy servant depart in peace"). Simeon's song came about because Simeon had been "inspired" to enter the Temple, discover the child and sing his confession of faith. A similar inference about the old prophetess Anna is to be drawn from 2:36, 2:38.

It is unusual that, with the possible exception of the Magnificat, these hymns were uttered by devout senior citizens. It is my opinion that they are representative figures, standing for the ancient people, Abraham's family. One old text, in a document that failed to get into the New Testament, says that God welcomed Jesus thus: "My son, in all the prophets I was waiting for you, that I might find rest in you. For you are my rest, and my firstborn son who will reign eternally."[6] There is a related tradition in John 1:32 where the Baptist says that the Spirit of God rested on Jesus. In other cases, the Judges and the prophets for example, the Spirit came on people but also left them, in keeping with Hebrew ideas. In the case of Jesus, the Spirit never left him. He is the God-inspired man *par excellence*.

As for John the priest's son, the Christian view was that he was the forerunner of the Messiah, the new Elijah. We should note his message about ethics and baptizing:

> *Repent, he cried, and have your sins washed away. Bring forth ... fruits worthy of repentance.... If you have two coats, give to someone who has none.... If you have meat, share with those who do not have any.... Tax collectors: exact only what is due.... Soldiers: Do violence to no man, neither accuse any falsely; and be content with your wages.*
>
> *I am not the Messiah. The Stronger One is coming, and I am not fit to loosen the latchet of his shoes. He will baptize with fire; I baptize only with water.*[7]

At this point, we shall return to 3:1–2a, where the beginning of Jesus' mission to Israel is narrated. Probably this was where Luke's gospel-book started at one time. In these verses, we are given a precise date for the appearance of John the Baptist, who marks the coming of Jesus. From the information given we can learn a number of things.

∆ Tiberius was Roman emperor from A.D. 14 to 37 and his fifteenth year was 28.

∆ Pontius Pilate was the prefect of Judea from A.D. 26 to 36.

∆ Herod, son of Herod the Great, was ruler (tetrarch) of Galilee from 4 B.C. to A.D. 39.

∆ Herod's brother Philip was tetrarch of Ituraea and Trachonitis from 4 B.C. to A.D. 34.

∆ Lysanias is said to be tetrarch of Abilene, but this seems to be a mistake. There may be a younger Lysanias whose name appears on inscriptions; he died between A.D. 28 and 37. There is a mystery about him.

∆ Caiaphas was the High Priest from A.D. 18 to 36, succeeding his father-in-law Annas who had ceased to hold office in 15. So Annas should not be listed like this.

When we coordinate all the references we get the year 27 or more probably 28 for the beginning of John the Baptist's mission. Everything to this point, however, is just a prelude to the story of Jesus.

IV
Part two of the content

There is an interesting section of Luke from 3:2 to 9:50. After telling about John, the baptism of Jesus and the spiritual experience Jesus had at the Jordan River while he was praying, it describes the Temptations of Jesus in the wilderness. At the beginning of the description of the Temptations, it says, "If thou be the Son of God ...",[8] evidently an allusion to Jesus' sense that God had called him to be his servant and in some way his "son." How that call was to be fulfilled was unclear. To test God himself and to magnify his own personality, Jesus wrestled, in imagination, with what he regarded as an evil influence. In the story of the temptations, the devil tested him with three trials:

Δ Could he make a stone into bread, like manna in the desert as the servant of God called Moses had done?

Δ Could he fulfil the prophecy in Daniel 7:14 or perhaps be a greater David by aspiring to be lord of a universal kingdom?

Δ Could he seize the high priesthood or be a messianic priest by working a mighty miracle at the Temple?

These temptations seem to suggest a programme for the mission to which Jesus was to set his hand. All his replies to the challenges came from the Second Law in Deuteronomy, which advises people to live by the word of God, to worship God alone and not the power of evil, and not to tempt God.[9] Jesus conquered every effort by evil forces to turn him from the route of service to God.

During his mission, Jesus attracted disciples, whom Luke called "apostles," a title used in the later Church. Jesus taught and preached to communicate his good news about God. People were healed and evil spirits were driven out by the power of the divine Spirit that operated through Jesus. When he went to a mountaintop with Peter, James and John to pray, Jesus was seen in a vision alongside "Moses," a dream-figure of the prophet who was to come, and "Elijah," a dream-figure of the priest who was to preside at a banquet in the messianic Kingdom (as we learn from the Dead Sea Scrolls). So Jesus was, to his dreaming disciples, the figure who must be the royal Messiah. If so, that dream was not to be realized. Jesus rejected the temptation to fulfil the prophecy in Daniel 7:14. What he did fulfil was in Isaiah 53:2–12: that he must suffer and die for the sins of others. When Peter cried out, at 9:20, that Jesus was "the Christ of God," it was not likely that he knew what Jesus' fate would be.

The account in 9:51 to 19:27 is ostensibly a travel narrative about Jesus' journey from Galilee to Jerusalem. In fact, very little happened and most of the space is devoted to teaching. There are also accounts of encounters that Jesus had with various people. Part of the section is centred in Galilee and tells of a mission of seventy disciples. There is no further information about them, so this seems to be legendary.

The most distinctive element in this section is how parable succeeds parable, as in chapters 14, 15 and 16. It is as if the author or editor had no setting for them, not knowing when Jesus used them or how often he repeated them. So they were gathered into an anthology at a much later time and given a setting that suited the author's own purpose of teaching in the church. Thus, the story of the Good Samaritan does not tell who one's neighbour is; it tells how to be neighbourly.

The elements in the Passion narrative and the stories about resurrection were noted above. According to Luke, while Jesus was on the cross, he cried: "Father, forgive them.... Today shalt thou be with me in paradise.... Father, into thy hands I commend my spirit."[10] There is doubt about the authenticity of the first saying, for it is omitted from several of the best manuscripts of the Gospels.

A notable feature of chapter 24 is that the risen Jesus is pictured as an interpreter of the Hebrew Bible, to which he gives a wholly Christian meaning. One can well imagine that in his teaching career, Jesus had indeed done something of this kind, making use of forecasts of his coming and serving (from Second Isaiah, for example). It is respectable to speak of a Christian "fulfilment" of the Hebrew scriptures. What was true of God in 1000 B.C. was still true in 4 B.C. and in A.D. 30.

Luke's book ends with an ascension scene at Bethany. The eleven who were there, this account says, worshipped Jesus and returned to the city "with great joy."[11] The Gospel begins and ends on a note of joy.

V

Major themes in Jesus' career and message, according to Luke

The first major theme in Luke is that Jesus preached "the Kingdom of God" and commissioned his pupils to do likewise. People should seek it.[12] I am often tempted to say that the word "kingdom" should not be used because of its associations now with taxes, frontiers, state politics and empire. Jesus was not interested in God's possessing that sort of thing, and in early Judaism there was conflict, as we have seen, between those who hoped for an earthly empire and those who longed for a new era of peace and wellbeing for all people. Sometimes, therefore, "God" should be substituted for "the Kingdom of God." It has been suggested, indeed, that the latter is a Church phrase and that Jesus did not preach "the Kingdom of God." That may be going too far.

The "kingdom" can be interpreted variously. It can denote the restoration of Israel in some manner or the messianic age. It may not refer to an earthly event at all but rather, perhaps, to one in heaven. As in the case of the messianic hope, there were many views but no certainty and no consensus about what the "Kingdom of God" should mean. The concept of kingdom refers to an "end." Jesus said, "Of that day and that hour knoweth no man ... neither the Son, but the Father."[13] Its coming is up to God alone. Human beings cannot build it: liberal views about being able to do so are beside the mark. God is the one in control. To be on God's side, as the Baptist knew, demands repentance. Moral and spiritual reformation are implied in the very notion of this new era's becoming a reality.

According to Jesus, the kingdom of God can be far off, close at hand or even present because people themselves help to decide how and when the new age becomes a real event for them. It's like leaven, one story in Q said (Luke 13:21): it is secretly present, bubbling up inside but not visible. From Luke, we learn that people may not have noticed that the coming of Jesus, God's inspired agent, meant the coming of God. People need to be childlike to receive him.[14] Though it cannot be seen, the kingdom of God is *entos humon*[15]: meaning either, "amongst you" (like the leaven and other images of the divine at work secretly) or "within your reach" (so that one merely has to stretch out and take it or take a single short step to be there).[16] In other words, God is to be met, and it is our business to recognize him and join his cause.

That idea allows the saying in 11:20 to be taken seriously: "But if I with the finger of God cast out devils, no doubt the kingdom of God is come upon you." The Greek original means "has arrived," with a flavour of "it has caught you by surprise." No wonder Origen, the greatest scholar of the first three centuries, said that "Jesus in himself is the kingdom."[17] Or one might say he was "Israel," the real and true Israel of God, a greater Jacob. He was "Adam," the true and real Adam, whose son he was, a human person in the image of God.

A second theme may refer to a new Exodus. The episode involving John the Baptist depicts the water of a river to be entered and, perhaps, crossed. As old Israel escaped through water, so the new also would escape divine judgment by the sacrament of water-baptism. Yet "water" is not good enough. What the people of God needed was not just cleansing but a purging and a spiritual destruction of the evil and sinful. "Fire" is required, and John predicts that the Coming One will burn up the chaff. The L saying at Luke 12:49 may be related to this concept, or it may belong with words about the split that Jesus causes between those who hear God's word and see God's presence through him and those who reject him and seek his death.

In spite of 9:31, where Moses and Elijah speak of Jesus' death as an "exodus," it does not necessarily follow that Jesus is to be the leader of a new Exodus bringing liberation, spiritual reconciliation and purification to the people of God. It is true, of course, that the stone-to-bread temptation may recall the manna-in-the-wilderness episode of the Exodus narratives. On the whole, however, Exodus themes in the mission of Jesus can be discounted.

A third theme, the theme of Jesus as the Prophet, is found when he was in Nazareth (4:24), in Nain (7:16), in the home of Simon the Pharisee (7:39) and on the road to Jerusalem where prophets are fated to die (13:33) and on the road to Emmaus (24:19). This is a rather astonishing set of references, not to be dismissed too quickly by those who think that "prophet" is not as wonderful a title for Jesus as "son of God" or "saviour."

Another theme is that of the Messianic king. Jesus says that his Father has appointed a Kingdom for him, and he does the same for his faithful disciples.[18] At the crucifixion, there is an inscription in Greek, Latin and Hebrew, "This is the king of the Jews."[19] But I have indicated already that Jesus refused the temptation to seize kingship. The words on the cross are contradicted by the words from the cross, where God's servant speaks.

Jesus as the servant of God is another theme. He was, as I have repeated several times, the servant of God according to Luke 4:18–21; 6:20–21; and 7:22–23. He himself probably looked back to Second Isaiah for inspiration, and many in the early Church followed suit (see 1 Peter 2:24–25). By emphasizing this motif of Jesus as servant, Luke makes it plain that Jesus had not been a threat to Caesar and that neither Pilate nor Herod had found fault in him. As a result, members of Christ's congregations would be no menace to public security.[20]

Jesus as a man of prayer represents a final theme, consistent with his position as a servant of Yahweh, as a teacher with a prophetic duty and as a person who had to live under the same conditions as Simon Peter, Mary Magdalene, Simon the Pharisee and all his other contemporaries. They were in a land that was under alien occupation where social problems abounded. Prayer was an appropriate activity for all who believed in Yahweh. Examples of Jesus praying are numerous:

Δ alone with God in the wilderness (5:16);

Δ on a mountain, the place of revelation, lasting all night prior to selecting twelve men to accompany him (6:12);

Δ on the Mount of Olives prior to his betrayal and arrest, when he was so distraught that, according to the story, he cried, "Father, if thou be willing, remove this cup from me: nevertheless not my will, but thine, be done" (22:41 – 42);

Δ "Father, forgive them ..." (23:34); and

Δ "Father, into thy hands I commend my spirit" (23:46).

The name "Father" is significant. Writing for a Greek-speaking public, Luke uses the word *pater*, meaning "O Father." In Mark 14:36, Galatians 4:6 and Romans 8:15, however, which all antedate Luke, the original Aramaic of Jesus is retained: *Abba*. It is a form of intimate affection (though not to be translated by "daddy"), and its use indicates that the concept of being a son was important to Jesus. Yet he says, "But love your enemies ... and you will be children of the Most High.... Be merciful, just as your Father is merciful."[21] Thus Jesus plus his disciples and their children constitute a family for God. This could lead one to think that the Genesis 1 story of creation, which Jesus would have known very well, encouraged the thought that human beings are indeed, by divine grace, to become godlike!

VI
The parables of Jesus

Jesus had a humble position as teacher, preacher and healer. Yet that was how he carried out his vocation to tell of the Kingdom of God. It is surprising that the leader of a religious reformation or revolution within Judaism was not a warrior, or at least a politician. The gospel-books do not permit us to consider Jesus in such positions. It is possible that their accounts minimize the social and economic upheaval threatened by the message and personality of Jesus with an overemphasis on piety, on the otherworldliness of the gospel and on religion.

Jesus is famous for his parables. "Parable" is a translation from the Hebrew *mashal* or the Greek *paroimia* or *parabole*. It has various meanings: a commonplace, a taunt, a riddle, a byword, an oracle, a comparison or simile in the form of a short story. Very seldom, if ever, is a parable to be likened to an allegory in which images and characters are analogous to other people or to certain truths. Allegory illustrates what would otherwise be abstract. Bunyan's *Pilgrim's Progress* is an allegory; the story of the prodigal son in Luke 15 is not. Jesus' parables actually contain major segments of his message, and the interpreter has to find ways in which to translate that message into a useful context. Sometimes the interpretation becomes an allegory, as in the case of the parable of the sower interpreted as an allegory of the soils in Luke 8:5–15 (borrowed from Mark).

The importance of parables is indicated by their number and distribution in the first three Gospels:

Δ in Mark, eight, two of which occur nowhere else;

Δ in Q, six, therefore in both Matthew and Luke;

Δ in Special Matthew, eleven;

Δ in Special Luke, fourteen.

The Distribution of Parabolic Stories

```
    Special                              Special
  Matthew 11                             Luke 14
         \                               /
          \        Mark 8               /
           ---Two are found only in Mark---
          /                              \
   MATTHEW                                LUKE
   11 + 6 + 6                           6 + 14 + 6
          \                              /
           \          Q 6               /
            _____ _/
```

Luke retells six Marcan parables as follows:

Mark 2:21–22,	the old and the new	in Luke	5:36–39
Mark 4:3–8,	the Sower		8:5–8
Mark 4:21–22,	the lamp and the bushel-basket		8:16–17
Mark 4:30–32,	the Mustard Seed		13:18–19
Mark 12:1–11,	the Wicked Husbandmen		20:9–16
Mark 13:28–29,	leaves on a fig tree		21:29–30

and the parables of the common tradition (Q) as follows:

Luke 6:47–49,	building a house
Luke 12:42–48,	the faithful or unfaithful servant
Luke 13:20–21,	the leaven
Luke 14:15–24,	invitations and excuses
Luke 15:4–7,	one sheep lost out of a hundred
Luke 19:12–27,	the talents

The parables that occur only in Luke are fascinating, and in the classic KJV they are particularly memorable. They may be grouped in different ways, but their meanings are too rich and varied to be limited to an arbitrary grouping that suits one particular interpreter. Usually there is a single point that Jesus wanted to make and it often has to be puzzled out: a challenge to the reader.

Here is one possible grouping:

A Grouping of the Parables

A. How one should act

1.	The Good Samaritan	10:30–37
2.	The rich fool	12:16–21
3.	The rich man and the poor man ("Dives and Lazarus")	16:19–31
4.	The Pharisee and the tax-collector	18:10–14

B. One should be humble

5.	Seats at a banquet	14:7–14
6.	The farmer and his slave	17:7–10

C. One should be wise

7.	Count the cost	14:28–33
8.	The shrewd rascal	16:1–8

D. Repent: and do it with love!

9.	Two debtors pardoned	7:41–43
10.	The unfruitful fig tree	13:6–9
11.	The lost coin	15:8–10
12.	The lost son(s) ("The Prodigal Son")	15:11–32

E. Pray: all the time!

13.	The impertinent friend (at midnight)	11:5–8
14.	The widow and the unjust judge	18:2–8

Luke's Life of Jesus

These stories should be read in the magnificent English of the KJV or the contemporary language of the NRSV or the REB. A summary in my own colloquial version may be useful, however.

A. How one should act

1. A man travelling from Jerusalem towards Jericho fell among brigands, who robbed him, beat him and left him for dead. Along came a Jewish priest who passed by on the other side of the road. Next came a Levite of the Temple who also passed by. Then came a Samaritan who noticed the poor fellow in the ditch. He took pity on him, dressed his wounds and took him to the nearest inn. There he paid to have the traveller looked after, promising to pay more, if necessary, the next time he passed that way. And he was an outcast and a heretic! (10:30–37)

2. A wealthy farmer said to himself, "I'm doing so well I'll have to build bigger barns. Then I can sit back, eat and drink, and enjoy life." "Stupid you," said God. "Tonight your life will end. What will you do then with your crops and barns?" (12:16–21)

3. A rich man died and went to hell. A poor beggar, who used to lie at the rich man's gate, also died; he went to heaven. Although the rich man called for the poor man to help him in his discomfort, it was not possible since there is no way to get from heaven to hell. Neither could the poor man fulfil the request of the rich man to go back to warn the family about their fate if they did not change their ways. Didn't they have their Bible? If they ignored that ("Moses and the prophets"), they would not change, even if somebody were to rise from the dead to teach them. (16:19–31)

4. A pious Pharisee and a tax collector went up to the wall of the Temple to pray. The Pharisee bragged to God that, unlike the corrupt taxman who also came to pray, he was a fine fellow. The taxman had no illusions about himself: he stood far off and cried, "Mercy, Lord. Lord, have mercy!" And mercy is what he got. So he went home, accepted by God and justified. The Pharisee was none the better for the exercise. (18:10–14)

Opening the Scriptures

B. One should be humble

5. When you're invited to a wedding party, take the lowest seat. Maybe your host will promote you to a seat at the top table. (14:8–10)

6. A farmer expects his ploughman or shepherd to prepare a meal at the end of the day's work and does not thank him for it since it is part of his duty. Since no one thanks a servant for doing his duty, do not expect praise for serving God. (17:7–10)

C. One should be wise

7. If you mean to build a house, wouldn't you get an estimate for the cost and see if you could afford it? If a king had ten thousand soldiers, would he not reckon carefully whether he could successfully fight his enemy who had a hundred thousand under his command? If he couldn't, he would sue for peace, wouldn't he? (14:28–33)

8. On hearing that his estate manager was squandering the property in his charge, a certain rich man demanded an accounting. The manager decided to make the best of things. He called in the master's debtors and told them how to falsify their bills. "You owe a hundred jugs of olive oil? Put down fifty. You owe a hundred barrels of wheat? Put down eighty." The result? The boss praised the rascal for his shrewd policy. (16:1–8)

D. Repent — and do it with love

9. Who will love a benefactor more: one who has been forgiven a debt of fifty thousand dollars or one who has been forgiven a mere fifty dollars? (7:41–43)

10. "This fig tree of mine," said its owner, "has been no good for three years. No fruit at all! It's just an obstruction, so cut it down." But his gardener pleaded with him: "Sir, one more chance! Just let me tend it for one more season. Let's see if it gives us fruit next year. If not, then of course you should get rid of it." (13:6–9)

11. A housewife lost a single piece of her ten-piece silver necklace. She looked everywhere for it. She turned the house

upside down and wouldn't stop searching until at last she found it! You are the lost, and God is out looking. (15:8–9)

12. A man had two sons, and he agreed to divide his estate between them before he died. The younger one then went off with his share, converted it into cash and proceeded to squander it. Then a famine came. He was broke and starving, so he hired himself out to a pig farmer. He still did not have food, though, and remembered that the slaves at his home had fared better than he now did. Although his elder brother might be lawful owner, he resolved to ask his father to let him be a servant. He arrived home with a speech ready about his folly, his sorrow and his desire to be a servant. But his father came running out and greeted him joyfully. A party was held to welcome him home. His elder brother, however, who had stayed dutifully at home, refused to welcome him and was so angry about the father's rejoicing that he would not join in the fun. (15:11–32)

E. Pray — all the time!

13. At midnight one day a man battered at his neighbour's door, asking for bread to feed an unexpected guest. He was impertinent and insistent, continuing to be an awful nuisance for a long time. The neighbour had everything shut for the night and wanted to be left in peace. But his friend went on and on. He wouldn't take "no" for an answer. At last he got satisfaction. That's how to pray. (11:5–8)

14. Once upon a time, in a certain town, there was a man who was a judge and a woman who was a widow. The judge was a scoundrel who neither respected people nor feared God. The widow had a case in his court, but he refused to hear it. She persisted, however, pestering him until she wore him down and he settled her case. (18:2–8)

VII

Concluding comments

It is difficult to do justice to the Gospel of Luke, which was once described as the most beautiful book in the world.

Attention has been drawn only to some episodes in Jesus' short career and to some examples of his wit, humour, satire and profound teaching about duty and the love of God.

Luke ends with legends about the risen life of Jesus: that theme dominates the New Testament literature. Resurrection was first handed on as a "tradition," for example to Paul of Tarsus who, in turn, handed it on to his congregations. In 1 Corinthians 15:3–8, he recounts the "sightings" of the risen Lord. They are "visions," and he claims to have had one himself of the same sort as those of Peter and others. It can be assumed that the vision showed Jesus as a living presence, glorified in the radiance of his life in and with God. Such sightings are never reported from people other than disciples or chosen people, like Paul or James the Lord's brother. Hence, resurrection was not in the public domain.

Resurrection was real, however, and Christianity depends on the claims made for it. It was not something that happened to the disciples: it happened to Jesus. He truly died; that is fundamental. But, says the Gospel, there was a unique act of God by which Jesus, the Servant of God, inspired by the Spirit of God, came alive: one might call it a re-creation, because the death was a real death. He was raised from the dead by God. Paul might have said that thereafter Jesus had a "spiritual body"[22] suited to eternal life.

After the Resurrection, new spirit was put into the fearful disciples and the women of the company (compare John 20:19). The Christian Church was born, the work of the Spirit. This birth is told in Acts.

thirteen

The Church Story in the Acts of the Apostles

I
What we can expect to learn from Acts

In the previous chapter, we learned that there is a unifying theme to the Gospel of Luke and the same author's Acts of the Apostles. It can be defined as the movement of the Holy Spirit in the first two or three Christian generations. That is the story that unfolds in Acts.

It has also been observed that the sequel to the resurrection of Jesus was the birth of the Church. In Acts, we see that birth taking place at the festival of Pentecost that came seven weeks after the crucifixion of Jesus. To understand what "Church" means is important to every Christian and useful to those who wish to appreciate how the Church has influenced Western civilization.

In Acts, there are tales of martyrs and heroes of the new faith movement but also evidence of some laxness in the moral life of early congregations. So Acts is an invaluable record. At the very beginning, there is a reference to the author's first volume followed by Jesus' commission to his disciples: "Ye shall receive power ... and ye shall be witnesses ... unto the uttermost part of the earth."[1] The gift of divine power, the Spirit, had been promised at Luke 12:11–12 and 21:15 (cf. also 10:16) so volume two (Acts) will presumably tell of the course of that witness and the witnesses themselves.

The author is not, however, an unrealistic romantic, for he records a warning said to have been delivered by Paul to the leaders of the church in Ephesus: that after his death "wolves" would enter and not spare the flock of God; there would be heresies, strange teachings that deviated from the original tradition.[2] In reading Acts, one discovers disunity, infidelities and power struggles within the early churches. Theophilus and others had to be warned, therefore, for there were some who held that, once baptized and made a member of the Church, there could be no restoration if one sinned against God and his people.[3]

Luke's work was to remind everyone of the spiritual realities that had been stressed by Peter and Paul, loyal witnesses to Jesus the Christ of God. After his preface, Luke tells how Matthias was chosen to take the place of Judas the traitor. Then he concentrates on Peter and the first beginnings and next on Paul and his remarkable missionary travels.[4] The itinerary of the Church-witness was from Jerusalem to Rome, from one capital to another. That was to be a pattern for the whole history of Christian missions.

II

The Spirit motif

The Spirit motif begins at 2:17–18 with the birthday of the Church at Pentecost and one of the speeches that are so prominent in Acts. Peter spoke with assurance, rehearsing what became the Christian gospel, and the results were overwhelming: three thousand converts in one day! Next we have the significant figure of Stephen whose spirit of wisdom annoys those who refuse to believe that Jesus was the Messiah. The controversy led to the first martyrdom.[5]

When the message of Jesus was spread to the northern city

Albrecht Dürer (1471–1528), *The Four Apostles*, on wood, 1526. Munich, Old Art Gallery.

The four apostles (from left to right) are John, Peter, Paul and Mark, and their choice is significant: they may be taken to represent tradition and reform in the German Church of the Renaissance.

Peter ("the Prince of the Apostles" for Catholic and Orthodox Christians) still carries his symbolic keys (see Matthew 16:19) and Paul (the Apostle of the Gentiles) his sword (see Ephesians 6:17), as they do in giant sculpture outside St. Peter's Basilica in the Vatican. But for Dürer, and the Reformed church with which he identified, the sword had become afresh a symbol of the living Word of God by which Martin Luther had set about liberating Christians from the medieval papacy of Peter's Roman successors.

His apostles are human individuals, saints who lack haloes and yet are transfigured by the Word and Spirit of the God revealed in Jesus Christ. The eyes of John and Peter meditate on the gospel; those of Paul and Mark flash with the energy of dynamic evangelists. Dürer shows us the eminent position of the Bible in the sixteenth-century Reformation.

Reproduced by courtesy of Bayerischen Staatsgemaldesammlungen, München.

of Samaria, centre of the despised Samaritans, the preaching apparently produced strange phenomena: signs and wonders, healings and spirit-gifts.[6] People fell into ecstasy and cried out in penitence as the Holy Spirit brought wonderful healings and transformations in the moral and spiritual lives of the converts. After a sermon by Peter in the town of Caesarea, similar phenomena happened in the home of a Gentile soldier,[7] leading to amazement that they happened among the Gentiles and to wonder about whether that was God's intention. There may be some exaggeration in the reports, but the existence of such phenomena can be verified in Church history.

A landmark statement came in Syrian Antioch as a congregation met for prayer and, perhaps, a regular service of worship. The Spirit, presumably through one or more of the local "prophets," directed that Barnabas and Paul should be sent off on a mission.[8] They went quite far, sailing to Barnabas's homeland in Cyprus and areas close to Paul's native town, Tarsus. Many spiritual, joyful conversions took place.

Another turning point came about when a Jerusalem meeting considered the question raised by Peter's experience at Caesarea and perhaps also considered the results of the mission by Barnabas and Paul. The decision was put as follows: "It seemed good to the Holy Ghost [Spirit] and to us."[9] This became a formula for later Councils and Synods — even when it might have been very hard to detect the presence of God's Spirit!

There are other examples at 18:24–28 and 19:1–7, which indicate that on some occasions at least, the ecstatic gifts of the Spirit, like "speaking in tongues," did not become evident until apostles "laid hands" on people. Here let me add that "speaking in tongues" did not mean "talking in foreign languages" as Acts 2:8 implies. There is a great deal of evidence, for example in 1 Corinthians,[10] that such speaking was ecstatic speech or speaking in a trance; "prophecy" was also ascribed to this phenomenon. Inspired preaching refers both to the speaker and to the listeners who responded. In Acts 21:11, Agabus prophesied that Paul would be seized by the Jews if he proceeded to Jerusalem.

Paul did not deny the reality of speaking in tongues, but he clearly downgraded it and preferred to pray, sing and preach with his mind. Prophecy demanded reason as well as inspiration. In Acts, Paul admitted that the Spirit warned him about his fate,[11] and he cited the admonition in Isaiah that we have noted several times: that people will hear but not understand, they will see but not perceive. Paul added that Isaiah had been inspired by the Holy Spirit to say that.[12] It is on the basis of all this evidence that Acts has been characterized as a "Gospel of the Holy Spirit."

III
The meaning of "Church" (ecclesia)

English *church*, Scots *kirk* and German *Kirche* probably are derived from Greek *kyriakon*, the Lord's house or community. French *église* is closer to the original Greek *ecclesia*, an old term for a local assembly called for diverse purposes, used in Greece and in synagogues of Greek-speaking Jews. In Hebrew, there are two corresponding words: *'edhah* and *qahal*. *Ecclesia* could be used of a Jewish synagogue — the people, not the building. In the translation of the Hebrew Bible into Greek, the Septuagint, we find that *ecclesia* represents *qahal* or a Hebrew word of the same root. It is very frequent in the literature of the Second Temple age and becomes virtually a technical term for God's people Israel, the covenant community that worshipped him. But *'edhah* also meant Israel in this sense, so that *ecclesia* was not limited to worship assemblies.

Moreover, the Greek equivalent for *'edhah* was *synagoge*: this proves that "church" *(ecclesia)* and "synagogue" (the people) were synonyms for a long period. Gradually synagogue became limited to a quite local group and to its meeting-place; whereas *ecclesia* was claimed by Christians and denoted (a) the whole Church of God and (b) every local congregation or church. In the second century, people began to define (a) as the "orthodox" or "catholic" Church and also as the "catholic" or "universal" Church. All these meanings came to be of immense importance in the growth of Christianity. Part of the evidence is in Acts.

The first congregation in Jerusalem grew rapidly,[13] and an unusual phrase in the Greek (not *ecclesia*) may be an equivalent for "community," a word explicitly claimed by the people of the Dead Sea Scrolls (in Hebrew *yachad*). It is quite possible that the feast of Pentecost, a harvest thanksgiving celebration, had become a time to "renew the covenant" with Yahweh. Since Jesus' disciples participated, it is not surprising that the event triggered an outpouring of spiritual energy and hope. For the disciples, the Messiah was known and would come to reign. The new covenant of Jeremiah 31 had been inaugurated, if not at the Last Supper of Jesus and his friends on the night on which he was betrayed, then at the Pentecost festival. Christians ate together, listened to the tradition of the first eyewitnesses, and were joyful.[14]

There is an attractive suggestion, although one that cannot be wholly supported by evidence, that the appearance of the risen Jesus to five hundred friends, mentioned in 1 Corinthians 15:6, may have happened at the first Pentecost. Such a vision could well belong with other Spirit phenomena.

"Church," therefore, is to be defined as "congregation of the new covenant" or as "the fellowship of the Holy Spirit," for it was the Spirit that created the Church just after the resurrection of Jesus. The covenant ideas, the usage of Holy Spirit, and above all the status of Jesus within Judaism as son of the *torah* and peerless prophet affirm a continuity between Judaism and Christianity. The Church was a daughter of Israel and became a new or spiritual Israel for its adherents. Yet many Jews did not accept the claims for Jesus and the Church, and before the end of the first century Christians were excommunicated from Jewish synagogues.

Related to the notion of catholicity referred to above, there is another dimension to "Church." As the genealogy of Jesus in Luke shows, Jesus could be thought of as "son of Adam," and thus as "son of man," in the last words of the martyr Stephen.[15] Hence his people, the body of all those who were baptized into his *ecclesia*, could be viewed as the new humanity (following the image of Adam) that God was restoring for an eternal Eden, "in his kingdom." So partially for that reason, the witness of the apostles and others had to be taken quite literally to the ends of the earth, to everyone: for God, as Paul said at Athens, "hath made of one blood all nations of men for to dwell on all the face of the earth."[16]

To sum up:

Δ On the basis of the evidence adduced here, the Church should be described as "missionary", "evangelical" and "catholic." So the Church became a worldwide fact, and its sacred writings have been translated into some two thousand languages, one of the most recent being Inuktitut for people of the Canadian Arctic.

Δ Both Jews and Gentiles were baptized, originally just the adults, though children did "belong."

Δ According to Acts 15:20, Gentile converts were instructed to eat only kosher food, not meat that had been dedicated to the deities of Greco-Roman society. They were not to be guilty of fornication, which in this case may refer to marriage within the forbidden degrees listed at Leviticus 18:6–18. They were not to partake of blood (in meat? or in taking human life?). Such ritual requirements may have been necessary in Palestine to allow Jews and Gentiles to eat together. The rite of circumcision was not asked of Gentile males. The text of Acts 15:20 is a bit dubious. Some authorities substituted a statement of the Golden Rule in its negative form, "Do not do to others what you do not want to be done to yourselves," for the kosher rule. The Jerusalem instruction of 15:20 is never mentioned by Paul in his correspondence, so one must be suspicious of its historicity and authority.

IV

The martyr motif

One of the more moving elements in the Church story in Acts is that of the believers who had to suffer for the faith.

John the son of Zebedee and Peter were arrested and taken before the rulers, elders and scribes who described them as "unlearned and ignorant men." Yet Peter eloquently insisted (as had the Three Children before Nebuchadrezzar) that "whether it be right in the sight of God to hearken unto you more than unto God, judge ye. For we cannot but speak the things which we have seen and heard."[17] There is an echo of his words in those of Martin Luther before the emperor at Worms: "Hier stehe ich/ich kannn nicht anders/Got hilffe mir. Amen." (Here I stand. I cannot do otherwise. God help me. Amen.) And a second time Peter and the apostles defy the Jewish council: "We ought to obey God rather than men."[18]

The first person to suffer martyrdom was Stephen, "a man full of faith and of the Holy Ghost [Spirit]."[19] Stephen's defence may have been composed by Luke, in typical Greek historical style, and it follows a pattern. He related Israel's history up to the building of the Temple by Solomon, no doubt because part of the indictment was that Stephen had blasphemed against Moses and God, spoken against the Temple and the Torah and said that Jesus of Nazareth would destroy the Temple and subvert the customs established by Moses.[20] Then Stephen turned accuser and drove his listeners into a frenzy.

What a wonderful story Luke told about this spiritual and spirited leader. Stephen's fate, however, was terrible: he was cast out of the city and stoned to death. As he died, he followed the example of Jesus, calling out, "Lord Jesus, receive my spirit.... Lord, lay not this sin to their charge."[21]

The Acts account became the model for the story of many martyrs during the first centuries of Roman persecution and, more recently, during the Second World War when Christians were martyred in Burma. One of the heroes of a Japanese prison camp was the former Olympic champion, Eric Liddell, whose story was told in the movie *Chariots of Fire*.

The next martyr was James the son of Zebedee, who died at the hands of Herod Agrippa, a grandson of Herod the Great.[22]

Even before the story of James's death, Acts tells us of Paul the persecutor turned advocate. When his life was threatened in Syria, he had to be let down over the city wall of Damascus to escape his foes.[23] In the second part of the book, Paul and his colleagues are featured. Persecution, beatings and prison sentences happened at almost every place the missionaries preached. Finally, Paul was arrested in Jerusalem, was tried in Caesarea, appealed to the supreme court of the emperor in Rome, and was executed (though in Acts his death is only forecast).

The Greek word *martus*, English *martyr*, normally meant a witness; but after the publication of Acts the meaning was narrowed to describe one who had witnessed with his or her lifeblood. About A.D. 200, a famous North African leader called Tertullian declared in a sentence that has echoed throughout Church history, "As often as you mow us down, the more numerous do we become; the blood of the Christians is the seed."[24] One could enter the kingdom of God only through much tribulation, as Barnabas and Paul told the new converts in Lystra, Iconium and Pisidian Antioch.[25]

V

The heroes of the faith

As we read Acts today, it becomes clear that the author was not interested only in the distant past of the churches. His own time was about A.D. 80–90, almost sixty years after the crucifixion and resurrection, and Luke was concerned with people like Theophilus and those in the congregations he knew well. Peter, James son of Zebedee, John, Paul, James the Lord's brother and many others were, for Luke, great leaders in the past whose example was to be honoured and followed in the present and future.

There are a number of people who put a human face on the story of the early Church. They deserve at least a brief mention. First, there are some who brought shame to the

Christian cause. Ananias and his wife Sapphira sold some property and pretended that they had given the proceeds to the Jerusalem church. For this deception, they both died because they had "lied to God."[26] Another person who became infamous was Simon of Samaria. Impressed by the miracles done under the ministry of Philip, he was converted. Then he coveted the power of Peter and John who, by the laying on of hands, seemed to communicate the Holy Spirit. He offered the apostles money so that he could exercise the same power but was bitterly reproached by Peter.[27] From this Simon, we get the word "simony," which means buying or selling religious powers or privileges.

There are some women to be remembered. Damaris, a convert in Athens, is only named. Dorcas of Joppa, famed for good works, was said to have been raised from the dead by Peter. Lydia, or "the Lydian" of Philippi, a dealer in dye, came from Thyatira in Asia Minor. Perhaps quite well-to-do, she gave hospitality to Paul and Silas and another.[28] It is possible that she was Euodia, mentioned by Paul in Philippians 4:2. Mary, the mother of Jesus, is named for the last time in the Bible at Acts 1:14; this implies that she and some of the brothers of Jesus joined the first church in Jerusalem. Another Mary, the mother of John Mark, lived in Jerusalem.[29]

We come now to a fairly large group of men, one very distinguished woman and four virgins who are described as prophetesses but are unnamed.[30] There is Apollos, a former Baptist, who was instructed in the Christian message at Ephesus and then became a popular preacher and leader in Corinth. He seems to have been a Jew with some expertise in the scriptures.[31] The teachers of Apollos were a Jew named Aquila and his wife Priscilla[32] (she may not have been Jewish). Expelled from Rome, they had gone to Corinth where Paul joined them. With Paul, they travelled to Ephesus and there met Apollos. They were probably in trade, making leather goods, possibly tents. Paul plied the same trade, so their travels may have been partly for commercial reasons. It seems, given the evidence here and in Romans 16:3, that they played a prominent role and were people of notable spiritual stature. This is often thought to be true especially of Priscilla: unfortunately there isn't more evidence about her.

Two men share a name: Joseph Barsabbas who is said to have been a companion of Jesus (yet there is no record of him in any of the gospel-books) and Judas Barsabbas, a prophet and member of the church in Jerusalem who was sent to Antioch about the decree respecting Gentiles in the Church.[33] We do not know whether the two men were brothers or whether there was only one person.

One of the romantic figures in Acts and the New Testament letters is John Mark, son of Mary of Jerusalem.[34] He was a companion of Barnabas and Paul on a missionary trip but left them. Since Paul did not want him on the next journey,[35] Paul and Barnabas separated and Barnabas took him. It has been conjectured that Colossians 4:10 refers to this man as the nephew of Barnabas and that he is also named at Philemon 24 — apparently, therefore, after reconciliation with Paul. He appears at 1 Peter 5:13 as son of Peter, probably using "son" in a figurative sense. None of the identifications is certain, however.

Another person who flits into the record and out again at once is the Matthias who was chosen to take the place of Judas as one of the Twelve. The Gospels have no record of him. Another of the Twelve who is mentioned once is Philip.[36]

Seven men, including Stephen the first martyr, appear at 6:3–5 in charge of seeing that Greek-speaking widows in the Jerusalem church were looked after. This was an *ad hoc* arrangement, in my view, and not appointment to a permanent office. It is possible that Luke thought otherwise, and it is frequently held that the Seven were deacons or elders. They were Stephen, Prochorus, Nicanor, Timon, Parmenas, Nicolas, and another Philip (not to be confused with apostle Philip). This second Philip is called "the evangelist,"[37] a term that is most unusual in the New Testament. With others, he fled from Jerusalem after the murder of Stephen and preached with great success in Samaria, Gaza, Azotus and Caesarea.

Two other facts are interesting: that his four daughters were virgin prophetesses and that he encountered an Ethiopian, "an eunuch of great authority under Candace queen of the Ethiopians," who had visited Jerusalem, perhaps as an adherent to Judaism. He asked Philip to interpret Isaiah 53:1–8 and as a result was baptized, "and he went on his way rejoicing."[38] For black Christians today, Africans and African-Americans, this conversion of an Ethiopian has special significance. It is a reminder that Christianity made remarkable progress very early in North Africa, from Ethiopia to Cyrene.

We may end this list of names with Silas and Timothy, two of the most faithful companions and colleagues of Paul.[39] The lives and examples of these men and women have inspired many. To that list could be added names of the outstanding missionaries, theologians and saints, some well known, some obscure, who have carried on the tradition of Christian discipleship. Suffice it to name Augustine of Hippo (Tunis); Columba of Iona; Augustine of Canterbury; Francis of Assisi; the Wesleys; Brébeuf and his fellow martyrs in Huronia, Canada; Kanzo Uchimura of Japan; Pandita Ramabai of India; and John R. Mott of the United States. The hero cult of the Church has contributed much that is of lasting value and importance in the story of Western civilization.

VI

The Christian message

The message presented to the Jews and Gentiles is important and influential. It is found in many of the speeches and summaries in Acts. There are two texts that can serve as a summary of the gospel that was proclaimed in Greek to people in the Roman Mediterranean: "How God anointed Jesus of Nazareth with the Holy Spirit and with power: who went about doing good, and healing all that were oppressed of the devil"[40] and "Of David's seed hath God according to his promise raised unto Israel a Saviour, Jesus.... Be it known unto you therefore, men and brethren, that through this man is preached unto you the forgiveness of sins."[41] This reference to sins and their forgiveness means that "Saviour" is being used in a nonpolitical sense, a point that Luke repeatedly makes for his Roman readers.

So far as Luke was concerned, the chief herald of that message was Paul of Tarsus, himself a Roman citizen whose dramatic conversion on the road to Damascus is narrated three times: at 9:1–22, 22:1–21 and 26:1–23. Set side by side, the three exhibit subtle changes, with nuances meant to be appropriate to each situation. The last one, however, may be unhistorical.

According to Acts 25:13, Agrippa II had come to Caesarea with his sister, Bernice, a notorious woman who may have been his consort and who later became the mistress of Titus, the son of the emperor Vespasian. There is a theatrical scene in a great assembly hall before dignitaries — a setting devised by the author of Acts. There Festus, the prefect of Judea who (it is said) did not believe that Paul had committed a capital crime (Acts 25:25), allowed the prisoner to speak. It was not a law-court setting at all, but a way in which Paul could be shown as making a public witness before royalty and other leading men. Luke intended his readers to see how well Paul was esteemed by an important Roman official. The next time Paul gave a legal testimony, it would be in the Supreme Court at Rome, for he had appealed to Caesar (Acts 25:11). It is very doubtful that these speeches were authentic transcripts. More likely, they were composed by Luke or someone else to fit each situation, in Hellenistic style. It has to be conceded, however, that there may be authentic bones beneath the Lucan garb!

Paul's career, as outlined in Acts and as ascertained from his letters, warrants special attention. He was chief organizer of congregations in many areas and a tireless preacher and pastor. He knew that local churches should be taught to understand that the Church is one, universal, and deserves to be called by the old sacred title for God's people, "Israel," a spiritual and not a genetic Israel.

It is odd that in Philippians 1:1 he speaks of local leaders as "bishops and deacons," while in Acts we read that he elected (or had elected) leaders known by a familiar Jewish name, "presbyters," also translated as "elders."[42] It is very plausible that the first local *ecclesiae*, churches, were also known as synagogues and that they were organized on the model of the Jewish synagogues. Acts 20:28 helps us to reconcile the usage, for there the presbyters of Ephesus are told by Paul, "Take heed ... to all the flock, over the which the Holy Spirit hath made you bishops." (The English versions have "overseers" for the Greek *episcopi*, "bishops.") Paul will be discussed further in the next chapter.

VII

A power struggle?

Luke's history, as it may still be called, stresses the great success of the early Church, yet beneath the surface one can detect serious tensions. The existence of these tensions is corroborated by Paul's letter to the Galatians.

When Paul came back to Jerusalem, a convert to the Christ movement, he tried to join the disciples, "but they were all afraid of him, and believed not that he was a disciple."[43] One man knew better. He was Joses Barnabas, whose name means "the son of consolation." A Levite and thus connected with the rites of the Temple, he was the same man noticed above as Paul's senior colleague on a missionary trip. However it happened, it was he who informed the local church in Jerusalem that Paul really had been converted and that he had already preached in Jesus' name in Damascus.[44]

As we have seen, the so-called apostolic decree from Jerusalem about eating kosher and living a blameless moral life may have permitted Jewish and Gentile Christians to associate and share the Church's common meal, the "lovefeast," with each other. Luke shows much interest in the issue. But the idea that there had been unanimity on this vexing question is directly challenged by Paul in Galatians 1:15–2:10. There he insists that there was a concordat about the missionary enterprise. It was designed and accepted by James the

Lord's brother (a leading figure in the Jerusalem church), Peter (always regarded as in some fashion the chief person among the original Twelve), John, and also Barnabas and Paul (who had been engaged in missions to Gentiles). The concordat was to the effect that Barnabas and Paul were to lead a mission to the Gentiles, while James, Peter and John would do the same among the Jews. It seems strange that Acts 10 and 15 represent Peter as the missionary to the Gentiles, although that may be due to a thesis held by Luke and his own church.

Yet we find in Acts that Paul regularly entered synagogues first. After rejection there, he went to the Gentiles, asserting that this abandonment of Jews for Gentiles had been prophesied by Habakkuk 1:5 in the Greek version (the LXX). This behaviour seems to be at odds with the concordat of Galatians. We should take Paul's word for such matters in preference to the later Luke.

It is also difficult to understand the place of James the Lord's brother in Jerusalem. There is no evidence that he ever led a mission of any sort, least of all to the Jews. Like Paul, he is said to have had a "sighting" of the risen Jesus and he presided over the meeting that ruled on the question of admitting Gentiles. There is a hint here that he was something of a legalist. Later tradition represented him as a very devout Jew, inoffensive to the Jewish authorities. His death in the late sixties or just before the capture of Jerusalem in 70 is reported in traditions that are not very reliable.

For an unbiased reader, there emerges a picture of the early Church as tending towards a split into three parties: one led by James, one led by Peter, and one led by Paul. Unfortunately, the evidence of Acts is ambiguous. Later histories follow an idealized view that Christians always loved one another and that, as Tertullian asserted, even the pagan world acknowledged this with awe and wonder.

Luke downplayed the tensions and was anxious, as we noted earlier, to show that the Christian movement and its "Saviour" were in no way threats to the peace and security of the Roman empire. Moreover, I am inclined to think that Luke really believed in Christian heroism, the basic unity of the churches and the success of the faith under the sure guidance of the Holy Spirit. So we may read Acts with pleasure, for it is rather like a television documentary. The churches appear as enthusiastic new groups, not sectarians but people of catholic sympathies. They regarded themselves as the heirs of father Abraham, revered Moses and all the prophets but above all were devotees of Christ Jesus, the present, living Lord, their Head and true King. They all had to live in the Jewish and Roman centres of civilization, the real world with its rival mystery cults and pagan polytheism, its dreadful institution of slavery, its busy commerce and its constant need to face political and military conflict. To live there with dignity and humility as well as conviction about a divine destiny, Christians truly had to depend on the power, wisdom and love of God's Holy Spirit.

Michelangelo da Caravaggio (1573–1610), *The Supper at Emmaus*, ca. 1598. London: National Gallery.

The resurrection story of the walk to Emmaus and the supper there with Cleopas and his companion is found only in Luke 24:28–35. It is possible that the artist and the tradition in which he was reared regarded this event as a form of the original Eucharist (Mass or Holy Communion), a supper with the Risen Jesus in remembrance of the Last Supper before his arrest, trial and crucifixion. The biblical account simply mentions bread and the recognition that came with the Lord's "breaking the bread." Caravaggio clearly sees it as a real meal, served by the family servant, and by no means confined to symbolic bread and wine.

It should be noted that the Lord is young and beardless, a reversion to the earliest Christian representations of Jesus (of whom no portraits exist). To some critics the Christ is somewhat effeminate.

One disciple leans forward astounded. The other has flung out his arms, presumably in a gesture of surprise: his open left hand answers Jesus' right hand of blessing and consecration. The scene is rustic and realistic, the table groaning with fruit as well as the bread and wine. In fact the fruit basket sits precariously at the very edge, ready to fall over. The humanism exhibited here is typical of many interpreters of scripture at the time.

One should note also how the scene is bathed in light. As Walter Friedlander has written, "Light is the most powerful agent for transmission of the 'magic realism' of Caravaggio."

Reproduced by courtesy of the Trustees, The National Gallery, London.

fourteen

Paul the Christian Jew

I

A Hellenistic Jew

One soon discovers that most of the New Testament in the King James Version seems to consist of "Epistles of Paul the Apostle to...." There are fourteen! In the NRSV, however, Hebrews is removed from that list, leaving thirteen. I myself would exclude Ephesians, and many would do the same with Colossians and even 2 Thessalonians. But the fact remains that, after Jesus, Paul is the dominant figure. In 1 Corinthians 15:3–8, Philippians 3:4–11, Galatians 1:11 to 2:14 and Romans 7:5–25, much authentic tradition can be discovered about Paul and about the way he regarded himself as a typical human being and a fairly typical Christian.

A Roman citizen by birth, Paul was reared in a city that rivalled Athens as a cultural centre by the first century of the Christian era. Like some other Jews, he had both a Jewish name, Saul, and a Roman or Greek one, Paul. He probably had some acquaintance with Greek rhetoric, philosophy, literature and religious life, and he used the Septuagint (LXX), the Greek version of the Hebrew

Paul the Christian Jew

Bible. Paul always insisted on his Jewishness and his right to be considered a son of the *torah* and the covenant: "Circumcised the eighth day, of the stock of Israel, of the tribe of Benjamin, an Hebrew of the Hebrews; as touching the law, a Pharisee; concerning zeal, persecuting the church; touching the righteousness which is in the law, blameless."[1] These are large claims:

Δ born and bred a Hebrew, probably from a family that still spoke Hebrew;

Δ not a priest's son and not an expert like the scribes;

Δ yet by the standards of goodness as defined in the Torah, a youth who scored 100 per cent!

II

A nationalist Jew

This good young man persecuted Jesus' followers fanatically because they threatened the pillar beliefs and basic practices of his faith.

At that time, Judaism was not homogeneous. It was held together by the universal acceptance of the Torah, the central role of the cult in the Jerusalem Temple and the unique vocation of Jews to be the covenant people of Yahweh. There was considerable tolerance in other matters. Then the Christian Stephen appeared, arguing in the very synagogue that Paul probably attended and attacking the Torah, the Temple and the customs.[2] Stephen's message was about a man who had recently been crucified as a criminal and false pretender.

Paul reacted violently. He was a nationalist like many, if not most, of his contemporaries. He was revolted by the very thought that a criminal, hanged on a tree, could be proclaimed as his Messiah. Paul knew the Second Law, which says that "he that is hanged is accursed of God" (he quoted that text in writing to the Galatians later on).[3] To him the Nazarenes, as the early Christians were known, were a menace and not to be tolerated, and yet he had doubts.

III

A Jew arrested by God

In no account of Paul's dramatic switch from being a Pharisee to being a disciple of Jesus is there any reference to his having been instructed in the Nazarene way of life and faith. The change shattered the complacency of a deeply devout man, whose mind was disturbed by a nagging "and yet...." Of course, in the synagogue of the Cilicians he may have heard something from Stephen: stories about Jesus, stories Jesus had told and the last story of a cross and a resurrection. One can only speculate.

His own version of these events is in Galatians 1:11–24. According to his story, he had devastated "the church of God." Then Paul had had a religious experience. In his grace, God had called him to reveal his Son in and to Paul. Looking back, Paul affirmed that God had intended him for his service even while he was a mere embryo. (This echo of Jeremiah 1:5 underlies Paul's conviction that he too had been called to be a prophet or the equivalent, an apostle.) Paul knew what he had to do, his account continues; he had not consulted other people about it.

The duty of this new prophet-apostle was to preach among the Gentiles about Jesus, Son of God: probably like the Servant of Yahweh depicted in Second Isaiah. Thus, he did not go to Jerusalem or consult the church leaders there. Conversion was followed at once by a trip to "Arabia," possibly the Yemen. Thence "he returned to Damascus." In the third year after his return to Damascus, he visited Jerusalem. He went to interview Peter and also saw James the Lord's brother but no other apostles. After that he went to Syria and Cilicia, presumably to preach. That was why he was not known personally to the churches in Judea. All they knew was that the persecutor had become a preacher among them. Dramatic enough!

Clearly he had not been converted in Jerusalem. He said that he "returned" to Damascus, so his conversion must have taken place there before he left for Arabia. As we saw, the tradition in Acts held that the conversion happened on a road near Damascus. All this highlights the fact that, in Acts, Luke never refers to this autobiographical material and, indeed, shows no knowledge of the fact that Paul had written many letters, like this one to the Galatians.

IV

A Christian Jew

From his letters, we can tell a lot about Paul's beliefs. He "received" traditions and "delivered" them to his converts: for example, about the resurrection "sightings" and about the supper celebrated by congregations, when they recalled the Last Supper of Jesus with his disciples.[4] One traditional formula he quoted is from Romans 1:3–4, about the Son who is the Messiah, the Jesus who had been hanged on a tree. We can set out the formula in three parts, using quotations from the REB.

Δ "On the human level he was a descendant of David," and so the king-Messiah. But Paul never clothes this idea in political or military garments.

Δ "On the level of the spirit — the Holy Spirit — he was proclaimed Son of God." This refers, I think, to Jesus' baptism when the Spirit "descended like a dove." Jesus was the Lord's anointed.

Δ "By an act of power that raised him from the dead ... [he is] Jesus Christ our Lord." Not Caesar, nor a cult deity, only Jesus is *kyrios*, lord. As the anointed he is Messiah in some sense. And his name as a Jew from Nazareth was *Yeshua*, Jesus. Every title is significant.

I suspect that the resurrection "sighting" claimed by Paul was indeed the cause of his conversion and vocation to preach in Gentile lands. His faith was still in Yahweh, but he began to live his life and practise his faith in a new way. He taught that even as he had learned to really love Yahweh and had received power of the Spirit, so his converts would also be raised to new life and given powers and graces of the same Spirit. It was not obedience to the regulations of the Torah that had enlightened and satisfied Paul, it was trust in God's promises and the discovery that God is indeed to be "loved" with all one's life, possessions and intellect.

In Romans 7, he seems to speak of himself both as a Jew of the first century and as another "Adam," a typical person with ordinary dilemmas: "The good that I would I do not: but the evil which I would not, that I do."[5] Paul implies that everyone repeats the "Fall" as told in the story of Eden. It is rather like music. The ground bass of the Pauline symphony is that everyone falls. But then we hear, "Who will rescue me from this body of death? Thanks be to God through Jesus Christ our Lord!"[6] That reminds me of the early part of Gershwin's *Rhapsody in Blue*, which seems to sing about confusion and distress; then that wonderful melody starts in the second half! Meaning comes. Joy comes. There is to be sunshine after rain, and a new day will dawn. Light shines, and with light comes what is nothing less than a new creation, as Paul wrote in 2 Corinthians.[7] This Christian Paul had experienced in his own life; because of it, he changed our world.

V

The man who changed the world

Historians who study the ancient world acknowledge Paul's enormous influence: it can be traced in the formation of orthodox Christian theology from the second to the ninth centuries. A rediscovery of his message sparked the Reformation in the sixteenth century, the Wesleyan movement in the eighteenth and the Barthian orthodoxy of our own century. His doctrine of the church is fundamental to the contemporary ecumenical movement. But why?

He wrote letters in which he deals with all sorts of spiritual and moral problems, and usually his advice is helpful. His letters came to dominate the New Testament, Christian scripture. In them, he could be quite systematic in thinking, but he

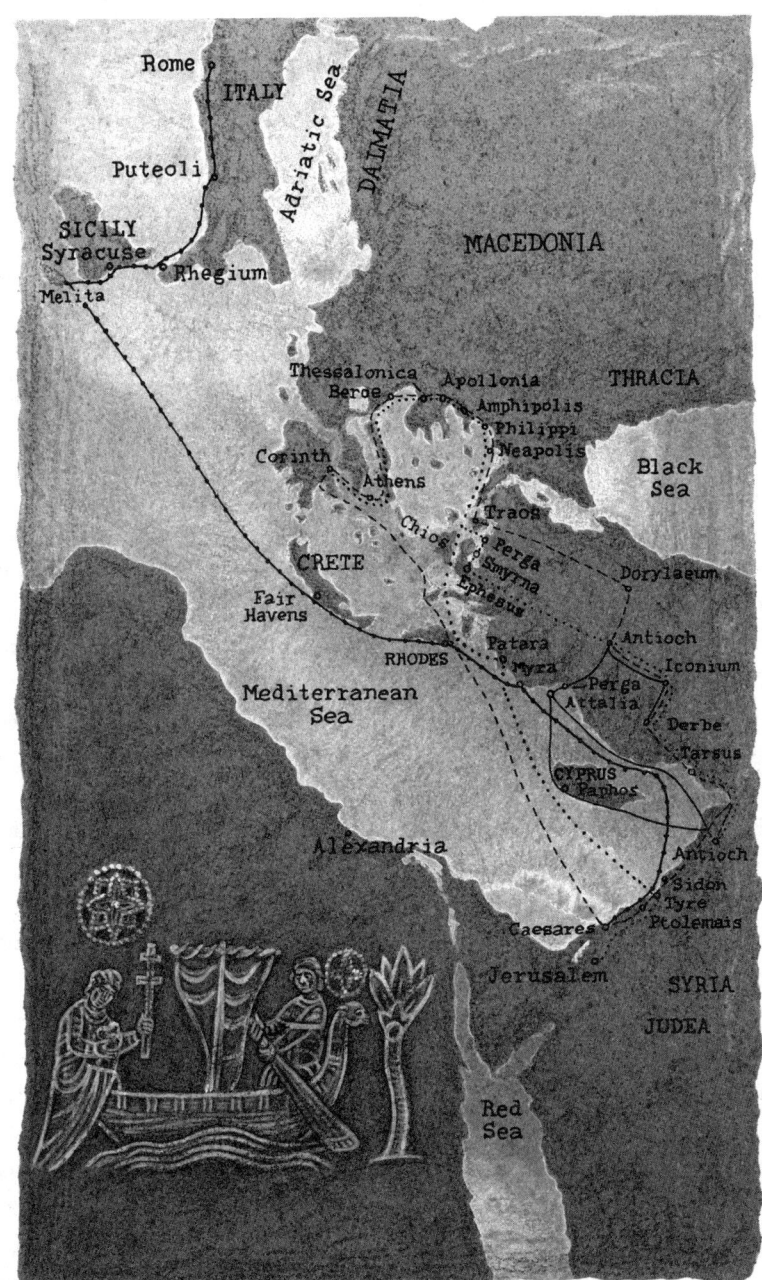

The Journeys of Paul

The gospel under sail would be an apt description of this map. The good news moves out to the larger world. The sketch is from a twelfth-century casket, the cross on a sea journey to France.

was not a professional philosopher. The letter to the Romans, if no other, has had an enormous influence on theology, on the relations of church and state, and on human rights.

The letters were transformed by becoming scripture. Paul wrote in the present tense; therefore the Bible is a living, speaking voice. He told about sin and forgiveness, about baptism and the Lord's supper, about magistrates and paying taxes. While doing so, he kept in mind an "end" that was to come, perhaps soon. It has been suggested that as he neared the close of his life, he was much less sure of that "soon."

He was influential because the secret of his life as a man and a Christian was hidden in his faith in Yahweh, God of his fathers and mothers in Israel, now to be known, loved and commended to others as "the God and Father of our Lord Jesus Christ." This secret was verbalized in the frequent phrase "in Christ." It has a mystical ring to it, for it can describe the spiritual marriage of a convert to the Master. Often the correct translation of the phrase is "Christian," sometimes it is "Christlike." Because Paul was a Christ-intoxicated person, he became and remains one of the greatest personalities in the human story. This Christian Jew was a giant among the early Christians because of his devotion to and inspiration by the Holy Spirit through Jesus of Nazareth.

As we shall see in the next chapter, Paul was a man with immense concern for children, women, men and even runaway slaves. Over the centuries, what he taught was not always acceptable: that is the case in our time. For he was a passionate man and occasionally — some say often — an opinionated man. His language does, in fact, betray his agitation. Yet he was wise and kind: always very concerned about the spiritual health of the congregations he had founded. He told them that he was their father and mother, he had travailed at their birth.[8]

A word or two must be said, however, about the frequent charge that he was misogynous. The most objectionable passages are in 1 Timothy 2:9–15, 2 Timothy 3:6 and Titus 2:4–5 in which female members of the church were forbidden to teach and speak in public. The writer enjoins them to remember Eve, the first sinner and mother of sinners, and be glad that salvation is possible for them by "childbearing." Although there are genuinely Pauline traditions that got into these documents, there are excellent reasons, based on style, vocabulary and doctrines, for believing that Paul did not write these letters to Timothy and Titus. Their message is not necessarily his teaching. The final editing of these letters may be dated about A.D. 125.

Texts in the authentic Paul that are controversial are in 1 Corinthians 11 about women's hair and the need for them to cover their heads at prayer. Paul was probably familiar with Jewish ideas that it was shameful for women to uncover their heads under certain circumstances (see Numbers 5:18 and Isaiah 3:16–17 and 3:24). In Paul's day, men did not cover their heads during worship services. The apostle seems to have believed in a hierarchy in which power descended from God through Christ to men and then to women. This belief would have come from his reading of Genesis 2:22. Hence there were elements in the heritage of Paul as a Christian Jew that prejudiced him against too much freedom for Christian women.

There were other factors influencing his admonition to women to cover their heads. In Corinth, prostitutes went about unveiled and Corinthian women in general had a reputation for licentiousness. In Paul's time, the reputation of this large, busy seaport, with its cosmopolitan proletariat, was such that for centuries "to corinthianize" had meant to indulge licentiously in sex. According to the geographer Strabo, the favourite goddess in Corinth — and especially in the dockside area — was Aphrodite, the goddess of love.

Recent studies of the Dead Sea Scrolls have found other beliefs, attributed to St. John Chrysostom, that may have influenced Paul. Some Jews, it appears, believed that angels were actually "present" at worship services. So with an eye to the legend in Genesis 6:4 (that the Nephilim were children of angels and mortal women), Paul and other leaders may have thought that women at Christian worship should be veiled and have their hair covered lest the angels present should lust after them. At any rate, one can read between the lines and see reasons for Paul's concern that the behaviour of female Christian converts should not be too lax.

It is my view that a later editor inserted 1 Corinthians 14:34–37, in which it is said that women cannot address the congregation. Those verses contradict what we find in 1 Corinthians 11:5: that women could not only pray, they could prophesy. That must have been possible in church assemblies where men prophets also spoke. Thus women, too, must have had gifts of the Spirit.

Too much must not be read into Galatians 3:28 about the unity in Christ of Jew and Greek, slave and free person, male and female. Unity did not carry with it equality of status even in a church. More notice should be taken of the ten or so women friends named in Romans 16, which is actually a letter to the Ephesians, among whom Aquila and Priscilla had gone to live and to whom a notable woman called Phoebe was going on some business. Rufus's mother had been like a mother to Paul. Persis was "beloved" and Stachys too was "beloved." Paul had very high regard for these and other women and that counts for a lot.

I have left to the last this verse from 1 Corinthians 11:3: "I want you to understand that Christ is the head of every man, and the husband is the head of his wife, and God is the head of Christ."[9] If this text means that the wife or woman is in a position of subjection, then it means that Christ is in a position of subjection too: ultimately both are subordinate to God. That position is not shameful for women nor for Christ. Neither is being put down.

Today one might wish that there had been a stronger emphasis on the equal partnership of men and women in the Church and society. Paul shared many of the attitudes of his times, but we should be ready to defend him against the charge that he was nastily prejudiced against women.[10]

Rembrandt (1606–1669), *The Descent from the Cross*, 1634. St. Petersburg, The Hermitage.

This is a very moving depiction of the event, rather unlike another rendering done as an official painting for a royal patron. Emotional elements are emphasized. A fair number of spectators are assembled at the foot of the cross, especially women of Jesus' company. One can see their sorrow and profound awe. The manipulation of Jesus' dead body is realistic and the entire scene is presented frontally. It is addressed to us, the viewers. That means that the viewer is to be drawn into the spiritual meaning of the Crucifixion. One becomes a participant at Calvary in a way that is reminiscent of black Gospel music: "Were you there when they crucified my Lord?" The biblical narrative is probably John 19:38–40, but see also Luke 23:49–55.

Reproduced by courtesy of Novosti Photo Library (London).

fifteen

Paul's Pastoral Advice to his Churches

I

Some real-life moral issues

Over the years, specific events have highlighted for me some of the issues that cause concern to pastors and teachers in the Church.

∆ Statements about allowing prostitution because it is a useful way of making money lead to concerns about what standards of sexual morality should be recommended to youth and parents in our society.

∆ When a Pentecostal preacher tells a Presbyterian minister that the only way to be a proper Christian is to experience the joy of the "second baptism" and the accompanying ecstatic gifts, the definition of a Christian person needs to be clarified.

∆ Some people have complacently said that the discrepancy between the rich and the poor is simply part of the system, that if there are poor people, it must be their own fault because no one in our economic system needs to be poor. They seem to think that since society ought to produce wealth, it is just fine that some people are millionaires and billionaires. That view leads to concerns about such self-centred indifference to the undeserved plight of millions in our world.

∆ Some people hold the view that reuniting the Christian churches is unnecessary because denominational differences actually enrich Christianity. That opinion leads to a number of questions: Why have schisms been so bitter throughout church history? Was the Inquisition due to false claims by one particular denomination? Why is nothing like a denomination found in the scriptures? How relevant are the spiritual teachings of the separate denominations, many of which excommunicate the members of rival sects (always in the name of one Lord Jesus Christ!)?

∆ Questions about why Jesus, who lived so far away and so long ago, should exercise moral authority over the behaviour of Christians today raise concerns. Christians must learn that Jesus is a living presence in the Church, and obedience to his way of life is essential to faith and discipleship.

Virtually all of these issues relate to domestic matters within the Church and have parallels in the life of Paul's congregations. Paul addressed these questions at length. Some of his writings are found in 1 Corinthians 5, 7 and 11–14 and Galatians 5:16–6:10.

II

On moral purity

Paul listed six types of people who should not be tolerated in a Christian congregation: sex offenders, avaricious or lustful people, idol worshippers, abusive slanderers, drunkards and violent robbers.[1] Sex offences appear first. The apostle noted a case of incest at Corinth:[2] it may have been marriage with a widowed stepmother, something that was illegal in Hebrew and Roman law. Paul demands that the local church confirm his verdict of guilty by enforcing a form of excommunication.

As for prostitution, Paul reacted with horror at the very thought of it: "Do you not know that your bodies are members of Christ? Should I therefore take the members of Christ and make them members of a prostitute? Never! Do you not know that whoever is united to a prostitute becomes one body with her? For it is said, 'The two shall be one flesh.' [Genesis 2:24]"[3] That is a very biblical and religious standard, derived from Paul's Jewish heritage. Today one might wish to add that the trade of prostitution depersonalizes and degrades women.

Paul exhibited a preference for celibacy. Part of his reasoning was based on the expectation that Jesus Christ would come soon to bring about vast changes in the human situation. He insisted, however, that marriage was lawful and in certain cases was to be recommended; he wrote that marriage would be better than cohabitation.[4] The apostle said husband and wife have equal rights in the matter of sexual intercourse. Divorce was not to be allowed, for the reason that the Lord, not Paul, had said so. Paul was quite careful not to impose his own commands on the local church; rather, he said, Christian morality depends on total dedication to Jesus Christ as Lord.[5] Remarriage was permitted after a spouse had died but with the proviso that the next partner should be a Christian.[6]

These concerns had been raised directly with Paul by the Corinthians, and he replied frankly. He was writing to people in a city where sexual licence prevailed. His injunctions were meant for a Greek city congregation about the year A.D. 55; Christians today may follow other advice in certain matters. Nevertheless, there are many important points in this teaching on moral purity.

III

On charismatic gifts

Baptism with the Holy Spirit had been predicted by John the Baptist.[7] There is a significant reference in Paul: "For in the one Spirit we were all baptized into one body ... and we were all made to drink of one Spirit."[8] Jesus said, on more than one occasion, that his disciples would receive the power and wisdom of the Spirit to face accusation; they would be defended, guided and empowered. But nowhere in the New Testament is there a "second baptism" that conveys the Spirit and its gifts. There was only one such act: the regular rite of Christian initiation. Paul made it clear that specific gifts or endowments would result from that initiation. These could be any of a number of things: wisdom, knowledge, fidelity, healing powers, miracle-working, prophecy, ability to interpret spiritual realities, or glossolalia (speaking in tongues) and its interpretation.[9] Glossolalia was indeed one of the gifts, but its place in the hierarchy was at the bottom; love (*agape* in Greek; *caritas* in Latin) is always at the top of the list. Paul would rather speak five words in the church service of worship "with his mind" than ten thousand words "in a tongue."[10] Love is what counts: love that is unselfish, Christlike and inspired by God himself who is loving.[11] The conclusion is that charismata are of little importance.

IV

On rich and poor church members

In Paul's remarks about the Corinthian celebration of the Lord's supper, there is a powerful, pungent criticism: "For when the time comes to eat, each of you goes ahead with your own supper, and one goes hungry and another becomes drunk."[12] His advice was to eat at home if you are hungry, so that, at the rite commemorating the Lord's last supper, everyone will share and help to "proclaim the Lord's death until he comes."[13] The rite would then have a proper place in the liturgy. It is by no means certain, however, that the advice was meant to abolish a real fellowship meal or "love-feast" as part of normal congregational assemblies.

In Paul's advice, there are no economic or political philosophies. The apostle was well aware that, unlike himself, few of his followers held Roman citizenship. Not many Corinthian Christians were powerful or of noble birth,[14] and so it was not feasible to expect major social change then and there. Paul advocated letting life be as it was.

But the religious message is blunt enough. Slaves, the prosperous and the poor all belonged, through baptism, to one Lord Jesus Christ. Therefore, they made a single body, and each member had to take care of each of the others.[15] That was what love meant. The poor were not to be despised; the better off were not to be complacent or smug.

V

On church unity

At the very beginning of the letter to Corinth, Paul indicated that reports had reached him in Ephesus about squabbles in Corinth. The people were divided in their loyalties: "I belong to Paul" or "I belong to Apollos" or "I belong to Cephas (Peter)" or "I belong to Christ."[16] Differences at the Lord's supper also demonstrated that unity was in short supply at Corinth. Although "Christ is the body," these people had not accepted the mystical union created by baptism and the gift of the Holy Spirit. So 1 Corinthians is an epistle of church unity, written to a divided, disunited congregation.[17]

The congregations founded in Palestine, Syria, Asia Minor, Macedonia, Greece, Italy and other areas not evangelized by Paul also needed to be unified. One local congregation was called "the church of God in Corinth" and every other one was likewise "the church of God in...." There was, however, only one real Church, since Jesus Christ risen and present in the Spirit possessed only one body. That is why reunion of divided Christendom today is an imperative of the gospel, a word of God to the faithful, and therefore to be neglected at terrible peril. However it is done, unity must be expressed.

VI

On sowing and reaping

Paul gave a great deal of ethical advice to the churches he founded and to the one in Rome, which he had not founded. It has been possible to cite only some of it that is relevant to contemporary issues. There is also, however, an astonishing list of virtues given in the letter to Galatia: "The fruit of the Spirit is love, joy, peace, patience, kindness, generosity, faithfulness, gentleness, and self-control."[18] All the virtues are simply aspects of the first one, the *agape*, the *caritas*, the love that is the primary effect of the Holy Spirit in the life of a Christian: it will always be the same.

"If you sow to the Spirit, you will reap eternal life from the Spirit"; but "if you sow to your own flesh, you will reap corruption from the flesh."[19] That is at the heart of Paul's Christian ethics.

Paul taught that God is not to be mocked, for he is the covenant God whose rules apply throughout the universe. One of the rules is that evil breeds evil, that "flesh," the sinful nature of men and women living outside of Eden, is opposed to the Spirit of God. There is a war going on between the forces of good and the powers of evil. It is visible in the world of nations and within every person's own life.

For Paul and the Church, the norm of moral behaviour is Jesus. He is not only the teacher but also the example. God himself is held up as a spiritual and moral example. Jesus is no dead, out-of-date teacher and prophet. He is the living Lord of the Church, and so his way of life is to be followed in every time zone and in every place where he is acknowledged. In the moral life, one sows and one reaps. God has ordered the life of people in such a way that results inexorably follow the sowing. Good is not the fruit of wickedness; it is the fruit of the divine Spirit.

sixteen

The Christ as High Priest in "To the Hebrews"

I

The symbolism of "Bethel"

Sometimes, in a small and rather bare church sanctuary, there is a banner painted on the wall above the central pulpit inscribed with the following words: "This is none other but the house of God, and this is the gate of heaven." These words come from Jacob's exclamation after he dreamt of a ladder.[1] Another saying often found is from Psalm 29:2: "Worship the Lord in the beauty of holiness." In a plain and otherwise unadorned place, these words can create an atmosphere of worship.

There are similar scrolls and motifs in hundreds of cathedrals and medieval sanctuaries as well as in contemporary buildings. Among the most moving and glorious are the magnificent Byzantine basilicas that are decorated with glowing mosaics. In the basilica of San Vitale in Ravenna, for example, on the left in the chancel Abraham is depicted entertaining three angels unawares, while on the right Abel is shown offering his sacrifice, and Melchizedek his. In the vault, a garland frames the Lamb of God, and a beardless Christ sits in royal purple on a globe, "crowned with glory and honour."[2] The basilica is awe-inspiring, numinous and evangelical. Christians have worshipped there for 1,400 years, so "a cloud of witnesses"[3] surround the worshippers who can sense the divine presence. In such a temple, the barrier between earth and heaven is all but dissolved: it is a "thin place."

In a sanctuary, a prophet would face the congregation, to read scripture, to pray and to preach. A priest, though, is needed to present a holy sacrifice — whether money, fruit or the bread and wine of the Lord's supper. With his back to the congregation, he faces God who is assumed to be high and lifted up above an altar or a holy table. Priests approach God to represent his people, while prophets address the people in the name of God.

God, of course, is invisible; he is not in the sanctuary as if it were a dwelling-place. Everything there, the building and the furnishings, is an earthly manifestation of heavenly realities and of the ceaseless adoration that is offered in heaven where there is no temple. In heaven, Jesus Christ is "seated at the right hand of God"[4] — figurative language to state the Church's conviction that Jesus is alive in and with God, therefore a real presence in the life of the worshippers. To understand at least a little of how that liturgy and symbolism developed in the Christian movement, only Hebrews in the New Testament needs to be read, particularly 1:1–4, 2:1–18, 4:14–5:10, 7:11–10:25 and 13.

II

The meeting place

We do not know who wrote Hebrews, which is called a "word of exhortation,"[5] but it is evident that the author was very familiar with the Hebrew Bible and had searched its text for wisdom about the Christian faith, its worship and way of life. He was certain that the old covenant with Israel had been abrogated and the new one that Jeremiah prophesied was in effect.[6] He made use of many contrasts between the life of old Israel, especially in its desert wanderings after the Exodus, and the church of Jesus the Nazarene. For him, the early rites in the tent or tabernacle were portents of the reality brought by the Christ. So there was to be no wilderness tent for the new pilgrim people on their journey, like father Abraham's, to the heavenly city of God, "the city that has foundations, whose architect and builder is God ... the city that is to come."[7]

Jesus, it was reported, had spoken of a temple that would replace the Jerusalem Temple: it would be one "not made with hands."[8] The idea is followed through in Hebrews 9, which says that Christ, through the shedding of his blood as a great sacrifice, entered the real, the true place of worship: in heaven, before the very face of God.[9] He is the mediator of the new covenant, the representative who gave himself on behalf of humanity and thus the person who suffered for sinners.

It is not easy to understand this way of describing the significance of Jesus. It takes the Resurrection seriously and depicts Jesus as interceding for his brothers and sisters on earth. So those who come together to worship God do so in the name of Jesus, seeking to imagine that they are really and truly in the divine presence. Hence the temple or church building is to be thought of as an earthly image of heaven itself. It is a "Bethel," a house of God.

III

The chief celebrant

When the author of Hebrews examined the regulations for worship, particularly for the Day of Atonement, Yom Kippur, he noted that there were two tents one inside the other: the second, inner one could be entered only by the high priest. Once a year, the high priest was to go there and offer penitential sacrifice for his own sins and the sins of the entire nation of Israel.[10] In Hebrews, tradition seems to be followed in prescribing that atonement be made only for inadvertent sins. The high priest, like all the lesser priests, had been appointed, called by God. Thus even the high priest was a man among men, an erring man, who would therefore be able to deal gently with weak men and women.[11]

The high priest, so important under the older covenant, became, in Hebrews, the symbol of the living Christ. He was tested like every one of us, yet had not sinned.[12] Sinless though he was, he could and did sympathize with people. He had been called and appointed by God to the office. To prove the point, the author of Hebrews cites Psalms 2:7 and 110:4, which he regarded as inspired oracles.[13]

Hebrews begins by calling Jesus the Son of God, "the reflection of God's glory and the exact imprint of God's very being."[14] It is therefore surprising that in the days of his flesh, Jesus offered up prayers and supplications that were not answered by deliverance from sorrow and death: "He learned obedience through what he suffered."[15] No passage in the New Testament equals that for a picture of the suffering, wounded, despised servant of God. The painting of the crucifixion by Mathias Grünewald for the Isenheim altarpiece is equally poignant.

IV

The benefits of worship

The book of Hebrews seems to have been addressed to a community that may have been threatened with apostasy, neglecting the gospel that had reached it through the disciples of Jesus who were confirmed by God himself "by signs and wonders and various miracles, and by gifts of the Holy Spirit...."[16] The community had fallen so far that they needed teachers, when they should have been teaching others. They therefore needed a lot of encouragement, which could come from Jesus their Prince (*archegos*), the perfecter of faith.[17]

These people had been baptized, "washed with pure water," and their consciences were clean.[18] When they assembled for worship, then, they could "provoke" one another — an interesting concept! — "to love and good deeds."[19] This was all the more important because they believed that the future Day of the Lord, the day when Christ would return to reign as the true Messiah, was approaching. His Church was to "receive" an unshakeable kingdom.[20] This appears to be the writer's way of describing the culmination of the salvific purposes of God. Worship was intended to bolster faith and hope, and it should not be neglected.

V
A final blessing

This unusual presentation of the significance of Jesus in terms of a temple cult, sacrifice for sin, an annual atonement ceremony, and a Lord who is in heaven acting as a new and eternal High Priest reads rather strangely in our contemporary Church. Some have emphasized the insistence in Hebrews that a sacrifice for the sins of humanity was offered by Christ "once for all,"[21] so that it can never be repeated, only remembered. This remains a difference between Catholic and Protestant theology and worship. It is, therefore, appropriate that, at the close of a sacramental act called variously the Lord's supper, the Eucharist, the Mass or the Holy Communion, often a prayer from Hebrews sends the worshippers into the world to bear witness to the gospel:

> *Now may the God of peace, who brought back from the dead our Lord Jesus, the great shepherd of the sheep, by the blood of the eternal covenant, make you complete in everything good so that you may do his will, working among us that which is pleasing in his sight, through Jesus Christ, to whom be the glory forever and ever.*[22]

Those who receive that blessing will know that they have also received "mercy and grace to help in time of need."[23] Surely that is what the worship of God should provide for the faithful.

Albrecht Dürer (1471–1528), *The Four Horsemen of the Apocalypse*, woodcut, 1498. Munich, Old Art Gallery.

This is one of eight woodcuts to illustrate texts from the book of Revelation. They suggest something of the contemporary terror in Germany about the possible early "end of the world" and the arrival of the millennium mentioned in Revelation 20:4. Dürer may well have shared the popular fears, just a few years before the explosion of the Lutheran Reformation in 1513.

The woodcut before us illustrates Revelation 6:1–8 accurately and fearsomely. First, a crowned rider holding a bow, on a white horse. Second, a horseman wielding a great sword, on a red horse. Third, a rider holding a pair of scales, on a black horse. Fourth, Death followed by Hades ("Hell") is the horseman who rides a pale, green horse ("sickly pale" in the REB; "a pale horse" in the KJV). Unfortunately we cannot see the colours on a woodcut.

According to the vision of John of Patmos, the author of Revelation, these horsemen were commissioned to remove peace from the earth. They were given power to kill by sword and famine, pestilence and wild beasts. For the wrath of the Lamb of God is to be let loose among the peoples. The wicked will be put to death, the demonic destroyed, and at the last the righteous will be liberated for eternal life in the New Jerusalem.

The French scholar Marcel Brion has correctly called Dürer a naturalist, a seer and a devout Christian. But one should take the visions of the apocalypse with much caution. Dürer gives very powerful expression to the literary source in Revelation and this expression has spoken to the imagination of many generations.

Reproduced by courtesy of Staatliche Graphische Sammlung, München.

seventeen

John's Revelation: Dreams and Hopes

I
Is the end of the world at hand?

"Apocalypse now" is a slogan that has recently become popular, since we live in the atomic age and it is possible to foresee the annihilation of human civilization through a nuclear holocaust in a world war. So far as Christians are concerned, the slogan is associated with an expected return of Jesus Christ, his "second advent," amid signs and wonders in the skies and on earth. Some believe that at that advent there will be a "rapture" of the faithful who are alive, who will rise and meet their Lord Christ "in the air" and be with him forever.[1] It is held that such a rapture must take place because Paul predicted it and it has not yet happened. Many have tried to fix its date but have not succeeded.

Apocalyptic anticipations have been nourished chiefly by John's Revelation. According to John, earthly and demonic beasts will be beaten, some time in the future, by One who is "The Word of God" and the "King of Kings": the Christ. The vanquished will be cast into a lake of fire and sulphur. Satan will be in bondage for a thousand years while Christ comes to reign over the people on earth with resurrected martyrs as his corulers and cojudges.[2]

Since John has provided almost no detail about this future event, predicted to happen very, very soon after he wrote — near A.D. 100 — many have speculated on it and produced rival scenarios. Premillennialists say that Christ's return will precede the millennium and his kingdom. Postmillennialists argue that his coming must await due preparation by his faithful Church. St. Augustine denied the entire scheme, teaching instead that the Church on earth is the Kingdom of Christ; therefore Christ's reign began when he first came to earth. None of these positions can be justified by the text of Revelation. It is, therefore, important for those who are inclined to apocalyptic interpretations of history to see what John's actual dreams and hopes were. They can be read in Revelation 1–3, 7, 12 and 18–21.

II

Background information

Revelation was written by a man named John, who was a prisoner on the small island of Patmos. He was a visionary, a commentator on the life of the churches he knew. He also claimed to be a prophet who had dreams, visions and divine revelations. The book is not, however, a collection of infallible oracles and predictions. It is mysterious, for it is full of symbols about life in Christ and the ultimate glory of the Church.

Revelation was written for Christians in the Roman provinces and perhaps Rome itself, as "seven hills" in 17:9 suggests. Its date may be within the reign of the emperor Domitian (A.D. 81–96) or early in the second century, but not later than the death of the emperor Hadrian in A.D. 135.

The author was not the apostle John son of Zebedee, as the reference to apostles in 18:20 shows;[3] it is quite certain that he was not the person who gave us the Gospel of John and the three letters of John. Possibly, all these writings were related to a particular "school" or area, perhaps near Ephesus. John of

Patmos seems to have been a real person. His message was important to the congregations of Asia Minor because provincial leaders of the Roman province of Asia were demanding the worship of Caesar and his image. It cannot be emphasized enough that, as in the case of Amos and the great prophets of Israel as well as the author of Daniel, another apocalypse, John was concerned with the believers of his own time and place. The predicted "end" was thought to be coming in that time, not in the twentieth century or in any conceivable century still to come. That is why speculation can be dangerous. Prophetic preaching can be made to suit the views of interpreters who refuse to recognize the human limitations of biblical writers.

III
To the seven churches of Asia

In Revelation, John described a wonderful vision he had. He wrote of the glorified Jesus, "one like the Son of Man," holding seven stars in his hand, while from his mouth came a sharp, two-edged sword.[4] This divine Spirit commissioned John to send messages to the churches he was concerned about. He wrote to the seven churches of Asia, and to each he gave a particular message, summarized as follows:

Δ To Ephesus: You have abandoned your first love.

Δ To Smyrna: Be faithful unto death, and I will give you a crown of life.

Δ To Pergamum: You have compromised with pagan practices.

Δ To Thyatira: You are sinning by allowing that false prophetess "Jezebel" to teach and seduce your members.

Δ To Sardis: There are some saints among you! But you are not all perfect.

Δ To Philadelphia: There is an open door before you. Go in, and don't be afraid of the great Test that is coming.

Δ To Laodicea: I have to rebuke and chasten you, because you blow hot and cold. You'd better change soon!

There was a call to repent in every one of the messages and a reminder that churches have to be faithful to Jesus. John also promised the people rewards: registration in the roll of the citizens of the City of God, heavenly food or "manna" to eat, possession of an identity disc (a white stone with the Christian's new name on it that would be good in the new Eden, the new Jerusalem) and permission to eat from the tree of eternal life and so live forever.[5] He also promised that the Church and the churches would have both national and international influence and, most astonishingly, that the conquerors, the faithful witnesses to the cause of Christ, would be enthroned with their Lord.[6] This destiny will be linked later to the millennial hope.

IV

John's visions

John had visions that we shall summarize here. At 4:1–5:14, there is a throne vision. John "saw" the Lord God Almighty enthroned, receiving the worship of twenty-four elders. There was a sealed book that had to be opened, but at first no one could be found who was worthy of the task. Then John saw that there was one who could open its seven seals. He was the Lion of Judah and the Lamb of God, Jesus, the Head of the Church.

In chapter 6, the seals are opened. John wrote that four beasts had appeared in the midst of the throne: a heraldic or symbolic lion, calf, man and eagle. A voice (like a trumpet) bade the prophet, "Come and see," and what he saw first were four horsemen on a white horse, a red horse, a black horse and a pale green horse. To each rider was given a divine responsibility: to conquer, to destroy, to judge. There was a holy war afoot. Victims who had died were under the heavenly altar and were told to bide awhile until the full number of persecutions was complete. God would then put an end to Roman idolatry and tyranny.[7] The heraldic beasts in John's vision are like those in Ezekiel 1. The victims who had died in the holy war must have reminded John of some he had known who had perished at the hands of Roman authorities.

A new Israel and a new exodus are foretold in 7:1–11:19. In John's vision, there was a vast crowd, from every nation, clothed in white and holding palms of victory. They numbered twelve times twelve thousand. A seal was put on their foreheads to mark them as God's servants so that they would be spared when the destruction began and locusts and scorpions were let loose.[8] The vision ended with an account of two witnesses who suffered in the city of Rome but were miraculously lifted up into heaven. The passage about the witnesses may refer to Peter and Paul or two unknown martyrs. Another possibility is that they may represent the two legal witnesses who could testify in a court of law against the criminal, evil powers that oppressed the churches. The number of tribes is described using the symbolism of the ancient tribes.

In 12:1–17, there is a vision that might have been induced by reading the story of Hagar who was cast out into a desert with her son and rescued by an angel.[9] John related that he "saw" a woman, "clothed with the sun, with the moon under her feet, and on her head a crown of twelve stars. She was pregnant."[10] She gave birth to a son who was snatched up to God and to his throne (REB) pursued by a great red dragon that wanted to devour the child. In heaven, Michael and his angels fought against the dragon and were victorious, so there was joy at his overthrow. There was still no final triumph, however, for the dragon returned to earth. Persecution had not ended.[11] The dragon was Satan, the accuser and devil who turned the governments against the faithful. With its return to earth, the churches were in a precarious situation and had to stay on guard.

John's vision continued with the presentation of a beast that had seven heads and ten horns and was worshipped by many people. It represented the cult of the goddess Roma, the city, and of the divine Caesar, the living emperor, whose cult was inaugurated in Pergamum.[12] Another beast followed. There was a number associated with it that held the clue to his name: six hundred and sixty-six.[13] John used gematria, the representation of letters of the alphabet by numbers to make a puzzle of the name. Nobody knows for sure what the name is. It could be Nero (Nero Caesar) or, based on the initials of their names, one from a list of Roman emperors. The most likely is the tyrant Nero, who destroyed Rome and burned Christians (in A.D. 64). What is certain is that the number does not refer to later villains.

Next in Revelation comes John's vision of the Lamb of God standing on Mount Zion accompanied by the redeemed of the new Israel: pure and guileless men and women. Six angels appeared whose primary message was that divine justice was at hand, specially for Rome. The text uses "Babylon" to indicate Rome. Babylon was the ancient enemy of Yahweh's people.[14] John said that just as ancient Egypt had been punished by plague after plague, so too would Rome suffer a similar fate. The passage is 18:1 to 19:4, parts of which, from the New Revised Standard Version, follow here:

Fallen, fallen is Babylon the great!
It has become a dwelling place of demons, ...
a haunt of every foul and hateful beast....
Alas, alas, the great city,
Babylon, the mighty city!
For in one hour your judgment has come.
And the merchants of the earth
weep and mourn for her,
since no one buys their cargo anymore....
And all shipmasters and seafarers, sailors and all whose trade is on the sea, stood far off and cried out as they saw the smoke of her burning....

*For in one hour she has been laid waste.
Rejoice over her, O heaven,
you saints and apostles and prophets!
For God has given judgment for you against her.*

V

The millennium

At this point in John's Revelation, we read about the Lamb's wedding feast in the divine Kingdom; about the Logos, the Word of God, who is seated on a white horse; and about the binding of the dragon for a thousand years and the millennial reign on earth of the resurrected martyrs with Christ as their Sovereign. That is the first resurrection, John predicts.[15]

There are many Jewish and Christian sources behind this expectation: they may be left to the archaeologists and historians of religion. It may be more helpful to note that in the dreams and hopes presented by John, there is no date for an end to either history or the universe. As noted earlier, many have speculated that John was an infallible and God-inspired person through whom an exact timetable for God's plan would be given, albeit in riddles. The end has been predicted for 1830, 1937, and some year around 1991. These dates were chosen because they were times of unsettling events such as war or the appearance of the atomic bomb.

The destruction caused by atomic bombs, which can set whole mountains on fire as in the conflagrations at Hiroshima and Nagasaki, is associated by some interpreters with the strange biblical text that follows: "The second angel blew his trumpet, and something like a great mountain, burning with fire, was thrown into the sea. A third of the sea became blood, a third of the living creatures in the sea died, and a third of the ships were destroyed."[16] The clues in Revelation, however, cannot be made to fit our own times. Every date predicted has proved to be false and calculations have had to be redone many times. It is futile to think that God planned it all in advance and gave the secret to John of Patmos. If he had, there would be no freedom, no right and wrong, no good and evil; Providence would be responsible for every detail of life and the fate of everyone.

VI
The Christ-figure in Revelation

In the book of Revelation, Jesus Christ is presented as the glorified Son of Man who controls the Last Judgment. Together with God, he is the Light of the City of God and the Book of Eternal Life is his.[17] Although he is, symbolically, the Lamb of God, he is also, according to John's hopes for the culmination of God's plans, a mighty warrior whose field marshal is the archangel Michael. In several texts he is praised as the Lion of Judah, the King of Kings, the victor over pagan princes. He is also presented as the bridegroom of the Church, an old Israelite theme.[18]

Two other images are important. First, Christ is the World Ruler, universal Sovereign or *pantocrator*. John described him as wearing a golden girdle, his head and hair white like wool, his feet like burnished brass, his voice lovely like the sound of many waters. This was the resurrected Jesus, he who possesses the keys of hell and of death. Like his Father, he is the alpha and omega, the First and the Last.[19] Second, the Lamb is to be understood as a ram, head of the flock. He is very "powerful," but the power is spiritual and not to be confused with earthly definitions. Wrath is ascribed to him, but the wrath is not some sentimental emotion: it is the spiritual antagonism of the divine against the devilish, of love against everything that produces hatred, vice and ungodliness.[20]

This depiction of Jesus seems to be far removed from the gospel picture of the humble teacher, healer and preacher of Galilee. It is important, however, to remember the context in which John's dreams and visions took place. During his time, Peter, Paul, Antipas[21] and unknown women and men were martyred; there were horrifying tales circulating about the Roman siege of Jerusalem and Masada (A.D. 70 and 73); the eruption of Vesuvius in A.D. 79 covered the cities of Herculaneum and Pompeii in lava; a famine struck during Domitian's reign; and unrest in areas like Pontus and Bithynia came to a head in the reign of Trajan about A.D. 112. Revelation was an apocalyptic prophecy for a group of churches that faced the possibility of a holocaust. It is not altogether surprising that some Christians looked for divine vengeance to be wrought on persecuting Rome and its minions.

VII
The values and limitations of visionary prophecy

The evidence shows that the early Church was in a quandary about having the book of Revelation in the list of sacred literature. Such scripture was read in worship services and served as a reference for sermons on the future of the Church and God's intention in creating and redeeming his creatures. In fact, fairly early in the fourth century, the first historian of the Church recorded that either everyone accepted Revelation as scripture or else everyone rejected it. That was some quandary! In the Eastern churches, to this day, it is considered to be a difficult document, to be handled with great care and caution.

In times of warfare and persecution, beleaguered churches and their people have found encouragement in the dreams and hopes of the prisoner on Patmos. They too have cried, "How long, O Lord, holy and true, how long?"[22] There is, of course, guidance for congregational life in the letters to the seven churches in Revelation 2 and 3. As for the rest, many have been consoled and inspired by the final vision of the Jerusalem that according to John's book is to be adorned like a bride. In that Jerusalem, there will be no evil but there will be healing for the nations. Peter Abelard put the vision into a hymn:

> *Truly Jerusalem name we that shore,*
> *vision of peace, that brings joy evermore;*
> *wish and fulfilment can severed be ne'er,*
> *nor the thing prayed for come short of the prayer.*

Faith operates by translating its beliefs and hopes into myths, legends, poetry and liturgical make-believe in the festivals of commemoration like Advent, Christmas, Holy Week and Easter. What John of Patmos offered was a kind of theology of history, proclaiming the divine government of time and our destiny. Believers who are prepared to discount what is fantastic and dated in Revelation can still be assisted by sharing the audacity of his faith in the glorified Christ who died and was raised and who is the living Word of God by whose grace and spirit the Church still survives.

Conclusion

We have now come to the end of an exciting journey through the world of biblical literature. Not everything in that world has been visited and appraised: far from it! Anyone whose appetite was whetted and whose interest in old Israel and new Israel was quickened will surely want to follow up with a reading and examination of some books in the Torah (Pentateuch), the Prophets, the Psalter and the theological history found in 1 and 2 Chronicles. There is important material in the other Gospels (Matthew, Mark and John) and in some of the New Testament documents such as James and 1 Peter (to name only a few of the books). I hope that you will wish to continue on the journey.

It is my hope that you have come to see that one reads the Bible not merely to assist a private communion with God but also to understand and appreciate great religious beliefs, important moral directives and the biblical teaching about what makes human life worth living. There is profound truth in the view that the purpose of life on earth is that people should become authentically human — or humane. At the same time, the Bible would also maintain that people should realize their status as icons and images of God the Creator. Ideally, the humane is the godly.

Existence in the secular world both mystifies and exhilarates its inhabitants. The Bible sheds light on human existence: its abnormalities and mischances as well as its grandeur and joy. Read and pondered with imagination and spiritual receptiveness, scripture invites us to identify with the people in it. There, readers will discover the wretchedness and the magnanimity of the human race; they will hear songs they can sing, prophecies that may change their outlook and spiritual teachings that speak directly to their condition. Of course, one may welcome that singing and teaching or one may reject it.

The unifying factor in this book has been historical, the story line of the origins, identity and fate of the nation Israel and the career of Jesus that gave birth to the Christian Church. Israel was a small nation, sandwiched between Egypt and one of a succession of empires in the Tigris-Euphrates valley. Its economy was agricultural. Its political capital was Jerusalem, except during nearly two hundred years when it was Samaria in the northern kingdom. The Church was a cooperative of quite small congregations in the cities along the strategic routes of the Roman empire; rural churches were a later development. There were power struggles in both the nation Israel and the cooperative Church. Human societies inevitably have considerable individual and corporate selfishness. The sacred literature called the Bible should not be encased in a liturgical or religious cocoon. It belongs in the secular world of politics, commerce and personal relationships.

It may seem odd that warfare is a common theme in the Hebrew Bible but has no place in the New Testament. The Church had not become a political institution, armed with the tools and weapons of a secular organization. The Church is not a nation.

One can study the good and evil characteristics of nationalism in the story of Israel — a topic that is of special significance in the last decade of the twentieth century. Almost from the start, however, the Church aimed at a cosmopolitan membership. People were taught that even leaders should be godly and that one had to pray for emperors, kings and statesmen. These ideas are still important today. States need people who are inspired by the Spirit of God. Those people will make the welfare of others a priority. They will love their neighbours and genuinely care for resident aliens among them, whether immigrants or refugees (that profound message is in Leviticus 19). They will also follow the new moral rule announced by the Spirit through Jesus of Nazareth. They are told, "love your enemies," as a supplement to the great Hebrew rules to love God wholeheartedly and to love one's neighbour as oneself.

It must be made clear that the Bible is not a history book nor a repository of infallible divine oracles that map out an inescapable future for people. One must always take account of the figurative language in the Bible: the metaphors, similes and poetry. This use of figurative language can be illustrated briefly by listing the images applied to Yahweh by the prophet Hosea (all references are to the REB). Yahweh is the husband of Israel (2:2); the father of his son Israel (11:1–4) and its lawgiver (8:12). As the moral judge who must be revered and obeyed, not out of fear but out of love, he is likened to a festering sore and canker (5:12); a bird catcher (7:12); a lion (5:14; 11:10); a lioness (13:8); a leopard (13:7); a she-bear (13:8) and a panther (5:14; 13:7). More positively, he is compared to the spring rains (6:3; 10:12); the dew (14:5) and a sheltering pine tree (14:8). He is the healer of his people (7:1).

As Christians read the Hebrew Bible, they have to remember that the Church quickly learned to Christianize the promises and prophecies of the old covenant, as if the ancient writers had meant one thing while God, as "the real author," had intended Jesus' disciples to read a Christian interpretation into the texts. A rereading of Hebrew thought justified including the Hebrew Bible along with the New Testament in the Christian Bible, where it is called the Old Testament. The

Old Testament then came to be seen as a "promise," and the New Testament as a "fulfilment" in Christian judgment. There is a profound sense of completion in finding Jesus to be the Lord's anointed, the hoped-for King, Prophet and Priest. So the Israelite heritage was indispensable for understanding the significance of Jesus the Jew, and the value of the Hebrew Bible must never be underestimated. Similarly, the tradition of the original apostles and their witness to Jesus was preserved in the literature of New Testament Epistles, Gospels and, as the Church eventually decided, in John's Revelation also.

From that perspective, one can begin to perceive that both Testaments are needed for the unity of the Bible. The Bible must play an authoritative role in the ongoing worship and mission of the Church. In the scriptures, there is no infallible rule for faith and life, yet Christians can never relegate them to obscurity nor ignore their virtues and their limitations. "Authority," therefore, is a word that must be used with caution with regard to the scriptures. The real "Word of God" for Christian faith is Jesus of Nazareth. In different ways, Hebrew prophets, seers and poets and Christian apostles and disciples witness to him as God's Word to the nations.

appendix 1

The Forms of Biblical Literature

A. In the Hebrew Bible

I

The geographical context

The ancient people from whom, according to tradition, historical Israel descended were located in an area roughly defined as the Fertile Crescent, stretching from the Persian Gulf near Kuwait northwestward to the sources of the Tigris and Euphrates rivers. The area includes modern Iraq, goes beyond that to Syria and south into Canaan, southward again into the Negev (that is, "Sutherland") and on to Egypt. Its features include deserts, rocky highlands, fertile coastlands and deep gullies or wadis. In Canaan, the Jordan River valley debouches into the Dead Sea 392 metres (1,274 feet) below the level of the Mediterranean Sea. There were few towns of any size, but a certain amount of commerce went on even in those preindustrial times. Palestine itself (as the biblical land may be called for convenience) was a land bridge between

Appendix 1: The Forms of Biblical Literature

Africa and Asia. It was a great battleground where wars were frequent.

According to tradition, the Semitic forebears in that area first lived as nomads, then led a subnomadic existence and later an agricultural life. From the Israelites, there is an old ritual for a harvest thanksgiving: "A wandering Aramean was my ancestor; he went down into Egypt and lived there as an alien, few in number, and there he became a great nation, mighty and populous."[1]

Then there was a time when the Semitic Arameans travelled and had adventures that became topics for tales and poems. These would have been recited by seers, teachers and perhaps also by priests on many different occasions. In later, more settled times, the traditional stories and rituals would have been associated with shrines in different parts of the country: in Israel, at Kadesh-barnea, Beersheba, Gibeon, Gilgal, Bethel, Shiloh and Shechem. It is not at all clear, however, what precise links should be made between sections of the Hebrew Bible as we have it and those religious centres. It must always be kept in mind that the present text was edited and reedited to the form we have that dates from the fifth century B.C. One result is that traces of ancient polytheism have been modified or removed in the interest of the developed Yahwist faith that was strictly monotheist.

II

The forms of prose

In the prose of the Bible, there are narratives, law codes, wisdom sayings and proverbs, and some prophecies.

Narratives include the saga of Genesis 1–36 and a short "novel" that might be entitled, "The Life and Adventures of Joseph, the son of Jacob" (Genesis 37–50). We have already surveyed some of that material and the subsequent heroic tales about the judges, warriors, princes and prophets, from Moses to Ezra.

There is one fable ascribed to Jotham, brother of an upstart leader or king, which he proclaimed from the top of Mount

Gerizim: "The trees went forth on a time to anoint a king over them; and they said unto the olive tree, Reign thou over us. But the olive tree said unto them, Should I leave my fatness, wherewith by me they honour God and man, and go to be promoted over the trees?" The tale continues with the fig tree also refusing, then the vine, and then the bramble. The bramble said to the trees, "If in truth ye anoint me king over you, then come and put your trust in my shadow: and if not, let fire come out of the bramble, and devour the cedars of Lebanon."[2]

Black Gospel music has kept another wonderful prose passage alive. It is the vision of dry bones in Ezekiel 37:1–14. To get its full flavour, one should know that the Hebrew word *ruach* means breath, wind and spirit; all these meanings are employed in the vision to tell how a nation and its army that are spiritually and materially dead will be marvellously raised into life and military strength by the Lord God who speaks through his representative Ezekiel. It is the wind of the Spirit that is creative, that can work amazing miracles of divine grace.

Quite late in the history of Israel, the strange tale of Jonah, discussed in the text, appears. It is wonderfully depicted in early Christian mosaics in the double basilica of Aquileia, near Venice.

The law codes include the several versions of the Ten Words discussed earlier. There is also a Holiness Code in Leviticus 17–26. It is necessary to be aware that "law" in the Hebrew Bible refers to secular and sacred obligations, both of which would have been regarded as "religious," just as today Picasso's *Guernica* has to be classed as a religious painting, though it deals with war and peace.

The law came from the very being of God himself, so that obligations of the various covenants emerge out of his will. The obedience of the covenanted nation ought therefore to have emerged, not out of passive acceptance or anything like a slave mentality but rather out of the loving acknowledgment of a free people. Hence, in later ages, some Hebrew thinkers could say that the law or *torah* of Yahweh has always existed and always will.

In the so-called Wisdom Literature — *Ecclesiasticus* and the *Wisdom of Solomon* in the Apocrypha as well as Job, Ecclesiastes and Proverbs — the meaning of "wisdom" is not the same as sophistic wisdom in the Greek philosophical tradition. It is more pragmatic and down-to-earth, referring to skill.

Since Hebrew *hokhmah* and Greek *sophia* were both grammatically feminine words meaning wisdom, it was possible, especially in the synagogues of the Hellenistic world, for Jews to personify wisdom. She was regarded as the lady Wisdom, a divine aspect, integral to the being of God himself: the ultimate source of everything that is good, right and wise. It sometimes seems as if Wisdom could be used as a synonym for God, but orthodox Judaism firmly refused to turn Wisdom or any other aspect of God into genuinely divine beings, gods or goddesses.

Even more significant is the fact that *ruach*, meaning spirit, could also be feminine. It is possible, therefore, to imagine that the idea of feminine traits within the Godhead would not have been entirely strange or objectionable to at least some Jews. For Christians, the Wisdom of God was certainly identified with the Holy Spirit, one of the Holy Trinity, and Jesus Christ himself was sometimes called the "Wisdom of God."

III

Prose characteristics

The prose writing in the Hebrew Bible lacks the subtle use of clauses familiar to us in English and in the classical Latin and Greek. But there is a very rich vocabulary. Hebrew is moving, hortatory, terrifying or consoling and often quite magnificent: the KJV in English has retained much of its richness, and some of it remains even in the NRSV.

It is disputed whether there is humour in the Hebrew Bible, and admittedly there is a great deal that is didactic. But a few interpreters have found humour in such a passage as this:

Go to the ant, you lazybones; consider its ways, and be wise....
How long will you lie there, O lazybones? When will you rise from your sleep?
A little sleep, a little slumber, a little folding of the hands to rest,
and poverty will come upon you like a robber, and want, like an armed warrior.[3]

Another humorous story tells of King Eglon of Moab who was killed in his privy by a left-handed man called Ehud, the son of Gera.[4] It has a parallel in the story of David sparing the life of Saul, "the Lord's Anointed," when he was in a cave.[5] Also, Samson killing a thousand Philistines with the jawbone of an ass may be cited as humorous: "With the jawbone of an ass, heaps upon heaps, with the jaw of an ass have I slain a thousand men."[6] As a final text with humour in it let me quote Ecclesiastes: "A living dog is better than a dead lion."[7]

In the secular tale of Esther, there is delicious irony when Haman, who had ordered a gallows prepared for his enemy, Mordecai,[8] is exposed by Esther. He has to beg the queen to save his life but is doomed to die the death he had planned for Mordecai: "Then Harbona, one of the eunuchs in attendance on the king, said, 'Look, the very gallows that Haman has prepared for Mordecai, whose word saved the king, stands at Haman's house, fifty cubits high.' And the king said, 'Hang him on that.'... Then the anger of the king abated."[9]

Hebrew prose is colourful and easy to read, rich in puns, similes, metaphors and other literary techniques for embellishing a narrative. An example of hyperbole is the claim that Saul and Jonathan "were swifter than eagles ... stronger than lions."[10] There are very good short stories. It has been said that a Hebrew writer did his best work by crowding emotion and action into a few sentences.

Much of the prose would have been recited aloud; consequently, there are places where a pause or a longer silence needs to be inserted, as it were. The reminders for speakers I

Appendix 1: The Forms of Biblical Literature

have added in the following examples illustrate this characteristic:

Δ In Isaiah 6:8, after the voice of Yahweh wonders who will go for the heavenly court, [— silence —] Isaiah hears himself saying, "Here am I; send me!"

Δ In 1 Kings 19:12, God was not in the wind or the earthquake or the fire. "And after the fire [— silence —] a still small voice."

Δ In Judges 5:27, "Where he bowed, there he fell down [— pause —] dead."

IV

Images and symbols

Much of the Bible springs from the imagination of ancient writers, and it summons us to use our imagination too. So symbols and images are very important. Here is one about King David and his captains:

> *Now three of the thirty captains went down to the rock to David, into the cave of Adullam; and the host of the Philistines encamped in the valley of Rephaim.... And David longed, and said, Oh that one would give me drink of the water of the well of Bethlehem, that is at the gate! ... those three broke through the enemy lines and brought the well water to the king. But David would not drink of it, but poured it out to the Lord, And said, My God forbid it me, that I should do this thing: shall I drink the blood of these men that have put their lives in jeopardy?*[11]

Of course, it was truly water that the knights had brought, yet it had become "blood." That is sacramental imagery at its best. It was and remained water. In the spirited camaraderie of David and his brave men, however, it was also a kind of blood, carried at the real risk of men whose act betokened loyal love. It is an image that reappears when a different kind of king, "a son of David," said at the Last Supper, "This [bread] is my body.... This is my blood of the new covenant."[12]

Hebrew symbolism is very clear in such passages and one has to be careful not to destroy the truth of the idea that water can be, in certain circumstances, blood — in a spiritual sense. There was not any magical transmutation of the well water from Bethlehem, nor is there any similar change in the wine of the Christian Lord's supper. By using water, bread and wine in such rituals, people enter into communion with the unseen divine Spirit, for the sacramental image somehow allows participation in the heavenly reality. It is not merely a "sign" pointing to something else in the beyond.

V

The poetry

One third of the Hebrew scriptures is poetry. Like all great poetry, it has multilayered meanings that readers discover for themselves. Often it is figurative and metaphorical; it requires imaginative or, one may say, spiritual response from a reader. It differs from more recent poetry, for there are no sonnets, no long epics and few short lyrics. There is almost no rhyme. There may be chiasmus, a form of inversion in which the order followed in the first phrase is reversed in the second: A...B; B...A. Some rhythmic forms depend on the number of stresses in a line. The basic form, though, is two lines that are treated as parallel to each other. The second line may repeat the sense of the first, it may contradict it, or it may include but add to the meaning. Sometimes couplets can be built up into larger stanzas. The following are examples:

Δ Psalm 19:1 is an example of synonymous parallelism:
"The heavens declare the glory of God;
and the firmament showeth his handywork."

Δ Proverbs 10:7 is an example of antithetic parallelism:

"The memory of the just is blessed;
but the name of the wicked shall rot."

∆ Psalm 40:1 is an example of synthetic parallelism:
"I waited patiently for the Lord;
and he inclined unto me, and heard my cry."

VI

Poems ancient and modern

Some of the songs and poems of the Hebrew Bible may go back to the twelfth century B.C. Examples can be found at Psalm 113, "Praise ye Yahweh (the LORD)"; at Exodus 15:1–21, "Then sang Moses and the children of Israel this song unto the Lord...."; and at Judges 5:1–31, the Song of Deborah and Barak following Israel's victory over a Canaanite confederacy (there is a prose version in Judges 4).

Almost as old may be Genesis 49:2–27, where the elderly Jacob predicts what is to befall his sons "in the last days." As we now have it, edited much later, it is probably a collection of ancient oracles.

There is also a remarkable song ascribed to Hannah, the mother of the seer-prophet Samuel, as we noted in the text. Her Magnificat is the prototype and partly the source for the Magnificat in Luke 1:46–55, which is attributed either to Elisabeth, the mother of John the Baptist (by Irenaeus in the late second century A.D.), or to Mary, the mother of Jesus (by almost all other ancient sources).

Other single and collected poems can be found in Job and Deuteronomy 33 (the Blessing of Moses). Many other fragments and references have been unearthed in the literature, some dealing with what we would call secular affairs. The following are examples:

∆ *Boasting* (Genesis 4:23–24 NRSV): "Lamech said to his wives: 'Adah and Zillah, hear my voice; you wives of Lamech, listen to what I say: I have killed a man for wounding me, a young man for striking me. If Cain is avenged sevenfold, truly Lamech seventy sevenfold.'"

Δ *Drinking* (Isaiah 22:13 NRSV): "Let us eat and drink, for tomorrow we die."

Δ *Harvesting* (Isaiah 5:1–7 NRSV): "My beloved had a vineyard."

Δ *Taunting* (Isaiah 47 REB): "Sit in the dust, virgin daughter Babylon."

Δ *Law* (Micah 1:2–7): "The Lord God will be the witness."

Δ *Lamenting* (Jeremiah 9:17–22): "Summon the professional mourners."

Δ *Sexual loving* (Song of Songs 8:5 NRSV): "Under the apple tree I awakened you."

VII
The Psalter

The Psalter is a wonderful anthology of religious poetry from different authors widely separated in time, perhaps as much as four or five hundred years. Some of the Psalms were composed by King David in his court. Many are hymns of the Second Temple. They include songs of praise and thanksgiving, confessions of sin, petitions for Yahweh's pardon, laments over individual and national disasters and coronation odes. Their range of emotions is wide and their appeal universal. Often the piety is heart-rending and "speaks" to the depths of the souls and minds of readers.

Nevertheless, there are also poems that induce enmity and call for heavenly vengeance, based on the idea that evil deeds and wicked persons ought to be punished both by God and his agents. The following are some examples:

Δ Psalm 79:6, 79:12 NRSV: "Pour out your anger on the

nations that do not know you.... Return sevenfold into the bosom of our neighbors the taunts with which they taunted you, O Lord!"

△ Psalm 137:8–9 NRSV: "O daughter Babylon, you devastator! Happy shall they be who pay you back what you have done to us! Happy shall they be who take your little ones and dash them against the rock!"

△ Psalm 139:21–22 NRSV: "Do I not hate those who hate you, O Lord?.... I hate them with perfect hatred; I count them my enemies."

Psalm 109 expresses the hope that the days of a wicked man may be few and follows with a long list of punishments: that his children be orphans, that his wife be a widow, that his goods be confiscated, that his garment be a belt of cursing and that his very name be blotted out in the second generation (109:8–19). It is true that such sentiments were common enough in the turbulent Middle East in biblical times, but that is no excuse for sanctifying the brutal killing of children in wartime.

One should note that the "I" of the Psalter sometimes refers to a single person, sometimes to the entire people. The king, the high priest or others may represent the nation, as on the day of atonement, for instance, when only the high priest enters the holiest place in the temple to confess the sins of Israel.

Many of the poems are hymns that were to be sung or chanted at the great worship celebrations. Music and dancing accompanied the sacrifices and festival rites, for all the arts ultimately had to be related to divine inspiration. A classic statement of this is the case of Bezaleel.[13] At the same time, we have to remember that the fear of idolatry made it impossible to use human forms in painting or sculpture to represent God and his activities. Celebrations were colourful rituals, marked with the music of choirs, cymbals, trumpets and guitars, ritual shedding of blood and meals of communion and thanksgiving shared by God and his people.

B. *In the New Testament*

I
Its different types of literature

In the New Testament, there is really nothing comparable to the Torah of Judaism as recorded in the Pentateuch. Only the Acts of the Apostles could be likened to the historical books of the Old Testament. There is no collection of important prophets, and of course the time span is much less — one hundred years instead of about two thousand.

In the New Testament, one can trace the development of a Jewish sect that very quickly became an autonomous religious community and a rival to all other faiths. It was centred on the career of Jesus who was acclaimed by his pupils as the fulfilment of Jewish hopes (the divine promise reiterated many times in the Hebrew Bible) and, in fact, as the Saviour of the world. The gospel-books that tell his story are relatively late, and they appear to constitute a unique literary genre.

Since the Christian movement was furthered by travelling evangelists and organized by local elders under the guidance of important leaders called apostles, it is apostolic traditions that had to be preserved and expounded in semiofficial epistles and in personal letters. The former include Romans by Paul and 1 Peter ascribed to Simon Peter; the latter include Philemon and 2 and 3 John. Unfortunately, it is impossible to be certain whether those named as authors of the documents did, in fact, write them; the exception is some of the letters dictated or written by Paul. Of Paul's writings, possibly Colossians and, in my judgment, certainly Ephesians, 1 and 2 Timothy, Titus and Hebrews have been wrongly ascribed to him. The final editor of the Fourth Gospel (John) is not known; he is probably not the author of Revelation and perhaps not the author of the Letters of John either.

Matters of that kind belong to technical scholarship and need not prevent people from enjoying the literature of the New

Testament and using it according to their religious stance. For most people in a Christian church, the Word of God is in the Gospels and the Epistles.

II
Special forms of the literature

Affirmations of faith: These are found in 1 Corinthians 12:3, "No man can say that Jesus is the Lord, but by the Holy Spirit"; and in Romans 1:3–4, discussed in chapter 14. Paul inherited and passed on the traditions of the earliest disciples.

Sermons: The sort of sermon that contemporary congregations are familiar with does not appear in the New Testament. Instead, there are collections of teaching, for example the Sermon on the Mount in Matthew 5–7 and the Sermon on the Plain in Luke 6. There is an interesting example in John 6 about the Christ as "the bread of God," where there are resemblances to rabbinic homilies. Parables, as we have seen in the text, play a very significant role in Jesus' teaching; nothing further needs to be added at this point.

Lists of duties, virtues and vices: There is a summary in Romans 13:8–10 that defines Christian duty in the simplest, most direct and totally adequate manner: "Owe no one anything, except to love one another; for the one who loves another has fulfilled the law. The commandments, 'You shall not commit adultery; You shall not murder; You shall not steal; You shall not covet; and any other commandment, are summed up in this word, 'Love your neighbor as yourself.' Love does no wrong to a neighbour; therefore, love is the fulfilling of the law" (NRSV).

In Galatians 5:10–23, vices are called "the works of the flesh," that is, of the fallen, sinful nature of people. Virtues are "the fruit of the Spirit," for, Paul taught, people reap what they sow, and there is a single harvest of goodness in those who are guided by the spirit of God.

A list in 1 Timothy 6:11, cites "righteousness, godliness, faith [or is it 'fidelity'?], love, endurance, gentleness" (NRSV).

In 2 Peter 1:5–7, a very late document, there is a moving image of the stepladder that Christians are to climb diligently. They add virtue to faith, knowledge to virtue, temperance to knowledge, patience to temperance, godliness to patience and brotherly-kindness to godliness. To brotherly-kindness is added the *agape* which used to be translated as *charity* but is better called *agape-love* or, for those who still employ Latin in the liturgy or their moral teaching, *caritas*. It is almost impossible to rid the contemporary English word *love* of sexual sensuality.

A better-known list is the so-called Tables of Household Duties that can be found at Colossians 3:18, Ephesians 5:22 and 1 Peter 2:18. It is significant in demonstrating the considerable conformity of first century Christians to the ethical mores of Greco-Roman life.

These Tables state that there are people who are superiors — husbands, fathers and masters — and others who are inferiors — wives, children and slaves (Christians still possessed slaves at that time). Superiors are told to love the inferiors. The inferiors are never instructed to love their superiors: their duty is to "obey" or "accept the authority" of the others. I cannot be comfortable with such teaching. We do not treat women and children in that fashion. It has to be said quite firmly that, in this respect, the ethics of the New Testament are dated and are not a precedent for people today.

Testaments (as in "last will and testament"): One of the most moving testaments is Paul's address to the elders ("bishops") of the Ephesian church, delivered at Miletus according to Acts 20. Another, also ascribed to Paul, is in 2 Timothy 4, where it is affirmed that Paul had fought a good fight and had finished faithfully.

Perhaps the most important example is in the Gospel of John 13:31–16:31. For many Christians throughout the history of the Church, this section of John has been very precious, a holy of holies, for the Lord speaks on the night in which he was betrayed. I find that there are three versions of a single farewell address or Last Testament: (1) 13:31–14:31; (2) 15:1–

16:4a; and (3) 16:4b–33. The passage ranks among the masterpieces of New Testament literature.

Poems and hymns: Careful examination of the teaching of Jesus in the first three gospel-books as well as the retranslation of his sayings into Aramaic reveals that Jesus was a poet. Matthew 6:25–33 is an example. Here the couplets have been woven into stanzas, and one scholar believes that this was a unique contribution of Jesus to Hebrew poetry:

> *Therefore I say unto you,*
> *Take no thought for your life,*
> *what ye shall eat, or what ye shall drink;*
> *nor yet for your body,*
> *what ye shall put on.*
> *Is not the life more than meat,*
> *and the body than raiment?...*
> *Consider the lilies of the field, how they grow;*
> *they toil not, neither do they spin:*
> *And yet I say unto you,*
> *That even Solomon in all his glory was not arrayed*
> *like one of these.*
> *Wherefore, if God so clothe the grass of the field,*
> *which today is,*
> *and tomorrow is cast into the oven,*
> *shall he not much more clothe you, O ye of little faith?*

The apostle Paul, too, was either a poet or a man whose prose rhetoric took wings. Examples are in the *Hymn to agape-love* in 1 Corinthians 13; in the cry of faith in Romans 8:31–39, "If God be for us, who can be against us?"; and in the lyrical praise of the Christ in Philippians 2:6–11, as the Icon of God the Father, the Second Adam and the Suffering Servant of God.

There are also, in Revelation, texts that seem to belong to liturgical acclamations and other parts of early services of worship in Christian congregations:

Opening the Scriptures

Δ "The new song.... Thou art worthy to take the book, and to open the seals thereof ... [thou] hast made us unto our God kings and priests" (5:9–10).

Δ "We give thee thanks, O Lord God Almighty, which art, and wast, and art to come; because thou hast taken to thee thy great power, and hast reigned" (11:17).

Δ "The song of Moses the servant of God, and the song of the Lamb, saying, Great and marvellous are thy works, Lord God Almighty; just and true are thy ways, thou King of saints. Who shall not fear thee, O Lord, and glorify thy name? for thou only art holy: for all nations shall come and worship before thee; for thy judgments are made manifest" (15:3–4).

Autobiography: There are useful, indeed essential, autobiographical passages in Paul's letters to the Galatians 1–2 and to Corinth, 2 Corinthians 10–12. In Philippians 3:2–16, he speaks proudly of his cherished Jewish heritage and his new life in which he counted everything else "but dung, that he ... might win Christ."

III
The structure of tradition

As a final point, it may be noted that the structure of the earliest Christian tradition can be seen in the discourses of Acts 2:14–36, 3:12–26, 8:26–40, 10:38–48 and 13:16–41.

Tradition is an important term in the vocabulary of the New Testament. Tradition had been passed on orally for two or three generations, and the literary forms we have examined are, in a sense, the depository of tradition. An extended form of it is to be seen in the Gospel of Mark. Luke's preface informs us that there were many such collections of the tradition, the truth concerning the events that had been fulfilled among the members of the first Christian congregations. They were not scientific histories. What tradition meant was the Christian party line, its message or *kerygma*, its gospel. The gospel-books should not be called myths, though they do seem to have divine activity as their subject matter. Jesus of Nazareth, the agent of the Spirit of God, the person in whom the churches had "seen" a veritable icon and image of God, was human, a man and a Jew of one particular time and place. Miracle stories and resurrection legends were not intended to deprive Jesus of his historicity. For there would have been no gospel to preach had he not been born, reared in Nazareth, educated in the synagogue (perhaps even in the scribal knowledge of the time), committed to a mission and a ministry in the service of God, Israel and the world, and subjected to a cruel death. There was, of course, a sequel, and the Church lives in its glow. For the Church believed, and still believes, that God raised Jesus from death into the eternal life of heaven.

appendix 2

A Short Guide to the Signs and Symbols of Scripture

Almond

An almond in the form of a mandorla (a pointed oval) is employed in art as a halo, a sign of divine grace and favour. See Numbers 17:8: Aaron's rod budded and "bloomed blossoms, and yielded almonds."

Anchor

The hope set before Christians is an anchor of the soul "sure and stedfast" (Hebrews 6:19). So the anchor is sometimes found in the early frescos of the Roman catacombs.

Angels

In religious lore, angels are divine messengers. Originally they may have been gods in the Council of Heaven. See Matthew 2:13; Luke 1:11–20; John 20:12–13. Israel's Guardian Angel was Michael (Daniel 12:1). Gabriel was the Interpreter (Daniel 8:16; 10:5 ff.) and appropriately, therefore, the herald of the Annunciation to Elisabeth and to the young girl Mary (the Blessed Virgin). According to Tobit 3:17 Raphael was a

Appendix 2: A Short Guide to the Signs and Symbols of Scripture

healer. It is very rare to find names for angels in scripture. They became prominent in the era of the Second Temple, perhaps as a result of Persian or Parthian influence.

Angelic beings include the *seraphim* of Isaiah 6:1–9 (the only reference) and the *cherubim* of Genesis 3:24, which also appear on the Ark of the Covenant (Exodus 25:18–20), so that the Lord, Yahweh, can be invoked as "Thou that dwellest between the cherubims" (Psalm 80:1).

Ezekiel 1:4–28 tells how the glory of Yahweh was seen in a vision of four strange winged creatures having the faces of a man, a lion, an ox and an eagle. In Revelation 4:7–10, the four beasts have the same faces. From this came the use of them as symbols of the Evangelists: the Man for Matthew, the Lion for Mark, the Ox or a Calf for Luke, and the Eagle for John. These play a notable role both in art (for example in the Book of Kells) and in architecture, on many famous pulpits.

Man is the image of God. *Lion* represents the power of Judah and the Messianic King. *Ox/Calf* is a sacrificial victim that appeases God or helps to reconcile God and his people. *Eagle* was reputed to renew its wings by soaring near the sun. It had incredible strength and became a symbol for profound spiritual power.

Apple

Apple should probably be translated *Quince* or possibly *Apricot* in Song of Songs 2:3, Joel 1:12 and Proverbs 25:11. In the Song, it represents the male lover.

Note: The tree of the knowledge of good and evil was not an apple tree. Two explanations for the error are offered: (1) *malum* in the Latin Vulgate version means both *evil* and *apple*; (2) Song of Songs 8:5 seems to refer to the tree of Eden as an apple tree: "I raised thee up under the apple-tree; there thy mother brought thee forth." It seems to be impossible, however, to get people to stop referring to the tree as an apple tree!

Apple of his eye

This is an English phrase, not a Hebrew one. *Apple* here is the pupil of the eye, regarded as a round globular body. Three Hebrew words are translated by the phrase: (1) *ishon*, a little man, or one most dear (2) *babah*, a gate, or a tiny image reflected in the eye (3) *bath*, daughter, or pupil or tear of eye.

Ark

The Ark was a chest containing the Tables of the Law. It was a portable shrine. Note "Ark of the covenant."

Ark of Noah

The Ark of Noah is quite different. It was a boat, a refuge from the flood waters. It is a symbol of the Church amid the storms of this life.

Babel

Babel is the place (Babylon) of linguistic confusion, a punishment for human *hubris*, the arrogance that threatened the Divine (Genesis 11:9).

Bethel

Bethel means House of God. Originally, it was a Standing Stone or Sacred Pillar associated with Jacob. In Christian piety, it came to mean the Church or a sanctuary.

Bread

Various meanings are suggested for "our daily bread" in Matthew 6:11 and Luke 11:3, the Lord's Prayer. The phrase can mean "tomorrow's ration"; "enough food for today"; "bread of the Kingdom"; "our *essential* food" (spiritually).

Broken bread is the symbol of the crucified Lord. Personal communion with him is sustained by "eating the bread and drinking the cup" (1 Corinthians 10:16). Cf. the Manna. In John 6:35 Jesus is reported as claiming, "I AM the Bread of Life", the one who feeds the spiritual life of his members. The I AM is itself an echo of "YAHWEH" as in Exodus 3:14.

Bride

The bride is Israel, beloved of Yahweh, her husband (Isaiah 54:5; Jeremiah 31:32; Hosea 2:19–20). Or she is the Church (*Ecclesia*) as in Ephesians 5:23–32. Sacred marriage language was used by Paul about conversion to Christian faith and the holy life it requires (2 Corinthians 11:2). He also employs the vocabulary of sexual intercourse for fellowship with the risen Lord (1 Corinthians 6:17).

Burning Bush

The burning bush is the place of revelation and the promise of liberation by God (Exodus 3:2). In Jewish and Christian art, it may denote Moses. Presbyterian churches have adopted it as their logo.

Cedar

Cedar, especially of Lebanon, Song of Songs 5:15. The Song has been treated allegorically in the Church, and also in the Synagogue. So the beloved is Christ. (Headings in the King James 1611 version express that allegory.)

At Ezekiel 17:22–24, the high tree represents Babylon, the low tree, Judah. Christians applied this to the Messiah Jesus. And compare Mark 4:30–32 where the little mustard seed became a great tree.

It is not biblical to use the cedar as a symbol for the beauty of the Virgin Mary, as artists do.

Cock

The cock is the sign of Peter's denial (Mark 14:30).

Compass Points

East and west compass points appear in a variety of ways: the Garden was planted eastward in Eden (Genesis 2:8). Wise men (astrologers) came from the east at Jesus' birth (Matthew 2:1). Some people worshipped the sun towards the east, not to the prophet's joy (Ezekiel 8:16).

Ezekiel saw the Glory of Yahweh return to the Temple by

the east gate (43:1–4). The Dispersed of Israel will return to the Holy Land from the east country and the west country (Zechariah 8:7; cf. Matthew 8:11).

How far has Yahweh removed his people's transgressions? "As far as the east is from the west" (Psalm 103:12).

The land God promised or gave to Abraham lies northward, southward, eastward and westward in Canaan (Genesis 13:14).

The Babylonian enemy, which is Evil, comes from the north (Jeremiah 4:6, 13:20; Ezekiel 38:15).

The south is the Negev, the dry or south land, in the wanderings of the patriarchs. Ezekiel 21:2–4 is a prophecy against the Negev, that is, land of Israel. There will be total destruction, "from the Negev [South] to the North."

The porters of the Temple were at all four points of the compass. In the New Jerusalem there are twelve gates, three at each compass point (Revelation 21:13). East is, of course, the sunrise area and it is "up front." West is "to the rear"; and so North is on the "left" and South on the "right": scripture people are "oriented"!

Darkness, Light

Darkness and light signify the moral and spiritual: evil/goodness; the devilish or demonic/the divine or angelic. Hence blindness is a sign of spiritual deprivation, sometimes wilful. The Persian religion and the Qumrân community use the symbols of darkness and light a great deal. The latter were "The Sons of Light," echoed in Matthew 5:14, John 12:36, 1 Thessalonians 5:5, Philippians 2:15 and Ephesians 5:8. Other important references include Isaiah 9:2, 42:7; John 1:5, 3:19, 8:12; 1 John 1:5, 2:8; 1 Peter 2:9. In Matthew 22:13 the "outer darkness" is Hell, the place of the wicked and the rejected.

Day of the Lord

The day of the Lord or the day of salvation; the day of vengeance. It may denote either the coming vindication of Israel or, in the New Testament, the coming of Christ as victorious King, his Second Advent or *Parousia*.

Appendix 2: A Short Guide to the Signs and Symbols of Scripture

Its widespread use may be seen at Amos 5:18; Malachi 3:2; Isaiah 2:12; Zephaniah 1:7; Isaiah 49:8, 61:2; Mark 13:32 ("that day and that hour"); Acts 17:31; 1 Thessalonians 5:2; Romans 13:12 and Hebrews 10:25.

Desert

The desert may be a chaotic place: the wilderness into which the scapegoat was driven (Leviticus 16:10) or home of wild beasts (Isaiah 13:21, 34:14; Mark 1:13). It may be a place of safety (Revelation 12:6), where Israel wandered after the escape from Egypt. It can be a place of temptation (Mark 1:12–13) or a place of communion (Mark 6:31; Luke 4:42). The desert plays a special role in the development of monasticism.

Donkey (Ass)

The donkey is a humble beast compared with the horse and the camel. In Isaiah 1:3, it recognizes its master's crib, but Israel does not! Matthew 21:5 quotes Zechariah 9:9 where the Evangelist, or a source he may have used, uncritically misinterprets the original "upon an ass, *and* upon a colt the foal of an ass" (but the KJV "and" is to be omitted). There was only one donkey, but in Matthew there seem to be two! The event referred to is the Palm Sunday entry, a favourite topic in art. Possibly that entry took place six months earlier, for the leaves fit an autumn festival.

Dove

The dove with an olive leaf is the symbol of rescue, as in the story of Noah and the Flood (Genesis 8:11). Alone, it is the symbol of the Spirit of God, as in the account of Jesus' baptism. It can indicate the Spirit's descent in other cases, such as Annunication scenes. Seven doves represent the seven virtues of Isaiah 11:2–3. In art, doves may symbolize souls.

Dragon

The dragon represents evil, Satan or the Devil or the enemy of the Church (Revelation 12:1–17). Compare that with Isaiah

27:1 and 51:9 and Ezekiel 29:3, where it is identified with the Pharaoh of Egypt.

Eagle

The eagle is swift and high flying: Exodus 19:4; Proverbs 23:5; Jeremiah 49:16. The legend of its renewed youth lies behind Psalm 103:5.

It is the symbol of John the Fourth Evangelist, derived from Ezekiel 1:10 and Revelation 4:7. This is the case in St. Augustine, *On the Agreement of the Evangelists* I:6. But Irenaeus, *Against the Heresies* I.xi, 8, assigned the eagle to Mark.

End

In Hebrew, *end* is *kets*, a time of destiny, a time when things like childbirth come to term. Or it may be a real end, a finish or completion (Psalm 39:4, which is rather ambiguous). A very important usage is at Lamentations 4:18, because there "our end is near" can be said also as "our end is come," that is, it has arrived. This helps to explain Mark 1:15 and the teaching of Jesus about the Kingdom of God. Mark's Greek word is *kairos*, and it carries the same sense of a turning point in history, a time when God fulfils his purposes and ends one age, so that a new age may begin.

In the Hebrew Bible see Amos 8:2; Ezekiel 21:29, 35:5; and Daniel 8:17, 11:35, 11:40, 12:4, 12:9.

In the New Testament consult Matthew 10:22; Luke 1:33; 1 Corinthians 10:11 (the overlap of the ages); 1 Peter 4:7; and Revelation 21:6, 22:13.

God is the First and the Last, *the Alpha and Omega* (Isaiah 41:4, 44:6); but in Revelation 1:8 and 22:13, the glorified Christ has the same title. At the very end, Christ-in-God will be the Lord and there will be a new beginning, an eternal blessedness for the faithful.

Fig Tree

The fig tree is sometimes identified with the tree of the knowledge of good and evil, because of the fig leaves

Appendix 2: A Short Guide to the Signs and Symbols of Scripture

(Genesis 3:7). There is a weird story in Mark 11:12–14.

Fish

The one hundred and fifty-three fish of John 21:11 may be symbolic for all the nations of the Gentiles.

Fishing, common for people beside the Sea of Galilee, is used to mean preaching (Mark 1:17). So quite naturally *fish* came to represent Jesus, luckily, because the Greek letters in the word for fish made up initials for "Jesus Christ God's Son Saviour." In Greek IHS are the first three letters in Jesus. But in Latin they are an acronymn for *In Hoc Signo*, "in this sign," that is, the Sign of the Cross; often used by artists within a halo. The fish symbol was used in early Christian art, but rarely thereafter. (Note: IHS does not mean "in his service.")

See Whale (because of Matthew 12:40).

Grapes

Grapes represent Israel (Hosea 9:10). There was a cluster on the great Golden Vine on Herod's Temple. Israel is the vineyard of the Lord (Isaiah 5:7). In John 15:1–8, Jesus calls himself the True or Real Vine, no doubt because, as Messiah or Word incarnate, he embodies the Israel of God. So the Church as the body of Christ may also be represented by grapes.

Hand

The hand of God is the symbol of his creative and protecting power (Exodus 3:20; Psalm 31:5, 95:7, 139:10; Isaiah 45:12, 50:2).

In Revelation 1:17, the writer speaks of his vision of the glorified Son of Man who laid his right hand on him in blessing and reassurance.

A laying on of hands, for example by the Elders, means a commissioning, a handing over of authority and, perhaps, a communication of spirit to another (as in 1 Timothy 4:14). There is a considerable body of evidence in the scriptures about laying on hands in the sacrificial cult, in blessing, in healing and in passing on the Holy Spirit.

Hart

Psalm 42:1 (KJV) refers to a hart; in the Revised Standard Version, it is a deer; in the Revised English Bible, a hind. The verse gave rise to a favourite scene in early Christian art, seen in mosaics of rare beauty.

It is said that Isaiah 35, especially verse 6 ("Then shall the lame man leap as an hart"), was the source for *The Peaceable Kingdom* by Edward Hicks.

Heaven

It is the dwelling-place of God (not literally) and sometimes means simply the sky.

Hour

"My hour" or "my time" refers to Jesus, the Son who is the incarnate Word of God and doomed to die at the hour of his destiny (John 2:4, 7:6, 7:30, 17:1). Though it is the hour of Jesus' death, for the Evangelist it is also the hour of the exaltation or glorification of the Word.

Hyssop

Hyssop was used in a rite of purification (Psalm 51:7): dipped in blood, it would be sprinkled on a house or person. According to John 19:29, "they filled a spunge with vinegar, and put it upon hyssop, and put it to Jesus' mouth." This seems odd. It has been conjectured that the sponge was put on a spear (Greek *hysso*) or that a different plant was intended. It occurs often in paintings of the Crucifixion.

Jerusalem

Jerusalem is the City of Peace, Zion, the City of David and the City of God: virtually paradise on earth. It was the site of the Temple until A.D. 70 and was the cynosure of hope for exiles. Paul wrote that "Jerusalem which is above is free, which is the mother of us all" (Galatians 4:26), hence God's

Appendix 2: A Short Guide to the Signs and Symbols of Scripture

eternal home. New Jerusalem (Revelation 21:2) is paradise restored, the city in a garden. So the earthly city still represents the Divine and is sacred to Jews, Christians and Muslims. It is the thinnest of places, because there one is near God!

Lamb

Lamb may be the unblemished lamb of Passover (Exodus 12:3) or Christ, as the Lamb of God (John 1:29; Revelation 5:12, 14:1). Since it is John the Baptist who is quoted at John 1:29, the lamb is a symbol for him; the symbol is carried on a long staff. Twelve sheep represent the Twelve Disciples. In Christian art, a flock of sheep represents the Church (Psalm 100:3).

Note: a lamb or sheep on a shepherd's shoulder was a pagan motif, for example for Hermes *Criophoros*. For Jews and Christians, David was the Shepherd-King; for Christians, Jesus is the Good Shepherd. The Good Shepherd was very common in early Christian art, either on a sarcophagus or fresco or as a small freestanding statue (sometimes with a young, beardless Christ), but it died out soon after the fourth century.

Lion

The lion may be figurative for a beast of prey (Psalm 91:13). It was one of the winged beasts of Ezekiel's vision (see Eagle). Note "the Lion of the tribe of Judah" (Revelation 5:5). It became the symbol for the Evangelist Mark. Later, it stood for Mark's city, Venice, whose inhabitants seized sacred horses from Mark's original city, which was, according to Christian lore, Alexandria in Egypt. In Christian art, the lion is associated not only with Daniel but even more frequently with Jerome.

Lyre

In the KJV, the lyre may be called a harp: symbol for David and the saints in Heaven (1 Samuel 16:23; 1 Chronicles 13:8; Revelation 5:8). See also Genesis 4:21, 31:27.

The instrument of Daniel 3:5 was probably a four-stringed Greek lyre, ancestor of the guitar.

Mountain

A mountain may be the mount of the Lord (Genesis 22:14), identified by Jews as Zion (Jerusalem) with its famed Temple Mount, 811 metres (2,600 feet) above sea level. (Scripture does not identify it as the site of Abraham's aborted sacrifice of Isaac and, of course, knows nothing of it as the place whence Mohammed ascended into Heaven.) The mountain of God is Horeb or Sinai (Exodus 3:1, 19:11); it is the place of revelation and communion with God (cf. Luke 6:12). Jesus on the mount in Matthew 5–7 may be intended to be a counterpart of Moses on Sinai. Appropriately, the Transfiguration took place on a high hill (Mark 9:2), as did the Ascension (Matthew 28:16), but contrast Acts 1:9–12.

Myrtles

Zechariah (1:8) says, "I saw by night, and behold a man riding upon a red horse, and he stood among the myrtle trees..." (the man was probably an angel). Here there may be mistranslation, since the Greek version of the Hebrew Bible has "mountains"; but exegetes disagree. Some Christians identified Christ as the man on a red horse and Gentiles (myrtles) as the people he had to convert.

The only biblical source for myrtle as symbol of peace and love is Isaiah 55:13.

Night (see Darkness)

It has multiple meanings. "The day is thine, the night also is thine" (Psalm 74:16). It is a time for dreaming dreams and seeing visions (Daniel 7:1–2, 7:7, 7:13). Compare that to "weeping may endure for a night, but joy cometh in the morning" (Psalm 30:5). Jacob, Joseph (son of Jacob) and kings like Nebuchadrezzar and the Pharaoh had nighttime dreams that needed interpretation by one who possessed the divine spirit.

"Watchman, what of the night?" comes from an ambiguous prophecy (Isaiah 21:11–12); it may refer to the night of despair or oppression.

Night is a time to go about unseen. It is the time of all that is dark and therefore of the Devil, opposed to God's light. "Judas went out immediately: and it was night" (John 13:30). Nicodemus came to Jesus by night (John 3:2). One should "cast off the works of darkness and put on the armour of light" (Romans 13:12). Revelation 21:25 tells that in the New Jerusalem there will be no night, only everlasting day.

Olive (See Dove)

A dove with the olive leaf is a symbol of rescue and universal peace: in fact, peace between God and the descendants of Noah.

The olive tree has a part in Jotham's Fable, the only fable in the scriptures (Judges 9:7 ff.).

Palm (See also Donkey)

At John 12:13 *lulavs*, bundles of palm, myrtle and willow, were flung on the way as Jesus entered Jerusalem. These belong to the harvest festival of Tabernacles held in the fall. So Jesus may have entered six months before the date usually given. If so, the length of his ministry in Jerusalem would be much greater, which would make a lot of sense.

The palm is also a symbol of victory (Revelation 7:9 etc.).

Partridge

The partridge is a symbol of deceit and theft (Jeremiah 17:11).

Pearl

In Matthew 13:45, the pearl is used by Jesus in a parable as a symbol for the marvel of finding the Kingdom of God. Pearls, however, may be referred to without any spiritual significance (Revelation 17:4, 18:12, 18:16, 21:21). It is not usual to find them in Christian art.

Rainbow

The rainbow is a sign of the covenant with Noah (Genesis 9:12 ff.). There was a bow round the Throne of God in the vision of Revelation 4:2–3. In Chartres and Moissac cathedrals, the Christ of the Last Judgment is depicted as seated on a rainbow.

Reed

A reed is a type of rush, used at the Crucifixion (Mark 15:36).

Scorpions

Scorpions are denizens of the terrifying wilderness (Deuteronomy 8:15). They torment people (Revelation 9:3, 9:5). At 1 Kings 12:11 the scorpion is used figuratively, perhaps proverbially, for a scourge.

Sea

From Isaiah 27:1, Daniel 7:3, Nahum 1:3–4 and Revelation 13:1 we learn that terrible beasts may rise up out of the sea, where dragons live. It may represent the underworld or Sheol. Yahweh, though, is in control: he can rebuke it and dry it up, as at the Exodus. Revelation 21:1 says that the primeval abyss is going to disappear, and at the End, which is an eternal New Beginning, "there was no more sea."

Serpent

The serpent seems to be the Devil in animal form, the Enemy, as C.S. Lewis might call the Devil. Yet in Celtic art it is symbolic of wisdom, the Guardian of knowledge.

Numbers 21:8 and John 3:14–15 refer to a bronze serpent set up by Moses to be a healer for people bitten by serpents. The wounded Christ is the healer of people wounded by sin (1 Peter 2:24; cf. Isaiah 53:5). Hence in art, a pole with a serpent entwined is a symbol of the suffering Messiah. There may be a connection with Asclepius, the god of healing, who is in some way related to serpent-worship.

Star

The star of Bethlehem is the star of the Nativity with all its associations for the Church. It is identified with the Magi.

Appendix 2: A Short Guide to the Signs and Symbols of Scripture

There is a famous illustration in the Roman catacomb of Priscilla, referring to a prophecy in Numbers 24:17: "A Star out of Jacob, and a Sceptre shall rise out of Israel." This became a Messianic prophecy and was applied to Jesus: "I am the root and the offspring of David, and the bright and morning star" (Revelation 22:16). Later the morning star would be linked to Venus, both as planet and as the goddess of love.

The woman crowned with twelve stars (Revelation 12:1) is perhaps the personified Church as the community of the Messiah. Later she was identified with the Virgin Mary. According to a recent decree of Pope Paul VI, Mary is now *Mater Ecclesiae*, Mother of the Church.

Faithful Christians are to receive the morning star in the New Jerusalem where they will share and display the victory and everlasting glory of Christ (Revelation 2:28; the original source is Daniel 12:3).

A magnificent use of the Star image may be seen in the mosaics of the Mausoleum of St. Lawrence in Ravenna (it is usually called the Mausoleum of Galla Placidia).

Daniel 8:10 uses stars to represent pagan powers.

Temple

A remarkable use of the temple image will be found at Ephesians 2:12–22 and 1 Peter 2:4–5, where believers are "living stones" in the spiritual house or Sanctuary of God. One may compare Mark 14:58, which says that Jesus was to build another temple, made without hands, and John 2:19, "Destroy this temple, and in three days I will raise it up," where he was referring to his body, the temple of God's Spirit. A similar concept of a community as a temple appears in the Qumrân Scrolls from the Dead Sea caves. The *yachad*, their society, constituted the earthly dwelling-place of God.

Thistles and thorns

In Genesis 3:17–18 thistles cumber the ground because of the Fall. They may symbolize evil and sorrow: see Proverbs 22:5; Jeremiah 4:3; Ezekiel 2:6; Matthew 7:16 (though Scots would disagree!). In art, thistles are often, as symbols of pain, linked with thorns. Jesus' crown was a crown of thorns. They have other evil effects: see Proverbs 26:9; Judges 8:7; Mark 4:7, 4:18 (allegory of the soils).

Time(s) and seasons

Symbolically, there are times that are fraught with destiny like *kets* and *kairos*. See Numbers 9:2–3; Daniel 2:21; Mark 1:15; Luke 12:56; Acts 3:19, 17:26; John 7:6; Romans 13:11; Galatians 4:10; 1 Peter 1:5. "Kairological time" for Dr. Paul Tillich is a time when the divine Spirit breaks into human history to befriend believers and sustain their communion with God.

Tree

In Genesis 2:9, two trees are in the Garden of Eden: one of Life, one of the Knowledge of Good and Evil, whose fruit must not be eaten.

The Tree of Jesse is a genealogical tree, for the line of David and David's greater Son, Jesus (Isaiah 11:1–2; Romans 15:12).

Water

Water has various meanings associated with drinking, washing, drowning and irrigation. On drinking, see 1 Corinthians 12:13 (drink the Spirit). Regarding cleansing, sometimes formal and useless, sometimes sacramental, see Mark 7:4; Acts 22:16; 1 Corinthians 6:11; Hebrews 10:22. Regarding drowning the old Adam (that is, human nature) and being resurrected to new spiritual life see Romans 6:4; Colossians 3:1, 3:10. Regarding running waters from Jerusalem and waters from Christ or his disciples for spiritual irrigation, see Zechariah 14:8 and John 7:38.

Water has to be crossed, out of the land of serfdom into freedom (Exodus 15:8–10), where there is plenty of water (Deuteronomy 8:7). See also Psalm 23:2, Isaiah 12:3 and John 4:10–14 regarding "living water."

Sometimes water may seem to be less effective than fire, for example, in Christian baptism as contrasted with that of John the Baptist. But John's "fire" was destructive and judgmental. Baptismal water was a symbol of those who would escape the Judgment and sometimes of moral cleansing and spiritual rebirth.

To be born of water and spirit means to be born "from above," that is, from God, or "a second time" — there is a pun here (John 3:5).

In Ephesians 5:26, the Church as Bride has to be washed for her sacred marriage.

In 1 Peter 3:20, the reference is to the Ark of Noah by which eight people were saved in or by water: a prefigurement of Christian baptism.

In the new Eden of Jerusalem, the river of life is flowing and the blessed have *water* to drink in never-failing supply (in contrast to life in the desert). Psalm 1:3 is fulfilled (Revelation 21:6, 22:1–2).

Way

There is to be a *highway* for pilgrims and returning exiles, through the desert or the jungle.

Way (Hebrew *derech*) simply means daily behaviour. See Genesis 18:19, 28:20; Exodus 13:18; Psalm 25:9, 107:40, 119:30; Proverbs 3:17; Isaiah 40:3, 43:16.

Early Christians seem to have been called *This Way* or the *People of the Way*, that is, belief or faith in the dead and risen Jesus (John 14:4–6; Acts 9:2, 19:23, 22:4).

Whale

The whale is depicted by artists on the assumption that the Big Fish that swallowed Jonah was a whale (or a dolphin?). That reference is from Matthew 12:40 (KJV), and it is not to be relied on.

Wine (See above under Grapes)

Note: In the scriptures, people, too, may be symbolic. The following are examples: Noah the survivor; Abraham the Father of the faithful; Jacob who is Israel, but also the supplanter and the tither; Samson the strongman hero; David, the Once and Future King; Emmanuel, at first an expected Prince as prophesied by Isaiah, later as the Christ who is "God with us"; Elijah, the Forerunner who is to prepare God's Way or the Messiah's; Moses, whom the rabbis call the First Redeemer, prototype of the Prophet who is to come in the End; and Adam, the first human being, created in the image of God, type of the sinful disobedient people, type also of the humanity whom the Christ will raise out of Hell.

At 1 Corinthians 15:21–26 and 15:44–49, Jesus is called the *Last Adam (eschatos adam)*, not the *Second Adam* as in Cardinal Newman's hymn. He is Luther's *Proper Man*, humanity, the Adam of the final age, restored to the likeness and service of God his Creator. He is the ever-living *Icon of God* (2 Corinthians 4:4–6). Jesus the Christ and Christians embodied into his life by baptism are said by Paul to be a single entity, a single man or person (Galatians 3:28).

References

References are to the KJV unless otherwise noted.

Chapter 1

1. Isa. 40:28 NRSV.
2. Ps. 95:3.
3. Hos. 11:1, 11:9.
4. Jer. 31:32 NRSV.
5. Luke 11:2 NRSV.
6. "Ashtoreth" is the name given in the Hebrew Bible to a Canaanite fertility goddess. Her name should be "Asherah," because the vowels *o* and *e* of Hebrew *bosheth*, shame, were added to the consonants of the Canaanite name. She may have been worshipped by some Israelites: see W.G. Dever, *Recent Archaeological Discoveries and Biblical Research*, 1990, pp. 135–36. It is also of interest that, much later, a goddess Anath was worshipped in the Jewish colony at Elephantine, near Assuan, Egypt, as the consort of the Lord Yahweh who is named as Yahu. On that, see E.G. Kraeling, *The Brooklyn Museum Aramaic Papyri*, 1953. Canaanite cults probably did attract many of the Israelites during the so-called Conquest and Settlement and even during the monarchy; the cult of Anath was quite exceptional.
7. 1 Cor. 6:17 NRSV.
8. Gen. 2:4–3:24.

Chapter 2

1. Gen. 32:28, 35:10.
2. Gen. 2:4–3:24.
3. Gen. 3:22–24.
4. Gen. 4:1–16.
5. Gen. 6:5–9:17.
6. Gen. 8:22.
7. Gen. 9:2–7.
8. Gen. 11:1–9.
9. Gen. 9:18–19.
10. Gen. 3:22–24.

Chapter 3

1. Deut. 26:5 NRSV.
2. The most recent archaeological evidence is unable to justify the Israelite traditions about Abraham, Moses, the Exodus and the wilderness wandering. Yet the name *Israel* has been found on the Merneptah stela, now dated to 1207 B.C. This makes it possible to date an exodus to the thirteenth century B.C. (A photograph of the stela can be found in John Gray, *Archaeology and the Old Testament World*, 1962, at p. 96.) I am prepared to accept the tenacious tradition of a genuinely historical Moses, a historic escape from Egyptian slavery and, though less surely, an Abraham as the ancestral father of the people known as Israel. It now appears likely that many of those who were enrolled in the Twelve Tribes were in fact part of the mixed

population that lived in Canaan during the fourteenth and thirteenth centuries; they began to form a nation-state only about 1020 B.C. On this see: N.K. Gottwald, *The Tribes of Yahweh: A Sociology of the Religion of Liberated Israel, 1250–1050 B.C.E.*, p. 83; John Romer, *Testament: The Bible and History*, pp. 67–87; W.G. Dever, *Recent Archaeological Discoveries and Biblical Research*, pp. 24 ff. A fairly radical statement is the following by Romer in *Testament* (p. 26): "Presently the best that may be said of Abraham and his family is that, if, as the Book of Genesis asserts, the Patriarchs once had real existence on this earth, then they must have lived before the first-known record of Israel in Canaan — and presently, that is before 1207 B.C.... Abraham *may* have lived somewhere in the 1000-year period before that date, though no trace of him or his family has ever been found." I would still want to date Abraham to about 1800 or 2000 B.C., but certainly cannot be dogmatic about that.
3. Gen. 15:18–21.
4. Gen. 17:10–14.
5. Gen. 12:2, 12:7, 13:15–16, 15:18–21 and 22:17.
6. Gen. 18:20–21 REB.
7. Gen. 18:32. The story is found at Gen. 18:23–32.
8. Gen. 12:13, 20:2, 20:12.
9. Gen. 21:18.
10. Gen. 15:19–21.
11. Gen. 25:31–34.
12. Gen. 27:6–40.
13. One cannot avoid doubting the morality of polygamy and the use of servant-concubines. The use of handmaids has been defended as necesssary under the conditions of life in the second millennium B.C. Now, however, those practices are offensive, and we fear that the scenario of Margaret Atwood's *The Handmaid's Tale* might become fact. Contemporary societies should not be bound by biblical precedents in matters of this kind. The word of God speaks to us with different accents and to different effect.
14. Gen. 34:1–31.
15. "Rachel's theft of her father's *teraphim* ... is ... explicable in the light of the social conventions of the Hurrian community of Nuzu.... Such a case as this ... indicates the association of the Hebrew fathers with north Mesopotamia in the middle of the second millennium B.C." (John Gray, *Archaeology and the Old Testament World*, pp. 37–38). This association is contested by Moshe Greenberg in the *Journal of Biblical Literature*, 1962, pp. 239–48.
16. Gen. 32:28 REB.
17. Gen. 28:12–22.
18. Gen. 32:30.
19. Gen. 32:24–32.
20. Gen. 35:9–15.
21. 1 Cor. 15:22, 15:45; Rom. 5:15.
22. Gen. 46:27.
23. Gen. 37:5–11.

24. Gen. 37:23–36.
25. Gen. 44:28.
26. Gen. 39:7–20.
27. Gen. 47:13–26.
28. Gen. 45:1–15.
29. Gen. 45:7, 50:20.

Chapter 4
1. Exod. 1:8.
2. Exod. 2:5–10.
3. Exod. 3:2.
4. Exod. 5:1–2.
5. Exod. 12:12.
6. Exod. 15:1–21.
7. Exod. 12:11 NRSV in part.
8. Exod. 13:14, 13:8.
9. Deut. 18:22.
10. Deut. 21:5.
11. Deut. 6:13.
12. Jer. 7:10–11, 7:14; Isa. 43:7.
13. Ps. 135:13.
14. As long ago as 1935 W.F. Albright wrote that "it is now quite certain that a large part, perhaps more than half, of the Hebrew people remained in Palestine and did not enter Egypt at all" (*The Archaeology of Palestine and the Bible*, 1935, reissue 1974, p. 148).
15. On the history and reconstruction of the Ten Words (Commandments) see Henri Cazelles, in *The Interpreter's Dictionary of the Bible*, vol. 5 (Supplementary), pp. 876, 877.
16. Exod. 20:12 as it now stands; cf. Deut. 5:16.
17. Deut. 34:5–7.
18. Deut. 6:4–9 REB.
19. Jer. 31:33.
20. Deut. 18:15, 18:18.
21. G. Vermes, *The Dead Sea Scrolls in English* (London: Penguin Books, 1962), p. 245.
22. Num 32:8; Deut. 1:19, 1:46.
23. Exod. 40:38.
24. The quotation is from Mark A. Noll, "The Christianizing of America (1789–1880)", in *Christianity: A Social and Cultural History*, H.C. Kee and others, 1991, p. 687.
25. Isa. 43:19.
26. Isa. 40:3 NRSV; see also Mark 1:3.
27. Ps. 23:1.
28. Heb. 11:27 REB.
29. For an alternative reading of Hebrew faith and history that tends to discount the centrality of the covenant idea, see Samuel Terrien, *The Elusive Presence*, 1978.
30. Exod. 19:5–6.

Chapter 5
1. On the problems of Jericho and the impossibility of accepting the biblical account of its conquest see: K.M. Kenyon, *Digging up Jericho*, 1957; and John Romer, *Testament*, pp. 67–87.
2. Num. 13; 14; 21–24; 32.
3. Judges 11:39.
4. Judges 13–16.
5. Judges 4–5.
6. Judges 4:17.
7. Judges 5:25–27.
8. 1 Sam. 1.
9. 1 Sam. 2:1–10; cf. Luke 1:46–55.
10. Judges 21:25.
11. 1 Sam. 8:4–5.
12. 1 Sam. 9:16.

Opening the Scriptures

13. 1 Sam. 13:12–13.
14. 1 Sam. 8:7, 8:9.
15. 1 Sam. 10:17–27.
16. 1 Sam. 10:24. The Hebrew word is *melech*, meaning *king*, in contrast to 1 Samuel 9:16 or 10:1, where the word *nagid*, meaning *captain* or *prince*, is used.
17. 1 Sam. 12:22, 12:24.
18. 1 Sam. 15:3.
19. 1 Sam. 15:8–9.
20. 1 Sam. 15:33.
21. 1 Sam. 31:1–6.
22. 2 Sam. 1:8–9.
23. 2 Sam. 1:19–27.

Chapter 6
1. 1 Sam. 16:18–19 NRSV.
2. 1 Sam. 16:12 NRSV.
3. 1 Sam. 18:7.
4. 1 Sam. 28:16–17.
5. 1 Sam. 25:44.
6. 2 Sam. 4.
7. 2 Sam. 5:1–4.
8. 2 Sam. 5:13.
9. 2 Sam. 12:1–12 NRSV.
10. 2 Sam. 23:1.
11. 2 Sam. 18:32–33.
12. 1 Kings 2:11–12.
13. Isa. 9:2, 9:6–7, 11:1.
14. 2 Sam. 7:1–17.

Chapter 7
1. 1 Kings 3:13.
2. 1 Kings 18:21–40.
3. 1 Kings 19:12.
4. 1 Kings 19:18.
5. 1 Kings 19:11–16.
6. 2 Kings 9:3.
7. 2 Kings 2:11.
8. Mal. 4:5–6.
9. Mark 9:13; Luke 1:17.
10. Isa. 6:1–8.
11. Ps. 137:1–6 NRSV.

Chapter 8
1. Micah 6:8 NRSV.
2. Amos 7:14–15 NRSV.
3. Amos 5:21, 5:23–24 REB.
4. Isa. 6:9–10.
5. Jer. 9:4, 9:6 REB.
6. Jer. 9:1–2 NRSV.
7. Jer. 2:8, 34:13–22.
8. Jer. 19:8.
9. Jer. 20:7, 20:9 REB.
10. Jer. 32:6–15.
11. Ezek 1:1–3:11, 33:1–9.
12. Ezek. 34:11–16.
13. Ps. 23:1.
14. Isa. 40:11 NRSV.
15. Ezek. 37:24, 37:27.

Chapter 9
1. Marcus Aurelius, *To Himself*, 12:36–36.
2. Acts 21:39, 22:28.
3. Ezra 7:6 NRSV.
4. Ezra 10:10–12 NRSV.
5. *2 Macc.* 15:36 REB.
6. Esther 9:31 NRSV.
7. Esther 9:1–28.
8. Esther 7:5–10.
9. Matt. 12:40.
10. Jonah 1:17.
11. Jonah 2.
12. Job 42:10–11 NRSV.
13. Job 29:15.
14. Amos 3:6.
15. Ezek 18:4, 18:10–23.
16. Ps. 73:23–24 NRSV.
17. Isa. 26:19 NRSV.
18. *Wisd. Sol.* 2:23–3:4.

Chapter 10
1. Dan. 1:7.
2. Dan. 1:12.
3. Dan. 6:10.
4. Dan. 3:17–18.
5. Dan. 3:25 NRSV.
6. Dan. 2:48.
7. Dan. 5:5 NRSV.
8. Dan. 5:26–28.
9. Dan. 7:27.
10. Dan. 7:14 NRSV.
11. Ezek. 28:3 REB.
12. Dan 11:31.
13. Dan. 9:2, 9:24–27.
14. Dan. 7:4–8.
15. Dan. 7:13–14 NRSV.

Chapter 11
1. 1 Sam. 10:1; Ps. 89:20; *Psalms of Solomon* 17:4, 17:21–46.
2. 1 Kings 19:16.
3. Exod. 29:7, 29:21; Lev. 8:12.
4. *1 Enoch* xxxv. 3, one of the books in the Pseudepigrapha.
5. *Psalms of Solomon* 17:22, 17:36, 17:37, 18:7.
6. Isa. 40:9.
7. Isa. 40:1–2.
8. Isa. 47:1, 47:15.
9. Isa 49:11–12.
10. Isa. 49:6.
11. Isa. 41:21.
12. Isa. 42:1.
13. Isa. 40:28–31.
14. Isa. 51:15.
15. Psalm 22:1.
16. Dan. 3:17–18.
17. Isa. 53:10–11 REB.

Chapter 12
1. Luke 24:47.
2. Acts 28:30–31.
3. Luke 1:7.
4. Some scholars think that the phrase "as was supposed" was inserted into the text of Luke at a later time, to suit Christian orthodoxy.
5. The *Magnificat*, Luke 1:46–55. The reading of *Elisabeth* for *Mary* is to be found in some of the texts of the Old Latin version of Luke; also late in the second century in citation by Irenaeus of Lyon, a very important bishop, who could be described as "the first theologian of Mary the Virgin"; in Niceta of Remesiana, who died early in the fifth century; and some manuscripts referred to by Jerome or Origen (cited from the commentary on Luke by John Martin Creed [London: Macmillan, 1942], pp. 22–23). *Mary* is, however, the reading of all the best Greek manuscripts and other versions. The principle involved in choosing is to decide whether orthodox scholars and bishops would have altered, as early as the end of the second century or at any time after the Councils and Creeds of the fourth century, a reference to the highly revered Virgin Mary. It is virtually impossible! The same authorities would have altered, however, an original *Elisabeth* to *Mary* because of Mary's exalted position in faith, liturgy and private devotion. We know that such changes were made in texts regarded as unorthodox. For that reason alone one could

say that the original reading was *Elisabeth*. But also, the sentiments and the song itself suit a barren older lady, not a young maiden.
6. From the Gospel of the Hebrews, cited by St. Jerome in a comment on Isaiah 11:2.
7. Luke 3:4–17 (translation and summary by the author).
8. Luke 4:3.
9. Deut. 8:3, 6:13, 6:16.
10. Luke 23:34, 23:43, 23:46.
11. Luke 24:52.
12. Luke 4:43, 8:1, 8:10, 9:2, 9:60.
13. Mark 13:32.
14. Luke 18:17.
15. Luke 17:20–21.
16. See Mark 12:34, "you are not far...."
17. Origen, *Commentary on Matthew* XIV, 7, on Matthew 18:23.
18. Luke 22:29.
19. Luke 23:38.
20. Luke 23:4, 23:14–15.
21. Luke 6:35–36 NRSV.
22. 1 Cor. 15:44.

Chapter 13
1. Acts 1:2, 1:8.
2. Acts 20:29–31.
3. For this, see Hebrews 6:1–6.
4. Acts 1:1–4, 1:15–26, 2–12, 13–28.
5. Acts 6:10.
6. Acts 8:1–25.
7. Acts 10:44–48.
8. Acts 13:1–4, 13:52.
9. Acts 15:28.
10. 1 Cor. 12–14.
11. Acts 20:23.
12. Isa. 6:9–10; Acts 28:25–27.
13. Acts 2:47.
14. Acts 2:42–47.
15. Acts 7:56.
16. Acts 17:26.
17. Acts 4:19–20.
18. Acts 5:29.
19. Acts 6:5.
20. Acts 6:11–14.
21. Acts 7:59–60.
22. Acts 12:2.
23. Acts 9:25.
24. Tertullian, *Apology* 50.
25. Acts 14:22.
26. Acts 5:1–10.
27. Acts 8:9–24.
28. Acts 17:34, 9:36, 16:14.
29. Acts 12:12.
30. Acts 21:9.
31. Acts 18:24–28.
32. Acts 18:2, 18:18, 18:26.
33. Acts 1:23, 15:22 NRSV and REB.
34. Acts 12:25.
35. Acts 15:37, 15:39.
36. Acts 1:23, 1:13.
37. Acts 21:8.
38. Acts 21:9, 8:27–39.
39. Acts 15:40, 16:1, 16:19, 17:4–14.
40. Acts 10:38; cf. 3:12–26.
41. Acts 13:23, 13:38.
42. Acts 14:23.
43. Acts 9:26.
44. Acts 4:36–37 (in NRSV and REB he is called Joseph, and his name *Barnabas* is taken to mean *son of encouragement*); 9:27.

Chapter 14
1. Phil. 3:5–6.
2. Acts 6:9.
3. Deut. 21:23; Gal. 3:13.
4. 1 Cor. 15:3–8, 11:23–26.

5. Rom. 7:19.
6. Rom. 7:24–25 NRSV.
7. 2 Cor. 5:17 NRSV and REB.
8. Gal. 4:19.
9. 1 Cor. 11:3 NRSV.
10. On the question of the covering of the hair by men and women, see Cynthia L. Thompson, "Hairstyles, Head Coverings, and St. Paul: Portraits from Roman Corinth," *Biblical Archaeologist* 51, no. 2 (June 1988): 99–115. Male and female worshippers had to be distinguishable. Women had a choice, but Paul recommended that they cover their heads because there were angels watching them. 1 Corinthians 11:16 may refer to general church parctice in Arabia, Asia Minor and Syria as known to Paul. The Corinthian women may well have been a special case, and so the injunction was not necessarily applicable elsewhere. Nor is it still in force today. Paul the Apostle was neither tyrannical nor stupid!

Chapter 15

1. 1 Cor. 5:11, author's version.
2. 1 Cor. 5:1–5.
3. 1 Cor. 6:15 –16 NRSV.
4. 1 Cor. 7:4, 7:36–38.
5. 1 Cor. 7:10, 7:6.
6. 1 Cor. 7:39.
7. Mark 1:8.
8. 1 Cor. 12:13 NRSV.
9. 1 Cor. 12:8–11.
10. 1 Cor. 14:19.
11. 1 Cor. 13:4–13; Gal. 5:22; Rom. 5:5.
12. 1 Cor. 11:21 NRSV.
13. 1 Cor. 11:34, 11:26 NRSV.
14. 1 Cor. 1:26.
15. 1 Cor. 12:25–26.
16. 1 Cor. 1:12 NRSV.
17. 1 Cor. 12:12.
18. Gal. 5:22–23 NRSV.
19. Gal. 6:8 NRSV.

Chapter 16

1. Gen. 28:17.
2. Heb. 2:9.
3. Heb. 12:1.
4. Heb. 1:3, see also Psalm 110:1.
5. Heb. 13:22.
6. Heb. 8:8–13.
7. Heb. 11:10, 13:14 NRSV.
8. Mark 14:58 NRSV.
9. Heb. 9:11–15.
10. Heb. 9:7.
11. Heb. 5:1–4.
12. Heb. 2:17–18, 4:15.
13. Heb 5:5–6.
14. Heb. 1:3 NRSV.
15. Heb. 5:7–10 NRSV.
16. Heb. 2:3–4 NRSV.
17. Heb. 5:12, 12:2.
18. Heb. 10:22.
19. Heb. 10:24 NRSV.
20. Heb. 12:28 REB.
21. Heb. 9:26, 9:28 NRSV and REB.
22. Heb. 13:20–21 NRSV.
23. Heb. 4:16.

Chapter 17

1. 1 Thess. 4:17.
2. Rev. 13:11–18, 19:20, 20:1–6.
3. The reference to holy apostles and prophets is to martyr-figures in time past, not to living apostles.
4. Rev. 1:13, 1:16 NRSV.

Opening the Scriptures

   5. Rev. 3:5 ("the book of life"; but REB has "the roll of the living"), 2:17, 3:12, 2:7, 2:11.
   6. Rev. 2:26, 3:21.
   7. Rev. 6:1–11.
   8. Rev. 9:3–4.
   9. Gen. 21:9–20.
  10. Rev. 12:1–2 NRSV. See Appendix 2, "Star," for attempts to identify the woman.
  11. Rev. 12:17.
  12. Rev. 13:1–18.
  13. Rev. 13:18.
  14. Rev. 14:1–20.
  15. Rev. 19:9–20:5.
  16. Rev. 8:8–9 NRSV.
  17. Rev. 1:13–16, 14:14–16, 21:23, 21:27.
  18. Rev. 5:5, 17:14, 19:7–9, 19:11–13, 19:16.
  19. Rev. 1:13–18.
  20. Rev. 6:16, 19:11–16.
  21. Rev. 2:13.
  22. Rev. 6:10.

Appendix 1

   1. Deut. 26:5 NRSV.
   2. Judges 9:7–15.
   3. Proverbs 6:6, 9–11 NRSV.
   4. Judges 3:12–30.
   5. 1 Sam. 24:1–8.
   6. Judges 15:16.
   7. Ecclesiastes 9:4.
   8. Esther 5:14.
   9. Esther 7:9–10 NRSV.
  10. 2 Sam. 1:23.
  11. 1 Chronicles 11:15–19.
  12. Mark 14:22–24 NRSV margin.
  13. Exodus 31:1–5, 35:30–35.

Select Bibliography

Introductory

Alexander, D. and Alexander, P. *Eerdmans Handbook to the Bible*. Revised edition. Grand Rapids, Mich.: Eerdmans, 1983. Maps, charts, photographs, good illustrations.

Carey, George, ed. *The Message of the Bible*. London: Lion Publishers, 1988. Summaries of the books with outlines and references.

Charpentier, Etienne. *How to Read the Old Testament, How to Read the New Testament*. London: S.C.M. Press, 1983. A helpful Roman Catholic guide, also available in French.

Heike, E. and Toon, P. *NIV Bible Guide: An Introductory Handbook*. London: Hodder and Stoughton, 1989. Much useful information from a "conservative" viewpoint.

Metzger, B.M. and Murphy, R.E., eds. *The New Oxford Annotated Bible: With the Apocrypha, NRSV*. London: Oxford University Press, 1991. Introductions to the books of the Bible, essays on history and geography, maps, etc. Highly recommended.

Moffatt, James. *A New Translation of the Bible*. 1926. Revised edition. London: Hodder and Stoughton, 1935.

Romer, John. *Testament: The Bible and History*. London: Michael O'Mara Books Ltd., 1988.

Terrien, Samuel. *The Elusive Presence*. San Francisco: Harper and Row, 1978.

Dictionaries

Achtemeier, P., ed. *Harper's Bible Dictionary*. New York: Harper, 1985 Excellent scholarship; "conservative-liberal" approach.

Black, M. and Rowley, H.H., eds. *Peake's Commentary on the Bible*. London: Thos. Nelson and Sons, 1962. An excellent Protestant one-volume commentary, probably due for an update. "Liberal" Protestant point of view.

Brown, R.E., Fitzmyer, J.A. and Murphy, R.E., eds. *The New Jerome Biblical Commentary*. Englewood Cliffs, N.J.: Prentice Hall, 1990. A Roman Catholic volume of first-rate scholarship; more demanding perhaps.

Bruce, F.F., ed. *The International Bible Commentary*. Grand Rapids, Mich.: Zondervan, 1986. Excellent studies by the more "conservative" evangelical scholars.

Buttrick, G.A. and others, eds. *The Interpreter's Dictionary of the Bible*. 4 Vols. Nashville: Abingdon Press, 1962. Supplementary volume, edited by K. Crim, 1976. A more demanding set of books, but the best in the field. Some contributors are quite "liberal."

Young, G. Douglas. *Young's Compact Bible Dictionary*. Revised edition. London: Tyndale Press, 1989. Maps and charts and attention to archaeology.

Other

Albright, W.F. *The Archaeology of Palestine and the Bible*. Memorial edition. Cambridge, Mass.: The American Schools of Oriental Research, 1974.

Bernard, Bruce. *The Bible and its Painters*. London: Orbis Books, 1983. Of interest to all who are aware of the Bible's influence on artists.

Dever, W.G. *Recent Archaeological Discoveries and Biblical Research*. Seattle: University of Washington Press, 1990. An important new approach.

Selected Bibliography

Frye, H. Northrop. *The Double Vision.* Toronto: The United Church Publishing House and University of Toronto Press, 1991. Highly recommended as an introduction to the profound work of this writer.

Frye. *The Great Code: The Bible and Literature.* New York: Harcourt Brace Jovanovich, 1982. Difficult for the general reader.

Frye. *Words with Power: A Second Study of The Bible and Literature.* Markham, Ont.: Viking, 1990. In part a sequel to *The Great Code.*

Gottwald, N.K. *The Tribes of Yahweh.* Maryknoll, N.Y.: Orbis Books, 1979.

Gray, John. *Archaeology and the Old Testament World.* London: Thomas Nelson and Sons Ltd., 1962.

Kee, H.C.; Hanawalt, Emily Albu; Lindberg, Carter; Seban, Jean-Loup; Noll, Mark A. *Christianity: A Social and Cultural History.* New York: Macmillan, 1991.

Kenyon, K.M. *Digging Up Jericho.* London: Benn, 1957.

Mühlberger, Richard. *The Bible in Art: The New Testament.* New York: Portland House, 1990. Of great interest to all who are aware of the Bible's influence on artists.

Phy, A.S., ed. *The Bible and Popular Culture in America.* Philadelphia: Fortress Press, 1984.

A Guide for Study and Discussion

John and B.J. Klassen

Were there times when you were excited, angered or surprised by what you discovered here or by the author, George Johnston? Whatever your response, chances are that you are not alone. Dr. Johnston himself has some questions, and they are thought-provoking. We suggest you skim through this study guide, see the possibilities open to you, then return to this page.

As you read alone

Opening the Scriptures is written in a way that gives choices. You do not have to read from front to back; you can start with those parts that interest you most. Also, do make notes in the margins if you wish, and underline where you will. It's your book!

Here are some questions the author ponders. What questions come to mind for you?

Chapter 1: Introduction

1. Someone said recently, "We must allow the Bible to be itself: a collection of writings from other times which needs to be reinterpreted from our time rather than simply filleted." Is that possible for you? Can you say why?
2. "The linguistic form of a myth has a sacramental relationship to a truth or truths that lie hidden in the mythological story." How do you see this illustrated in the Garden of Eden myth?

Chapter 2: Beginnings

1. Roberta Bondar, Canadian astronaut, suggests we must care for our beautiful planet Earth. Chapters 1 and 9 of Genesis suggest otherwise. In what way might the Bible lose authority for us if we agree with her?

A Guide for Study and Discussion

2. How does one account for the presence of evil in God's good creation? This is one of the toughest questions. Don't expect fast or easy answers.

Chapter 3: Patriarchal Legends

1. The parallel between the near-sacrifice of Abraham's son and the death of Jesus as God's son is often noted. What value do you see in being aware of such parallels in the Bible?
2. The Hebrew Bible asserts that God gave the land from "Dan to Beesheba" or from the Euphrates to the Nile to the ancestors of the modern Israelis. Should modern Israel occupy this area? This is a complex question. What reasons do you have for your views?

Chapter 4: Exodus: The Escape

1. Should an observance of Passover become part of the Christian year? Why?
2. In what ways is God present or absent in the exodus and desert experiences of your personal faith journey?
3. Why is it important to know the Ten Commandments and obey them?

Chapter 5: Spirited Personalities

1. Ancient Israel, like ancient Greece, discovered that the institution of monarchy was essential for national life and survival. What would be the advantages for peace, justice and prosperity if modern nations all had monarchs who were "the Lord's anointed"? What would be the disadvantages?
2. Given the modern priorities of money, profits and individual enterprise, what are some of the problems the new democracies in Europe, Latin America and Asia are likely to face? Think of reasons for your opinions.

Chapter 6: David

1. Are there ways in which Bathsheba was more important than David for the history of Israel?

Opening the Scriptures

2. Why do the psalms of David and other Hebrew psalms have such continued and powerful use in Christian worship?

Chapter 7: Schisms and Exile

1. How does nationalism affect the well-being of the Global Village? This modern question has an ancient history.
2. In what ways does idolatry enter our practice of Christianity today? What would you say are some of the most powerful idols?
3. In what ways is antisemitism a factor where you live?

Chapter 8: Prophecy

1. What would an Amos say about the usefulness of Sunday worship for you and for your community? Do you find Amos a troublemaker?
2. In what ways do you find Jeremiah's new covenant being fulfilled in church life, belief and personal religious practice today?
3. Name two or three living prophets. What is it that makes you think of them as prophetic?

Chapter 9: Second Temple: Ezra

1. Why do good people have to suffer? This too is a difficult question with few easy answers.
2. What has caused the "loss of faith" and disillusionment characteristic of recent times?

Chapter 10: Daniel

1. Why have the miracle-stories in the book of Daniel been important?
2. What is ungodly about imperialism today?

Chapter 11: Climax and Threshold

1. Is the Messiah still "the One who is to come"?
2. Why is there so much emphasis on the "end of history" and "end of the world" in these writings?

3. Once a *canon* of authoritative scripture has been accepted, does that mean the end of divine revelation?

Chapter 12: Luke's Life of Jesus

1. What is lost if belief in the virgin birth is abandoned?
2. What evidence does Luke provide to support Jesus' preferential option for the poor?
3. In what ways is the concept of the Kingdom or Realm of God relevant to our secular life?
4. How would you describe what it meant for Jesus to have been "raised from the dead by God"?

Chapter 13: The Church-Story in Acts

1. How has the modern charismatic movement affected the lives of people in your congregations?
2. In what ways would ecumenical congregationalism be useful or not useful in your present church life?
3. What are the stories behind the national or local "saints" commemorated in the stained-glass windows in your church or in plaques on the wall?

Chapter 14 and 15: Paul

1. Would you describe Paul as sexist, antifeminist or misogynist? Why?
2. Did Paul, theologian and church organizer, change, corrupt or distort the message of Jesus?
3. Why does Paul's description of "agape-love" provide a useful distinction for today? (That Greek word for the love of God is pronounced *ah-gah-pay*.)
4. What qualities and gifts as described by Paul do you look for in a candidate for ordained ministry today?

Chapter 16: Christ in "To the Hebrews"

1. To what extent is the Lord's Supper (the Eucharist, the Mass, the Holy Communion) to be understood as a sacrifice or a commemoration of Jesus' sacrifice?
2. In what ways do ministers act as "priests" in your congre-

Opening the Scriptures

gation? What values are retained by this?
3. How does Dr. Johnston help us understand what we are doing on a Sunday morning? You may want to reread some paragraphs in this chapter.

Chapter 17: Revelation

1. Does the writer of this scripture help you understand your faith community?
2. "I know that my Redeemer liveth." Recall Handel's music. Play it if available.
3. Do you think visions still take place? What makes them authentic?

Some concluding thoughts to ponder:

1. What does it mean for human beings to be Godlike?
2. In what ways does historical, literary criticism assist or not assist your understanding of the Bible?
3. As a graphic way of reviewing this whole book, look again at the maps on pages 4, 14, 30, 49, 58, 67, 106 and 149.
4. At this point, what is the authority of the Bible for you personally?

As you see, one can have many questions about these stories and themes. In response to the question, "Why is the Bible such an important piece of literature?", George Johnston suggests: "In the scriptures, there is no infallible rule for faith and life, yet Christians can never relegate them to obscurity nor ignore their virtues and their limitations. Authority, therefore is a word that must be used with caution with regard to the scriptures" (p. 179). With such pertinent ideas and questions, there is a next step you can take: engage another person in conversation. If you would like to do this, here are some suggestions:

With a friend

Once a friend has accepted your invitation, let this book be the focus. However, it will also be important to find ways to have a conversation that leads to deeper understanding of your life experiences, as well as the concerns raised for you in the book. How will you do that? How will you share your personal journey? Here are some steps the two of you could take:

a) Share your first memories of Bible stories. Who told them? Why? What were your thoughts? Are songs and hymns among your early memories?
b) When did you first stop reading the Bible? Why? What was happening around you? In your life, school and work?
c) Which of your experiences has been brought back through your reading of *Opening the Scriptures?*
d) What are your responses to the suggestions in chapter 1 that stories, legends and myths may be a better way to describe religious experience than logical and intellectual propositions?
e) Does all the masculine language in the Bible hinder your reading? What can be done about that? How do you deal with it? Does the New Revised Standard Version help?
f) Do you think the author is too optimistic when he suggests that the Bible can still be useful in dealing with some of our most critical social problems? Or does the Bible itself contribute to these problems (environment, gender inequity, poverty, racism, etc.)?

There is no need to cover all these questions, of course. However, it is often helpful to start with your own experience. These questions may give a context for you and your friend to know where each is coming from as you move on. Some questions will no doubt remain unanswered or unacknowledged. That's quite appropriate. Strongly differing views may arise. That's also acceptable; don't strain for compromise or polite agreements. Let the responses to the reading and the discussions be vehicles for new discoveries about life, faith and each other.

In your living room

It could be rewarding and enriching to invite several people over to your house for some discussions on this book. Whom would you invite? Would it be a same-gender group? Mixed? Couples? What would you invite them to do? There are questions that have emerged for you. You could suggest them as starting points. Your discoveries, your puzzlements are a good place to begin. To get underway try three or four evenings. (Tuesdays are favourites.) If four to eight people say yes, you'll need a plan. Here are some suggestions:

a) Outline the session

Having indicated the purpose of the invitation, you now need to give some directions for the time together. You could say, after coffee or at the outset when all have arrived, "I have a few suggestions as to how we might spend the next hour or ninety minutes." Then give these headings as an outline of how the time will go, when you plan to end, and what to think about for next week's meeting.

    i) Some introductions around everyone's experience with the Bible.
    ii) Your queries and discoveries out of your reading.
    iii) Wrestling with a few questions, yours and others.
    iv) Next week.

b) Getting started

Give everyone a opportunity to talk about an early experience of hearing Bible stories or telling them. This could be quite brief, just a few sentences each.

Think back to what prompted you to read *Opening the Scriptures*. What is the question or issue that you most want to explore with the rest? Then you might simply make a list of the questions from everyone, avoiding discussion at this time.

When you have all the questions, take a quick look as a group (you will see that you are a group now) to see how many are the same. As a group, choose the one or ones with which to start.

When you have made your selection, let the person who raised the question rephrase or expand it. Now, what are some ways to explore the question? First, this is a time to make sure that all who want to get into the discussion. Second, remember that definitive and dogmatic answers are not as useful (they may even be conversation stoppers) as honest questions or thoughts or hunches that can be encouraging. Third, don't be anxious about periods of silence.

If you want some additional discussion starters, you might refer to the questions in the "read alone" section or some others that arise out of the book. (For instance, in chapter 2 it is stated that the power given to human beings over other creatures is "not acceptable in our time to those who worry about ecology and the environment." Do people agree with this statement?)

The illustrations in this book were carefully chosen by Dr. Johnston, as you can see from his notes. You could select one and have a photocopy made (at the church office, perhaps) for each person. Allow time for meditation and sharing.

Winding down

At the end of the evening take a few minutes to review what has happened. What helped the explorations? What hindered the discussion? What could be done differently next week? What question(s) would be a good place to start?

You may not feel comfortable providing this leadership. Fair enough. So, is there someone you are inviting with whom you could share it? Have a short discussion with that person ahead of time. Together, plan the evenings. Also, it is possible that people in the group may decide to take turns assuming leadership functions or even hosting the group.

In your congregation

House groups are rewarding, it's true, but congregational events can open things up. You know there are some members of your congregation who would enjoy a time of discussion around themes in *Opening the Scriptures*. Most prefer a limited time commitment — at least at the beginning of a group. A short contract is helpful. Suggest four to six meetings, asking people to contract for particular dates.

How could you initiate a gathering? Perhaps the Christian Education Committee, a book club or other existing group would be the place to start. It is important to go with a plan.

Purpose of the gatherings:

To explore some questions you have about the place of the Bible in your church and society. To challenge, and be challenged by, some of the statements that emerge from reading scripture (e.g., Is death the result of sin? [p. 16]), and from your reading and discussion of *Opening the Scriptures* by George Johnston. This author states: "In scripture there are no theoretical answers to questions of life and death" (p. 17).

Time: Might be Sunday mornings before church or an evening or afternoon when the group you want to attract could be available (ninety minutes is a good length for introductions, some input and discussion).

Place: A comfortable space, easily accessible to all, where people can sit in a circle.

Invitation: The church bulletin and announcements may be helpful, but you might want to talk personally to several people who might be interested.

Resources: This book, *Opening the Scriptures,* would be your main resource; along with the Bible (several translations, for comparison). You might also consult the bibliography on page 223 and look in your church library for atlases and other reference books — but not too many! Audiovisual resources can be powerful when carefully selected and well presented, with lots of time for discussion. See the list at the end of these notes.

A Guide for Study and Discussion

A weekend retreat

If you have found this book an adventure, would you like to spend a church-sponsored weekend with a group of people exploring points of interest and issues raised for you in your reading? Many people have found such a weekend fun and a source of purposeful fellowship. How do you start? A cottage? A retreat centre? How do you find out what is possible?

Well, this would be an opportunity to have a conversation with the minister or other leaders in your congregation, or with people in the Conference office or at the nearest leadership centre. Think through your own ideas first. It helps to develop a purpose, a time, a place, topics and resources. Consider additional resources. Not every group could afford to invite the author! But there are other people nearby who teach biblical studies, ministers (yours or others), educators in your community. These ideas and all such preliminary thoughts will, of course, change in dialogue and planning.

Some interesting themes for a weekend retreat present themselves in the book. For example, "No plaster saints found here" or "How does God mete out justice?" or any other theme that stood out for you. Keep notes of new themes that come to mind as you begin planning with others.

Think of particular blocks of time and how a programme might develop. This one could be adopted to your circumstances:

Session I (Friday evening):

7:30 Arrival (with appropriate background music), welcome and name tags (if necessary).
Take time for people to get settled in, if it is a cottage or retreat centre setting. To provide a sense of expectation you might have pictures of the symbols found in appendix 2 and photocopies of the illustrations posted around the room.
Introductions, singing, followed by a review outline of the weekend.
Invite people to pick a partner, "someone you don't know very

well." Share some background stories (place of birth, work, hobbies, etc.) and "Why did you come to this event?" (a chance for everyone to display some wit and wisdom!).

8:00 In the same twos, choose a symbol from those displayed around the room, or others from appendix 2, p. 196. Discover and discuss the meaning of this symbol and its connections with the scriptures.

8:30 Total group:
Suggest that each person tell why the other in their team came to the event.
Have each team show their symbol and share some of their impressions and discoveries.
Move into general discussion.
Close with prayer, reflection, meditation.

Session II (Saturday morning):

9:30 Opening, singing, and perhaps a few exercises to loosen up.
Introduction to themes.
Divide into groups of threes or fives. Each group chooses a theme. Possible choices are:
   Stories, Legends, Myths
   Prophecy
   God and Justice
   Early Development of Judaism
   Early Church
   Who is Jesus?
   A Time of Transition: Messages from the Seven Churches

10:30 Suggest ways in which groups could present information, stories, discoveries and connections with current times and issues. (Ways include art, drama, journalism, song, sermon, poem, mural, etc.)

10:45 Break (coffee, fruit juices, walkabout)

11:00 Groups meet to prepare presentations.

A Guide for Study and Discussion

Session III (Saturday afternoon):

2:30 Each group presents their material in the mode they have chosen. You could decide whether to have general conversation after each presentation or do them all and then have conversation. Divide the afternoon to allow time for all presentations and some general discussion.

Session IV (Saturday evening):

7:30 Film or video
See the suggestions at the end of this study guide.
In small groups, consider these three assignments:
1. Identify the religious themes.
2. Which themes can be related to the scriptures?
3. How does this film speak to the human condition?
Have some people give a summary or reflection on the experience.
End with recreation, informal fellowship.

Session V (Sunday morning):

9:30 Prelude of recorded music
Opening reflection, singing, brief worship
Personal journalling in this fashion:
Each chooses a place to be apart —
"One reads the bible not merely to assist a private communion with God but also to understand and appreciate great religious beliefs, important moral directives and the biblical teaching about what makes life worth living."

Each reflects and writes, asking themselves:
What stood out for me in this time together?
What would I like to continue alone? With others? In the congregation?
What new insights do I have now about the scriptures? The church? Myself?
What disappointments have I experienced in this event?
What would I recommend?
Total group then moves into general sharing and evaluation.
Closing remarks.
Closing worship.

Advent study: preparation, expectation, hope, future

The season of Advent provides the opportunity to celebrate again the birth of Jesus. It is a time that, as Dr. Johnston suggests, raises acute awareness both of the nature of story and of how "our present always includes a living past" (p. 31).

An Advent study can be based on themes found in *Opening the Scriptures*. So how might you initiate such a study group? You could invite people to your home or to the church. You could talk with a clergy person or some other members of the congregation. It is not necessary to think in terms of large numbers; eight to twelve people is a good size. Four weeks in Advent would be a good time. You could meet on a weekday, Sunday before church, or over a sandwich after church.

The invitation could be made through the bulletin or announced. Your personal announcement would be much more appealing than just another in the list on a Sunday morning. Share some of your questions and some of your excitement. Invite others to take this walk with you through the scriptures towards Christmas.

Here are some suggestions in broad outline. As you prepare, you will need to design each session with five steps: purpose, place, time, leadership, resources. Decide: will each person have a copy of the book? Will they be expected to read a specific chapter or certain pages before arrival? Will you read parts in the group? Each session might include these features:

Arrival, coffee, opening, conversation.

Introduction of the theme or topic.

Outline of time (how we have planned the time together).

A question or quotation, followed by discussion in twos or threes to get everyone thinking and talking.

Presentation of some new information or a reference to some particular section in the book.

General discussion, questions, insights.

Summary: What was helpful today? What wasn't?

A Guide for Study and Discussion

Assignments for next week.

Closing, prayer, singing, recorded Advent music.

So much for features of the meeting. Now, here are some general themes:

Session 1: Preparation
"Why bother with the prophets?" (chapter 8)
Did they really foresee the coming of Jesus?
Why do we read the words of the prophet Isaiah in a Christian context?
Which is more appropriate — to say "the Old Testament" or "the Hebrew scriptures"? Why?

Session 2: Expectation
"Climax and threshold" (chapter 11)
The world of Jesus' birth. (Refer to map on p. 106)
Messianic expectations (pp. 95 – 96)

Session 3: Hope
How is our hope connected with the Hebrew past?
Does the link depend on the virgin birth? (pp. 110 – 12 and Luke 1 – 2)

Session 4: Future
The Realm of God: What does it look like? Where are the models? Do we look back to see the future?
"Prophecy demanded reason as well as inspiration" (p. 131)
The vision of Peter Abelard's hymn (p. 174).

A Lenten study: parables to live by

The period leading up to Easter is another good opportunity to organize a special study group. *Opening the Scriptures* provides the resource. Invite others to take this walk through the scriptures towards Easter with you. This six-session series is based on chapter 12. It is planned for a group to meet weekly throughout Lent.

The group might gather in different homes or at the church for breakfast early on Sunday mornings. The suggestion here is that the group will spend most of the time looking at the fourteen parables unique to the Gospel of Luke. Among these are very familiar ones but also some less well known. Some members in the group may be willing to research information beyond what is offered by the author. Check the bibliography and the audiovisual resources.

It is recommended that you have copies of Luke in at least three versions for comparison: King James Version, New Revised Standard Version and Revised English Bible.

Each session could well include some informal conversation to begin with and perhaps a closing prayer that gathers together concerns expressed during the study time. For further practical suggestions, see the outlines of other events in this study guide. Here now are the six sessions.

Session 1: Introduction

It will be important to provide some background, along with chapter 5 of *Opening the Scriptures*, "The distribution of parabolic stories" and "A grouping of the parables" (pp. 132–33). Remember that for the first seventy years after Jesus, stories about him circulated by word of mouth. A movement had begun, as sayings and stories increased about this remarkable person. The stories included the variety of people he associated with, particularly women. They retold the miracles he was said to have performed. They remembered the choices he made when put to the test. With great detail, they spoke of his trial, crucifixion and resurrection. Also remembered and retold were the stories he used in his teaching. In time, many of these were recorded in each of the Gospels. (See "Distribution of Parabolic Stories" p. 121.) Surprisingly, however, Luke records fourteen not found in the other three Gospels.

In this first session you will want to discuss "Just what is a parable?" Although you may want to research more technical definitions, the author nevertheless provides a start (p. 120).

Now examine Luke 10:30–37. How does this parable exemplify the definition?

What variations in interpretation occur in the different translations? (Have people check KJV, NRSV and REB.)

What was the message for the hearers in Jesus' day?
What is the message for us today?
For our Lenten series, the fourteen parables have been grouped into six themes. Here they are with biblical references, one theme for each session.

Session 2 Theme: How one should act
  The Good Samaritan, Luke 10:30 –37
  The Rich Fool, Luke 12:16 –21
  The Rich Man and Lazarus, Luke 16:19 –31
  The Pharisee and the Tax Collector, Luke 18:10 –14

Session 3 Theme: One should be humble
  Seats at a Banquet, Luke 14:7–14
  The Farmer and his Slave, Luke 17:7–10

Session 4 Theme: One should be wise
  Count the Cost, Luke 14:28 –33
  The Shrewd Rascal, Luke 16:1– 8

Session 5 Theme: Repent — and do it with love
  Two Debtors Pardoned, Luke 7:41– 43
  The Unfruitful Fig Tree, Luke 13:6–9
  The Lost Coin, Luke 15:8 –10
  The Lost Son(s), Luke 15:11–32

Session 6 Theme: Pray — all the time
  The Impertinent Friend at Midnight, Luke 11:5 – 8
  The Widow and Unjust Judge, Luke 18:2 – 8

An intergenerational event, ages 5 and up: Finding symbols of our faith

What fun! A gaggle of families arrive to discover that the agenda is *a scavenger hunt*. There are symbols hidden in many and various places. The object is to find a symbol, then have conversation about the meaning of these in the life of the Christian community. Using appendix 2 of *Opening the Scriptures*, here is a list of symbols for your preparation.

Angel	Anchor	Ark
Ark of Noah	Bread	Burning Bush
Cock	Compass	Desert
Donkey	Dove	Eagle
Fish	Grapes	Hand
Lamb	Lion	Mountain
Night	Olive	Palm
Rainbow	Star	Tree
Water	Way	

As a variation you could divide the gathering. In each group, have one preschooler, one primary school child, one teenager and two adults (parent, grandparent or single person). These groups of five then go and find two symbols. After the hunt, have a conversation about the meaning of these symbols in the Bible. Each group should have at least one copy of *Opening the Scriptures* as a resource. You might also talk about what these symbols mean in daily life. Each group would be asked to prepare a skit, a pantomime, a drawing or an oral presentation, thus sharing with the entire gathering what they have discovered.

An intergenerational get-together like this could begin or end with a pot-luck supper. Some singing and prayers, as well as some very brief readings, could be included at the beginning and end. Simple? Yes. Rewarding? Yes, if you are mindful of the attention span of the youngest child and the energy of the eldest grandparent.

Graphics and audiovisual resources

Biblical stories, sagas, and themes are found in almost all forms of Western literature, art and music. The author of *Opening the Scriptures* has had a lifelong interest in this fact. The illustrations chosen by Dr. Johnston for this book are a small sampling, an encouragement to you to explore the continuing pervasive influence of the Bible.

In your private reading, or with a friend, books of religious art with reproductions in full colour will stimulate imagination and insight into what this book is about. Your local public library is a place to begin; librarians are friendly and helpful. So too your own minister, who likely has a small but impressive collection.

Charts and maps are good graphic resources, as you have discovered in this book. Your church library is a source, and recent printings of Bibles often feature such study aids. For use in groups, do large freehand outlines on a flip chart or chalk board.

A Guide for Study and Discussion

Biblical inspiration underlies so much of our music. That is immediately obvious in such classics as Handel's *Messiah*, perhaps the most recognized religious composition in the world. The ready availability of portable players for tapes and CDs opens up wonderful possibilities. Use music whenever possible with small and large groups. Contemporary "popular" music also draws on biblical themes, often in surprising ways. Your organist would welcome inquiries.

Film is a medium that combines all of the above, great themes, visual artistry, and all manner of music. Again, technology puts almost any film on call. Always, *always* preview films for suitability. Also, you may want to screen only certain scenes for discussion purposes.

Vision TV, Canada's religious channel, encourages people to use their VCRs for replay. This is an excellent resource for you as an individual or as planner for a small group.

Through AVEL (the audiovisual library of the United Church) depots across the country, a large number of films are available to enhance the study of this book.

Commercial video stores stock treasured older movies, as well as excellent new releases. Many make a powerful contribution to religious understanding and spiritual development, but do preview before using with a group.

These are seed ideas. Your imagination will help you open up the power of our scriptural heritage for today's world.

Here are a few suggestions as you begin to develop your own list:

Examples of items available in video stores:

Jesus of Montreal
a modern passion play

Chariots of Fire
standing up for principles

A Man for All Seasons
Christian character in high office

Whistle Down the Wind
children's religious imagination

Opening the Scriptures

Gandhi
nonviolent social action

Inherit the Wind
courtroom drama about the Bible

Field of Dreams
how does God communicate?

Crimes and Misdemeanors
contemporary ethical problems

Romero
Christian witness for justice

Amadeus
great gifts, human choices

Babette's Feast
estrangement overcome in a wonderful woman's dinner

The Company of Strangers
spiritual depths in senior women

Places in the Heart
present-day community of saints

Witness
clash of cultures and beliefs

The Chosen
Old Testament faith tested

Truly, Madly, Deeply
grief, loss and love

Trip to Bountiful
faith and faithfulness

Examples of items available in AVEL depots:

RSV Video Bible Study
A series that has great flexibility. Some books of the Bible are presented on one videocassette: for example, Genesis, Gospel of Mark, Gospel of John, Revelation. Discussion breaks are designed into the tapes. Other books of the Bible are offered in more depth; for example, the Gospel of Luke and Acts of the Apostles. This is a miniseries in itself, seven 27-minute cassettes. Details are available in all seven AVEL outlets across the country.

Here I Stand
The first two programmes in this series, *Process for Biblical Discovery* and *Biblical Literalism*, are useful extensions to Dr. Johnston's book.

The Prophets Speak
Old Testament prophets are reenacted by Canadian scholars. They do TV-style interviews! Throughout the eight-part series, there are panel discussions that could serve as models for your purposes. Excellent study guide available.

Questions of Faith
Interviews with church people, including one question that arises for every group, "What do you mean by faith?" This is the first of six cassettes.

Faith, Hope and Clarity
Programme six in this series is a 30-minute presentation of how Christians and Jews see biblical teaching on salvation. You meet representatives of both faith traditions.

A Guide for Study and Discussion

Where is that in the Bible?

Dr. Johnston has written *Opening the Scriptures* to encourage you to open your Bible and discover its riches for yourself. He has recommended passages for reading, even while he is presenting an overview. With your new confidence, you can now go on to make your own list of passages. It will increase your sense of "where things are" in the Bible. Here's a beginning:

Adam and Eve stories
Genesis 1–3

Beatitudes
Matthew 5

Birth of Jesus
Matthew 1 and Luke 2

Blind Men
Matthew 9

David
1 Samuel 16–31; 2 Samuel;
1 Kings 1–2

Feeding the People
Matthew 14, Mark 6, Luke 9,
and John 6

Good Samaritan, a parable
Luke 10

Growing Seed, parable
Mark 4

Hidden Treasures, parable
Matthew 13

Isaiah the Prophet
Isaiah 1–39

Jesus, Trial and Crucifixion
Matthew 26, Mark 14, Luke 22,
John 18

Job, a Drama
Job

Last Supper
Matthew 26, Mark 14, Luke 22,
John 13

Lazarus
John 11

Lord is My Shepherd
Psalm 23

Lord's Prayer
Matthew 6

Lost Son, a parable
Luke 15

Love
1 Corinthians 13

Moses and Burning Bush
Exodus 3

Paul the Apostle
Acts 9

Opening the Scriptures

Red Sea Crossing
Exodus 14

Rich Man and Lazarus
Luke 16

Ruth and Naomi
Ruth

Samson and Delaiah
Judges 16

Solomon
1 Kings 1–11

Ten Commandments
Exodus 20, Deuteronomy 5

Ten Girls, parable
Matthew 25

Water into Wine
John 2

Widow and Judge
Luke 18

Index

I Hebrew Bible (Old Testament)

Genesis

1	224	15:19–21	21
1–3	243	17:10–14	19
1–11	vii	18:19	211
1–36	181	18:20–21	19
1:1–2:3	15	18:23–32	20
2:4–3:24	10, 12	18:32	20
2:8	199	19:24–25	20
2:9	210	20:2	21
2:22	151	20:12	21
2:24	156	21:9–20	170
3:7	203	21:18	21
3:17–18	209	22:1–14	20
3:22–24	13, 17	22:14	206
3:24	197	22:17	19
4:1–16	13	25:31–34	22
4:21	205	27:6–40	22
4:23–24	187	28:12–22	22
6:4	151	28:17	160
6:5–9:17	13	28:20	211
8:11	201	31:27	205
8:22	13	32:24–32	23
9	224	32:28	11, 22
9:2–7	15	32:30	23
9:12	207	34:1–31	22
9:18–19	15	35:9–15	23
10:5	15	37–50	23, 181
11:1–9	15	37:5–11	24
11:9	198	37:23–36	24
12–50	vii, 18	39:7–20	24
12:2	19	44:28	24
12:7	19	45:1–15	25
12:13	21	45:7	25
13:14	200	46:27	23
13:15–16	19	47:13–26	24
15:18	21	49:2–27	187
15:18–21	19	50:20	25

Exodus

1–3	27

Opening the Scriptures

1:8	27	17–26	182
2:5–10	28	18:6–18	133
3	243	19	178
3:1	206	26:14–34	89
3:2	28, 199		
3:14	31, 198	**Numbers**	
3:20	203	5:18	151
5:1–2	28	9:2–3	210
12–15	27	12:7	100
12:3	205	13	39
12:11	31	14	39
12:12	28	17:8	196
12:37	35	21–24	39
13:14	31	21:8	208
13:18	211	24:17	209
14	244	32	39
14:31	100	32:8	35
15:1–21	28, 187		
15:8–10	210	**Deuteronomy**	
19–34	27	1:19	35
19:4	202	1:46	35
19:5–6	38	5	27, 244
19:11	206	5:6–21	32
20	244	5:16	33
20–24	36	6	27
20:1–17	29, 32	6:4–9	34
20:12	33	6:13	32, 114
25:18–20	197	6:16	114
29:7	95	8:3	114
29:21	95	8:7	210
31:1–5	189	8:15	208
31:18	29	18:15	34, 35
32:15	29	18:15–18	95
32:19	29	18:18	34
34	36	18:22	32
34:1	29	21:5	32
34:11–26	2	21:23	145
35:30–35	189	26:5	18, 181
40:38	35	33	27, 187
		34:5–7	34
Leviticus			
8:12	99	**Joshua**	
16:10	201	24	39

Index

Judges
1	40
2:16–23	40
3:12–30	184
4–5	40
4:4–5:31	40
4:17	41
5:1–31	187
5:25–27	41
5:27	185
8:7	210
9:7	207
9:7–15	182
11:39	40
13–16	40
13:2–16:31	40
15:16	184
16	244
21:25	41

Ruth
1–4	244
4	47

1 Samuel
1	41
1–7	40
2:1–10	41
8	42
8:4–5	42
8:7	43
8:9	43
9:1–10:16	42
9:16	42, 43
10:1	43, 95
10:17–27	42, 43
10:24	43
11	42
12	42
12:22	43
12:24	43
13	42
13:12–13	42
14	42
15:3	44
15:8–9	44
15:26	47
15:33	44
15:35	47
16–31	243
16:1–13	47
16:12	47
16:14–23	47
16:18–19	47
16:23	205
17–31	47
18:7	48
24:1–8	184
25:44	48
28:16–17	48
31:1–6	44

2 Samuel
1–24	243
1:1–27	47
1:8–9	44
1:19–27	44
1:23	184
2–24	47
4	48
5:1–4	50
5:13	50
7:1–17	52
7:16	93
12:1–12	51
18:32–33	51
23:1	51

1 Kings
1–2	243
1–11	244
1:1–2:11	47
1:32–11:43	54
2:11–12	51
3:13	54
12–22	57

Opening the Scriptures

12:11	208	2:7	111, 163
18:21–40	59	8	46
19:11–16	59	10:7	186
19:12	59, 185	13	93
19:16	95	13:1–6	101
19:18	59	18	93
		18:1–50	101
2 Kings		19:1	186
1–25	57	22	93
2:11	59	22:1	101
8:13–15	59	22:1–31	101
9:1–3	59	23	46, 243
9:3	59	23:1	37, 70
22–23	35	23:2	210
		25:9	211
1 Chronicles		27	93
11:15–19	185	27:1–14	101
13:8	205	29:2	160
		30:5	206
Ezra		31:5	203
7:6	77	34	46, 93
10:10–12	77	34:1–22	101
		39:4	202
Esther		40:1	187
5:14	184	42:1	204
7:5–10	79	51	50
7:9–10	184	51:7	204
9:1–28	79	63	46
9:31	79	72	93, 94
		73:23–24	82
Job		74:16	206
1–42	243	79:6	188
3–31	80	79:12	188
29:15	81	80:1	197
32–37	80	89	93
38–41	80	89:20	95
42:1–6	80	89:20–36	94
42:10–11	80	91:13	205
42:12–17	80	95:3	8
		95:7	203
Psalms		100:3	205
1:3	211	103:5	202
2	93, 94	103:12	200

105:15	95	5:7	203
107:40	211	6:1–8	60, 63
109:8–19	189	6:1–9	197
110:1	161	6:8	185
110:4	163	6:9–10	64, 131
113	187	7:14	111
119:30	211	9:1–7	93
119:169–176	101	9:2	52, 93, 200
130	93	9:6	93
130:1–8	101	9:6–7	52
135:13	32	11:1	52, 93
137:1–6	61	11:1–2	210
137:8–9	189	11:1–9	93
139:10	203	11:2	112
139:21–22	189	11:2–3	201
146	93	12:3	210
146:1–10	101	13:21	201
		21:11–12	206
Proverbs		22:13	188
3:17	211	26:19	82
6:6	184	27:1	201, 208
9–11	184	28–33	64
22:5	209	34:14	201
23:5	202	35:6	204
25:11	197	36–39	64
26:9	210	40–55	71, 93
		40–66	77
Ecclesiastes		40:1–2	98
9:4	184	40:1–41:29	97
		40:3	37, 211
Song of Solomon (Songs)		40:9	97
2:3	197	40:11	70
5:15	199	40:28	7
8:5	188, 197	40:28–31	99
		41:4	202
Isaiah		41:8–10	100
1–23	64	41:21	99
1–39	243	42:1	99
1:3	201	42:1–4	100
2:12	201	42:1–49:12	97
3:16–17	151	42:7	200
3:24	151	43:7	32
5:1–7	188	43:8–13	100

Opening the Scriptures

43:16	211	4:6	200
43:19	37	7:10–11	32
44:1	100	7:14	32
44:2	100	9:1–2	66
44:6	202	9:4	66
44:21	100	9:6	66
45:4	100	9:17–22	188
45:12	203	13:20	200
45:14	98	17:11	207
47	188	19:1–20:6	65
47:1	98	19:8	68
47:15	98	20:7	68
48:12	100	20:7–15	65
49:1–6	100	20:9	68
49:6	98, 100	21:1–10	65
49:8	201	21:11–14	65
49:11–12	98	23:1–40	65
49:13–53:12	97	25:11–12	89
50:2	203	25:14–38	65
50:4–9	100	26:1–24	65
51:9	201	27:2–6	65
51:15	99	27:15–20	65
52:13–53:12	100	28:1–17	65
53:1–8	138	29:1–9	65
53:2–12	115	29:10	89
53:5	208	30:1–24	65
53:10–11	102	30:9	47
54–55	97	31	71
54:5	199	31:31–34	65
55:3	47	31:32	8, 199
55:13	206	31:33	34
58	71	32:1	65
60	93	32:6–15	68
61	71, 93	32:7–15	65
61:1	95	33	65
61:2	201	34:1–7	65
65:17–25	93	34:13–22	68
		35:1–11	65
Jeremiah		36:1–4	64
1–18	65	36:1–27	65
1:5	146	37:3–21	65
2:8	68	38:1	65
4:3	209	38:3–22	65

38:24–26	65	2:48	86
39:3	65	3:5	205
39:14	65	3:17–18	85, 101
42:1–6	65	3:25	86
43:1–13	65	5:5	86
49:16	202	5:26–28	86
		6:10	85
Lamentations		7–12	88
4:18	202	7:1–2	206
		7:3	208
Ezekiel		7:4–8	90
1–24	69	7:7	206
1:1–3:11	69	7:13	206
1:4–28	197	7:13–14	90
1:10	202	7:14	87, 98, 114, 115
2:6	209		
8:16	199	7:27	87
17:22–24	199	8:16	196
18:4	82	8:17	202
18:10–23	82	9:2	89
21:2–4	200	9:11–13	86
21:29	202	9:24–27	89
25–32	69	10:5	196
28:3	88	11:30	87
29:3	202	11:31	88
33–39	69	11:35	202
33:1–9	69	12:1	196
34:11–16	69	12:3	209
34:24	47	12:4	202
35:5	202	12:9	202
37	71		
37:1–14	182	**Hosea**	
37:24	70	1–3	64
37:27	70	2:2	178
38:15	200	2:19–20	199
40–48	68	3:5	47
43:1–4	200	5:12	178
		5:14	178
Daniel		6:3	178
1–6	88	7:1	178
1:7	85	7:12	178
1:12	85	8:12	178
2:21	210	9:10	203

Opening the Scriptures

10:12	178		***Zechariah***	
11:1	8, 111		1–8	77
11:1–4	178		1:8	206
11:1–12	64		6:9–14	93
11:9	8		8:7	200
11:10	178		9:9	201
13:7	178		9:9–13	93
13:8	178		14:8	210
14:1–9	64			
14:5	178		***Malachi***	
14:8	178		3:2	201
			4:5–6	59

Joel
1:12   197

II Apocrypha and Pseudepigrapha

Amos

3:6	81
5–9	64
5:18	201
5:21	64
5:23–24	64
7:14–15	63
8:2	202

Wisdom of Solomon

1–3	77
2:23–24	17
2:23–3:4	82
6–9	77
18	77
19	77

Jonah

1:17	79
2	80

Ecclesiasticus

1	77
10	77
15	77
19	77
24–26	77

Micah

1:2–7	188
6:8	63

I Maccabees
1–16   77

Nahum
1:3–4   208

2 Maccabees

7	102
15:36	79

Habakkuk
1:5   141

Tobit

1–14	77
3:17	196

Zephaniah
1:7   201

Haggai
1–2   77

1 Enoch
xxxv. 3	96

Psalms of Solomon
17	47
17:4	95
17:21–46	95
17:22	96
17:36	96
17:37	96
18:7	96

III New Testament

Matthew
1	243
1:1	47
1:23	111
2:1	199
2:13	196
2:16	91
5	243
5–7	191, 206
5:14	200
6	243
6:11	198
6:25–33	193
7:16	209
8:11	200
9	243
10:22	202
12:40	79, 203, 211
13	243
13:45	207
14	243
16:19	129
18:23	117
21:5	201
22:13	200
25	244
25:31–46	71
26	243
28:16	206

Mark
1:3	37
1:8	157
1:12–13	201
1:13	201
1:15	202, 210
1:17	203
2:21–22	121
4	243
4:3–8	121
4:7	210
4:18	210
4:21–22	121
4:30–32	121, 199
6	243
6:31	201
7:4	210
9:2	206
9:13	59
11:12–14	203
12:1–11	121
12:34	117
13:28–29	121
13:32	116, 201
14	243
14:22–24	186
14:30	199
14:36	119
14:58	162, 209
15:36	208

Luke
1–2	110, 237
1:1–4	107
1:7	110
1:11–20	196
1:17	59
1:27	111
1:32	112
1:33	202
1:34	111
1:46–55	41, 112, 187
1:68–79	112

Opening the Scriptures

2	243	10:30–37	122, 123, 238, 239
2:29–32	112		
2:36	112	11:2	8
2:38	112	11:3	198
2:48	111	11:5–8	122, 125, 239
3–23	110	11:20	117
3:1–2a	110, 113	12:11–12	128
3:2–9:50	114	12:16–21	122, 123, 239
3:2b–9:50	110	12:42–48	121
3:4–17	113	12:49	118
3:23–28	111	12:56	210
3:31	47	13:6–9	122, 124, 239
4:3	114	13:18–19	121
4:18–21	118	13:20–21	121
4:24	118	13:21	117
4:42	201	13:33	118
4:43	116	14:7–14	122, 239
5:16	119	14:15–24	121
5:17	104	14:8–10	124
5:21	104	14:28–33	122, 124, 239
5:36–39	121	15	243
6	191	15:4–7	121
6:12	119, 206	15:8–9	125
6:20–21	118	15:8–10	122, 239
6:35–36	119	15:11–32	122, 125, 239
6:47–49	121	16	244
7:16	118	16:1–8	122, 124, 239
7:22–23	118	16:19–31	122, 123, 239
7:39	118	17:7–10	122, 124, 239
7:41–43	122, 124, 239	17:20–21	117
8:1	116	18	244
8:5–8	121	18:2–8	122, 125, 239
8:5–15	120	18:10–14	122, 123, 239
8:10	116	18:17	117
8:16–17	121	19:12–27	121
9	243	19:28–23:56	110
9:2	116	20:9–16	121
9:20	115	21:15	128
9:31	118	21:29–30	121
9:51–19:27	110, 115	22	243
9:60	116	22:29	118
10	243	22:41–42	119
10:16	128	23:4	118

23:14–15	118	18	243
23:34	115, 119	19:29	204
23:38	118	19:38–40	153
23:43	115	20:12–13	196
23:46	115, 119	20:19	126
23:49–55	153	21:11	203
24:1–53	110, 116		
24:19	118	**Acts of the Apostles**	
24:28–35	143	1:2	128
24:47	109	1:1–4	128
24:52	116	1:6	107
		1:8	128
John		1:9–12	206
1:5	200	1:13	137
1:29	205	1:14	136
1:32	112	1:15–16	128
2	244	1:23	137
2:4	204	2–12	128
2:19	209	2:8	130
3:2	207	2:14–36	194
3:5	211	2:17–18	128
3:14–15	208	2:42–47	132
3:19	200	2:47	132
4:10–14	210	3:12–26	138, 194
6	191, 243	3:19	210
6:14	34	3:22–23	35
6:35	198	4:19–20	134
7:6	204, 210	4:36–37	140
7:30	204	5:1–10	136
7:38	210	5:29	134
8:12	200	6:3–5	137
11	243	6:5	134
12:13	207	6:9	145
12:36	200	6:10	128
13	243	6:11–14	134
13:30	207	7:56	132
13:31–14:31	192	7:59–60	134
13:31–16:31	192	8:1–25	130
14:4–6	211	8:9–24	136
15:1–8	203	8:26–40	194
15:1–16:4a	192	8:27–39	138
16:4b–33	193	9	243
17:1	204	9:1–22	139

Opening the Scriptures

9:2	211	21:8	137
9:25	135	21:9	136, 138
9:26	140	21:11	130
9:27	140	21:39	75
9:36	136	22:1–21	139
10:38	138	22:4	211
10:38–48	194	22:16	210
10:44–48	130	22:28	75
12:2	135	25:11	139
12:12	136	25:13	139
12:25	137	25:25	139
13–28	128	26:1–23	139
13:1–4	130	28:25–27	131
13:16–41	194	28:30–31	109
13:23	138		
13:33	111	***Romans***	
13:38	138	1:3	47
13:52	130	1:3–4	147, 191
14:22	135	3:12	201
14:23	140	5:5	157
15:20	133	5:14–21	17
15:22	137	5:15	23
15:28	130	6:4	210
15:37	137	7:5–25	144
15:39	137	7:19	148
15:40	138	7:24–25	148
16:1	138	8:15	119
16:14	136	8:31–39	193
16:19	138	13:8–10	191
17:4–14	138	13:11	210
17:26	133, 210	13:12	207
17:31	201	15:2	210
17:34	136	16:3	136
18:2	136		
18:18	136	***1 Corinthians***	
18:24–28	130, 136	1:12	158
18:26	136	1:26	158
19:1–7	130	5	155
19:23	211	5:1–5	156
20	192	5:11	155
20:23	131	6:11	210
20:28	140	6:15–16	156
20:29–31	128	6:17	9, 199

7	155	1:11–2:14	144
7:4	156	1:15–2:10	140
7:6	156	3:13	145
7:10	156	3:28	152, 212
7:36–38	156	4:6	119
7:39	156	4:10	210
10:11	202	4:19	150
10:16	198	4:26	204
11–14	155	5:10–23	191
11:3	152	5:16–6:10	155
11:5	152	5:22	157
11:16	152	5:22–23	159
11:21	157	6:8	159
11:23–26	147		
11:26	157	***Ephesians***	
11:34	157	2:12–22	209
12–14	130	5:8	200
12:3	191	5:22	192
12:8–11	157	5:23–32	199
12:12	158	5:26	211
12:13	157, 210	6:17	129
12:25–26	158		
13	193, 243	***Philippians***	
13:4–13	157	1:1	139
14:19	157	2:15	200
14:34–37	152	2:6–11	193
15:3–8	126, 144, 147	3:2–16	194
15:6	132	3:4–11	144
15:21–26	212	3:5–6	145
15:22	23	4:2	136
15:44	126		
15:44–49	212	***Colossians***	
15:45	23	2:10	210
		3:1	210
2 Corinthians		3:18	192
4:4–6	212	4:10	137
5:17	148		
10–12	194	***1 Thessalonians***	
11:2	199	4:17	166
		5:2	201
Galatians		5:5	200
1–2	194		
1:11–24	146		

1 Timothy
2:9–15	150
4:14	203
6:11	191

2 Timothy
2:8	47
3:6	150
4	192

Titus
2:4–5	150

Philemon
24	137

Hebrews
1:1–4	161
1:3	161, 163
2:1–18	161
2:3–4	163
2:9	161
2:17–18	163
4:14–5:10	161
4:15	163
4:16	164
5:1–4	162
5:5–6	163
5:7–10	163
5:12	163
6:1–6	128
6:19	196
7:11–10:25	161
8:8–13	161
9:7	162
9:11–15	162
9:26	164
9:28	164
10:22	163, 210
10:24	163
10:25	201
11:10	162
11:27	38
12:1	161
12:2	163
12:28	163
13	161
13:14	162
13:20–21	164
13:22	161

1 Peter
1–5	107
1:5	210
2:4–5	209
2:9	200
2:18	192
2:24	208
2:24–25	118
3:20	211
4:7	202
5:13	137

2 Peter
1:5–7	192

1 John
1–5	107
1:5	200
2:8	200

Revelation
1–3	167
1:8	202
1:13	168
1:13–16	173
1:13–18	173
1:16	168
1:17	203
2:7	169
2:11	169
2:13	173
2:17	169
2:26	169
2:28	209
3:5	169

3:7	47	18:20	167
3:12	169	19:7–9	173
3:21	169	19:9–20:5	172
4:1–5:14	169	19:11–13	173
4:2–3	208	19:11–16	173
4:7	202	19:16	173
4:7–10	197	19:20	167
5:5	173, 205	20:1–6	167
5:8	205	20:4	165
5:9–10	194	21:1	208
5:12	205	21:2	205
6:1–8	165	21:6	vi, 202, 211
6:1–11	170	21:13	200
6:10	174	21:21	207
6:16	173	21:23	173
7	167	21:25	207
7:1–11:19	170	21:27	173
7:9	207	22:1–2	211
8:8–9	172	22:13	202
9:3	208	22:16	47, 209
9:3–4	170		
9:5	208		
12	167		
12:1	209		
12:1–2	170		
12:1–17	170, 201		
12:6	201		
12:17	170		
13:1	208		
13:1–8	171		
13:11–18	167		
13:18	171		
14:1	205		
14:1–20	171		
14:14–16	173		
15:3–4	194		
17:4	207		
17:9	167		
17:14	173		
18–21	167		
18:1–19:4	171		
18:12	207		
18:16	207		

IV New Testament Apocrypha

Gospel of the Hebrews 112

Recycleable paper.
920204